DISCARD

Knowledge under Construction

Knowledge under Construction

The Importance of Play in Developing Children's Spatial and Geometric Thinking

Daniel Ness and Stephen J. Farenga

ROWMAN & LITTLEFIELD PUBLISHERS, INC.
Lanham • Boulder • New York • Toronto • Plymouth, UK

ROWMAN & LITTLEFIELD PUBLISHERS, INC.

Published in the United States of America
by Rowman & Littlefield Publishers, Inc.
A wholly owned subsidiary of The Rowman & Littlefield Publishing Group, Inc.
4501 Forbes Boulevard, Suite 200, Lanham, Maryland 20706
www.rowmanlittlefield.com

Estover Road
Plymouth PL6 7PY
United Kingdom

British Library Cataloguing in Publication Information Available

Library of Congress Cataloging-in-Publication Data

Ness, Daniel, 1966–
    Knowledge under construction : the importance of play in developing
children's spatial and geometric thinking / Daniel Ness and
Stephen J. Farenga.
        p.   cm.
Includes bibliographical references and index.
    ISBN-13: 978-0-7425-4788-9 (cloth : alk. paper)
    ISBN-10: 0-7425-4788-4 (cloth : alk. paper)
    ISBN-13: 978-0-7425-4789-6 (pbk. : alk. paper)
    ISBN-10: 0-7425-4789-2 (pbk. : alk. paper)
    1. Cognition in children.   2. Play—Psychological aspects.
I. Farenga, Stephen J., 1958–   II. Title.
BF723.C5N46   2007
155.4'13752—dc22   2006037989

Printed in the United States of America

♾ ™ The paper used in this publication meets the minimum requirements of
American National Standard for Information Sciences—Permanence of Paper for
Printed Library Materials, ANSI/NISO Z39.48-1992.

For Eric and to all young children who naturally demonstrate advanced cognitive abilities that go unrecognized by standardized tests.

Contents

Foreword

Receiving an invitation to write a foreword is first of all receiving an invitation to read a book. Writing a foreword is inviting others to read the book too. At first I was surprised with the invitation of Daniel Ness and Stephen Farenga. What do I know about developing children's spatial and geometric thinking activities? Very little. "The Importance of Play" and "Knowledge under Construction" sound sympathetic, but what can I say about it?

I read Daniel's and Stephen's book with a lot of interest. I might say the book is about the awakening of geometrical thought in early childhood, if I am allowed to paraphrase the title of the English language version of one of my own books *Awakening of Geometrical Thought in Early Culture* (Gerdes 2003). Both in early culture and in early childhood, geometry is, first of all, grasping space. At the end of my book, I summarized some of my conclusions in the following way:

> The capacity of human beings to recognize geometrical forms in nature and also in their own products was formed in activity. The capacity to recognize order and regular spatial forms in nature has been developed through labor activity. *Regularity* . . . is the *result* of human creative labor and not its presupposition. It is the real, practical advantages of the invented regular form that lead to the growing awareness of order and regularity. The same advantages stimulate comparison with other products of labor and with natural phenomena. The regularity of the labor product simplifies its reproduction, and in that way the consciousness of its form and the interest in it become reinforced. With the growing awareness develops simultaneously a positive valuing of the discovered form: the form is then also used where it is *not necessary*; it is considered *beautiful* (p. 168).
>
> The cylinder, cone, or other symmetrical shapes of vessels, the hexagonal patterns of baskets, hats, and snowshoes, etc., may at first sight *appear* to be the result of instinctive impulses or of an innate feeling for these forms or—in

another idealist variant—as generated by a collective "cultural spirit" or "archetype," or also, mechanically, as an imitation of natural phenomena—for example, of crystal structure or of honeycombs. In fact, however, humans *create* these forms in their practical activity to be able to satisfy their daily needs. They *elaborate* them. The *understanding* of these materially necessary forms emerges and develops further through interaction with the given material in order to be able to produce something useful: bows, boats, hand axes, baskets, pots, etc. From the *recognition of these necessities* and of the thereby acquired possibilities of employing them to achieve certain aims emerged the human *freedom* to make things that are useful and considered beautiful (p. 168).

With the reflection in art and games of shapes formed in activity, early mathematical thinking started to liberate itself from material necessity: form becomes emancipated from matter, and thus emerges the *concept* and *understanding* of form; the way is made *free* for intramathematical development.

In the interplay of the needs important to a society, material possibilities, and experimental activity, certain shapes—for example, symmetrical forms—proved themselves to be optimal. Thinking in terms of order and symmetry does not need a mythical explanation. It reflects the societal experience of production. Once this experience has established itself to the degree that the regularity has acquired an aesthetic value, then also *new* and, in a certain sense, ordered shapes could be created without an immediate, inescapable material compulsion existing for them. In this process, the early geometrical thinking develops further—that is, the capacity to create *thinkable or imaginable* forms (p. 169).

Societal-cultural activity and labor are the motor for the early development of geometry in human history. What I learnt from Daniel and Stephen's book is that playing with blocks and other objects is extremely important for small children to learn to "grasp that space in which the child lives, breathes and moves. The space that the child must learn to know, explore, conquer, in order to live, breathe and move better in it" (Freudenthal 1973, 403).

Let children experiment, let them construct their own buildings, let them concentrate and engage in playful space exploring activities, let them discover symmetry and balance, let them invent repeated patterns, let them draw, let them construct knowledge. Given the means, the freedom, the time, and the guidance, children—all children, independent of their origins—will lay the bases for their future geometry education. Playing is the motor for the early development of spatial and geometric thinking activities.

Reading Daniel and Stephen's book stimulates the reader to reflect. About what is grasping space at an early age. About what an early childhood educator may do to encourage the awakening and development of geometric thinking. About . . . discover it yourself!

May I invite the reader to read, absorb, and continue her/himself in *Knowledge under Construction*. Surely this pioneering work will stimulate further research.

> Paulus Gerdes
> Universidade Pedagogica
> Ethnomathematics Research Centre
> Maputo, Mozambique

Acknowledgments

We are grateful to Dr. Paulus Gerdes, Professor at the Universidade Pedagogica in Maputo, Mozambique, who has written the foreword to this volume. Paulus's work and dedication to the study of geometry, the influence of culture on spatial thinking, and human rights throughout the world has been a great inspiration for us. We would like to acknowledge our dear companions, Bonnie and Dale Johnson, who have served as models and exemplars of scholarship and social justice. In addition, we thank the many individuals who reviewed the manuscript for their input and suggestions. Finally, thanks go to those at Rowman & Littlefield—Alan McClare, executive editor, Alex Masulis, editorial assistant, and Katherine Macdonald, associate production editor—who have assisted us through all the stages of this project.

Introduction

We join spokes together in a wheel,
but it is the center hole
that makes the wagon move.

We shape clay into a pot,
but it is the emptiness inside
that holds whatever we want.

We hammer wood for a house,
but it is the inner space
that makes it livable.

We work with being,
but non being is what we use.

—Lao-tzu (6th century BCE)

We not only live in space: we live it. When we read, we do so in space; when we go to a store, we do so in space; when we construct apartment buildings, we do so in space; when we identify new discoveries, we do so in space; when we observe celestial bodies from earth or 250 kilometers above the earth's surface, again, we do so in space. This book is about space. More specifically, it's about space as the young child sees it, works with it, works in it, and manipulates objects within it in the everyday context of free play. It is also about how children construct knowledge associated with space—given that space is inextricably associated with mathematics and science concepts.

Given this intrinsic connection to mathematics and science, why, then, is it important for the adult—in particular, a teacher or parent—to know about space? First, our understanding of space serves as a prerequisite for our learning of numerous areas of inquiry, particularly in mathematics and the physical sciences. It is also very helpful in our understanding of some of the social sciences, such as geography and the movement of individuals or social groups from one area to another. Understanding space also helps us devise plans, as in architecture or engineering where the architect's or engineer's blueprint acts as the referent, that is, the representation of the actual building, roadway, or subway system. Our understanding of space also enables us to carry on everyday functions, like setting a dinner table, constructing objects and materials for daily use, or anticipating the area needed to write on a chalkboard or a piece of paper. Perhaps most important, without some knowledge of space, you would find it very difficult to survive in the everyday world. It would be quite difficult, for example, to operate a car if you were unable to judge and estimate spatial relationships (i.e., distances) between the car being driven and nearby cars, people, objects, or property.

We do not, however, cover all aspects of space. We cannot. To cover all aspects of space in the world, or universe for that matter, in a single text would be next to impossible. In fact, several volumes of an encyclopedia would be much too brief to cover all issues associated with space. Our intention, however, is to extrapolate necessary topics related to space to study how young children's everyday actions summon spatial characteristics and how these characteristics can serve as a springboard for later study in school and functionality in the real world.

This book serves several purposes. First, we demonstrate various methodologies for identifying spontaneous activity in terms of young children's cognitive processes regarding spatial, geometric, and scientific concepts. Based on videotaped analyses of young children's block play, we provide evidence of emergent mathematical and scientific behaviors that underscore the analogy of the young child as mathematician, architect, and scientist. Parallels are drawn among the traits associated with these professionals and the intrinsic cognitive propensities of young children. Second, we have created a system of measurement for the identification and categorization of children's spontaneous mathematical and scientific behaviors exhibited during block play. The measurement system, which provides the empirical evidence through the use of spatial-geometric-architectural (SPAGAR) codes, is provided for teachers and parents to support the value of block play—henceforth, construction play—in cognitive development. The measurement system goes well beyond narrative to quantify the field of naturalistic observation—a methodology to which, with the exception of his own children, Jean Piaget paid little if any attention—by breaking the code regarding young children's spatial, geometric, and architectural thinking. Third, we introduce methods for evaluating intelligence and everyday abilities in young children. These methods provide professionals studying in the fields of education and psychology insight into alternative methods of cognitive assessment.

Despite the modest number of works on children's encounters with blocks, little, if anything, has been written that examines children's informal block play as a means of determining and assessing cognitive ability. In this book, we use naturalistic observation to identify the emergent behaviors that children demonstrate while engaged in block constructions. At a time when the importance of high stakes testing is being questioned by parents, teachers, and educational researchers, this work provides the foundations to support an alternative form of assessment by demonstrating the relationship between young children's block play and the development of their cognitive abilities. We suggest that these emergent behaviors—or protobehaviors—are the basis for developing advanced mathematical and scientific concepts.

Teachers and parents often notice that young children start to spontaneously manipulate objects in their external environment. During infancy, parents are quick to notice that children often pick up objects and place them on top of one another. With these actions, early forms of building—or construction—behaviors commence. When given toys that come in large boxes, children are often seen playing with the carton or box in which the toy came after the novelty of the toy has diminished. Upon observing these children, the cartons or boxes are usually arranged in a manner that demonstrates some type of enclosure. Given additional building materials, like blocks or Legos, children continue with this trend and are often observed constructing houses, garages, and other forms of enclosure in a very similar manner. Interestingly, these behaviors appear to cross socioeconomic and transcultural boundaries, provided that the children are in an environment in which they can display them. These common childhood building experiences provide the impetus for questions that foster further inquiry.

Why a book on young children's spatial thinking and construction behaviors? One central problem to consider is not only what our study of spatial thinking and representation can inform us about young children's cognitive abilities—indeed, numerous studies tell us that (Bryant and Squire 2001; Newcombe and Huttenlocher 2003); rather, we must consider how our study of young children's spatial thinking can shed light on their future practical abilities both in and out of school and how this information can foster their success in everyday and formal tasks in the years ahead. In this book, we study the intrinsic value of spatial thinking and how it is demonstrated in construction play during the early years. Countless studies on children's spatial thinking, both theoretical and practical, have failed to demonstrate the intrinsic value of spatial thinking for young children. Moreover, there are numerous "what to look for" books on children's block play—most recently, those of MacDonald (2001), Church and Miller (1990), and Wellhousen and Kieff (2001)—that present various activities and intuitive connections between block structures and subject-matter skills but fail to identify and make connections among theoretical frameworks, empirical research in cognitive development, and practice.

Based on years of classroom and clinical experiences with young children, their parents, and teachers, it is clear to us that most people still do not grasp the value of block play and underestimate its importance in a number of areas of mathematical and scientific development. Consider the following scenario:

> Ms. Cruz allowed the preschool children in her class to work uninterrupted in the "block" center of the play area. During this time, children were encouraged to work together, develop stories, explain how and what they were constructing, and make picture books, one page for each day. This ensued for a number of weeks. Many parents approached Ms. Cruz with concerns that the children were spending too much time in play and wanted to know when they were going to learn something "real," in other words, something academic. Ms. Cruz explained to the parents that during free play, a variety of cognitive abilities are being developed, which relate to the school's pre-K curriculum. The content, process skills, and products are required components in the formal instruction of mathematics, science, and language. She also mentions the need to foster spatial, geometric, and scientific thinking. When pressed further, Ms. Cruz explained that a great deal of block play exhibits children's knowledge of balance, symmetry, problem solving, communicating ideas, reasoning, and a whole host of other interrelated concepts and process skills.

The above scenario raises a number of questions regarding children's free play, cognitive development, and formal instruction. To begin with, what kinds of spatial and geometric thinking do young children employ during block play, and what architectural principles underlie their constructions? Which aspects of spatial, geometrical, and architectural thinking are most prominent during young children's block play? What age, gender, or social class differences, if any, in spatial, geometric, and architectural activity exist while exhibiting building behaviors? What physical, social, environmental, or cultural conditions bring about spontaneous everyday spatial, geometric, and architectural activity? And perhaps most important, does our understanding of building behaviors, specifically as these behaviors tap concepts related to space and geometry, provide us with an indication of young children's belief systems regarding scientific inquiry?

Before these questions can be answered, we must consider the optimal environment in which researchers in the areas of cognition, developmental psychology, and education can tap spatial, geometric, and architectural activities taking place—namely, free play in the preschool setting. In advancing the role of block play in the preschool setting, adults, mainly parents and teachers, need to reconsider the role of play—more specifically, young children's play—and how it affects cognitive development. Unfortunately, it is common for adults to confuse children's play as nothing more than "fun and games" or trivial and banal activities, bereft of any cognitive and instructional value (Reifel 1984). However, we see play as the primary mechanism by which emergent cognitive behaviors—protobehaviors— serve to support the development of both process skills and cognitive abilities. The Protomathematical and Scientific Experience Model (discussed in chapter 8) places play at the core of the development of cognitive processes, which supports the emergence of basic process skills, cognitive readiness, and cognitive concept attainment.

Indeed, there are a number of texts and research studies that focus on cognition in spatial and geometric thinking (See Gattis 2003; Newcombe and Huttenlocher 2003). However, few, if any, examine the role of spatial and geometric cognition with regard to the everyday behaviors of the young child. A scant number of studies entertain the subject of young children's everyday cognitive behaviors related to spatial and geometric thinking, but the evidence is exiguous at best. This volume addresses and underscores the importance of these issues in terms of their psychological, social, and educational implications. Further, we propose a plan for promoting and fostering young children's cognitive development and growth that connects their engagement in free play construction activities with emergent protobehaviors that tap conceptual knowledge in academic studies.

For many years, cognitive psychologists and education researchers specializing in early mathematical and scientific thinking devoted themselves primarily to issues relating to the learning of arithmetic, the development of number skills, and the understanding of science concepts. This research is replete with studies on infants' (Wynn 1995; Mix, Huttenlocher, and Levine 2002) and children's acquisition and understanding of numerical skills (Baroody 1987; Geary 1994; Gelman and Gallistel 1978; Ginsburg 1989) and science-related concepts (Harlen 1985; Kamii and DeVries 1978; Paulu and Martin 1991; Wandersee, Mintzes, and Novak 1994). Historically, less attention has been given to the development of spatial, geometric, and scientific thinking than to arithmetic thinking in general. Moreover, this emphasis on the so-called three Cs—counting, calculation, and conservation—has served as the paradigm in studies on young children's mathematical development and as the predominant mathematics curriculum in early childhood and childhood (i.e., elementary) mathematics education at the expense of other mathematics- and science-related areas, such as space, geometry, and inquiry-related skills. Yet, the importance of spatial-geometric and scientific thinking in and out of school should not be underestimated. As Lao-tzu's verse above indicates, the roles of space and geometry in terms of their application to both purposes of pleasure and survival have been deemed important since early recorded history. But their place in research has been emphasized only in the last two or three decades. Prior to the late 1980s, most studies on spatial, geometric, and science concept formations have been undertaken by developmental and cognitive psychologists, and their research falls into several overlapping areas.

First, developmental psychologists have examined the role of search for missing or hidden objects in early childhood development (See Presson and Somerville 1985; Sophian 1984). It is in this domain that humans are faced with problem solving situations that require spatial thinking skills. Moreover, search involves a variety of aspects of space, such as location, shapes of objects, and direction. These studies also demonstrate that search is a universal characteristic among all people and all ages; all cultures possess and manipulate objects, and all individuals are faced with situations in which needed objects may not be in sight or are not readily available. Finally, psychologists whose work is devoted to this area believe that search, as it relates to spatial representation, can inform us a great deal about other areas of cognition, namely, the development of memory, intuition, and logic, and the role of planning and intention.

Second, developmental and cognitive psychologists have focused on the relationships between brain function and spatial cognition (See Stiles-Davis, Kritchevsky, and Bellugi 1988). Researchers have attempted to answer questions relating to the ways in which the brain processes spatial understanding as well as the biological underpinnings to spatial cognition.

Third, other researchers in the realm of developmental and cognitive psychology have attempted to advance the pioneering work of Piaget and his colleagues (Piaget and Inhelder 1956; Piaget, Inhelder, and Szeminska 1960), who claimed that an understanding of topological space emerges before Euclidean space (see chapter 2 for definitions of these terms). Some of the leading researchers who have advanced Piaget's topological primacy thesis include Lovell (1959), Page (1959), Peel (1959), and Laurendeau and Pinard (1970). In stark contrast to this widely held position, our research indicates that young children's everyday block play, and free play in general, shows little, if any, evidence of topological space but a great amount of evidence that young children have a powerful understanding of Euclidean space—entirely contrary to Piaget's topological primacy thesis.

Indeed, Piaget's theoretical framework for human intellectual development was subject to a great deal of methodology- and content-related criticism from the branch of cognitive psychology both during his lifetime and posthumously. The majority of the post-Piagetian researchers identified the limitations of Piaget's ideas. By attempting to fine tune some of his theoretical arguments and eliminate their shortcomings, post-Piagetians have extended their newly discovered research based on the core of Piaget's work.

Despite this tendency, however, neither Piaget nor the post-Piagetians have identified the essence of cognitive behaviors in children within the everyday context. It follows, then, that past and recent research in the field of spatial and geometric thinking has failed to account for the everyday goings on of the child. With few exceptions (Ginsburg, Inoue, and Seo 1999; Ginsburg, Pappas, and Seo 2001; Ginsburg et al. 2003; Ness 2001, 2002), cognitive research, as a whole, is devoid of studies that examine intellectual behaviors and development through children's everyday free play. Moreover, everyday ideas and activities having to do with enumeration and magnitude do not inform us very much about scientific phenomena and hypothesis testing that everyday spatial-geometric thinking activities do.

Fourth, research in the area of young children's science concept development has focused on prior knowledge, naïve conceptions, misconceptions, or alternate understandings (Bransford, Brown, and Cocking 2000; Novak 1995; Ormrod 1999; Wandersee, Mintzes, and Novak 1994). Young children often approach a new task with pervasive misrepresentations of how the world works (Farenga and Joyce 2002). It is evident that their science ideas are driven by a language of exploration, explanation, and generalization. It appears, then, that much of young children's thinking is perceptually motivated and is influenced by evidence and experience. This models a constructivist philosophy. As Farenga and Joyce suggest, "knowledge is constructed by a synergistic interaction of prior knowledge and newer learning experiences" (1997, 248).

Fifth, cognitive psychologists have developed computer simulations as a means of attempting to generalize the ways in which students learn geometric relations and use particular problem solving strategies. Some of the more well-known models of geometric cognition include J. R. Anderson's (1983) ACT*, Greeno's (1980) model of geometric problem solving, and Parallel Distributed Processing (PDP) Networks, developed by McClelland, Rumelhart, and their colleagues (1986).

This is not to say that mathematics education research before the 1990s was devoid of studies related to space and geometry. In fact, a handful of edited volumes published before the 1990s often included one chapter (and possibly two) on the subject. One such example is Lesh and Landau's volume (1983), which published a chapter on "Space and Geometry" by Bishop and another on Van Hiele's theories on geometric thinking by Thomas Hoffer. Finally, perhaps the most prolific researchers in the areas of space and geometry from a mathematics education perspective are Clements and Battista (Clements 1999; Clements and Battista 1992). Both Clements and Battista have examined the research in the development of spatial and geometric reasoning in the early years and students' understanding of the subject throughout elementary and secondary school. Further, much of their earlier work dealt with research in Logo programming and its benefits to children's geometric thinking skills, as well as their contribution to the idea of spatial structuring, which deals with the ways children manipulate mental schema as a means of solving problems in geometry.

Despite new insight in recent studies on preschoolers' mathematical and scientific thinking, a number of issues remain understudied in the research. First, there has always been, and still remains, a greater emphasis on preschool children's arithmetic development or number concepts than on their understanding of space and form. Second, most studies use specifically assigned tasks to examine mathematical performance. Few, if any, studies have examined preschoolers' informal mathematical and scientific thinking in the everyday context. Although educators often believe intuitively that block play promotes cognitive development, they often lack the evidence to support its significance in the classroom. In this book, we attempt to provide sound evidence and a rationale to support practices which are often misconstrued as "educational filler." Third, with the unfortunate onset of standardized testing at the preschool level as prescribed by the No Child Left Behind Act, in this book, we identify ways to assess young children's cognitive abilities, not by what inaccurate test scores show, but by what young children "inform us" as they engage in their natural everyday behaviors during free play. Fourth, even fewer studies have investigated the role of socioeconomic (SES) status in children's mathematical thinking (Ginsburg, Pappas, and Seo 2001). Finally, based on observations of children during free play, preschoolers demonstrate evidence of basic architectural principles during their involvement in Lego or block play. But in addition to the sorely understudied area of children's spatial and geometric thinking in the everyday context, research investigating the underlying architectural principles manifest during preschool children's free play are almost entirely lacking.

This book consists of eight chapters. Chapter 1 provides a foundational overview of the definitions involving space and geometry, as well as a discussion of the philosophical and psychological underpinnings of these areas of study. In chapter 2, we examine four theoretical models having to do with the development of spatial thinking and geometric thinking. We also propose our everyday model for the purpose of examining young children's spatial and geometric cognitive propensities. In the third chapter, we investigate children's emergent knowledge of basic architectural principles—a topic that is essentially devoid in the literature on mathematical thinking in the early years. The fourth chapter provides an examination of our methodology in the analysis of young children's emergent spatial, geometric, and architecturally related cognitive behaviors during everyday free play. In particular, we discuss the general benefit in the method of contextual observation as a means of measuring young children's engagement in spatial, geometric, and architecturally related behaviors. In addition, we define thirteen codes associated with young children's engagement in emergent spatial, geometric, and architectural (SPAGAR) activities. In chapter 5, we examine young children's spatial, geometric, and architectural activity in terms of age, gender, and socioeconomic status. A total of 90 preschool aged children were included in this study. Chapters 6 and 7 involve the use of case studies. In chapter 6, we selected two children—both exhibiting evidence of spatial, geometric, and architecturally related activity during nearly all their free play time—for two separate case studies, a boy in the first study and a girl in the second. Both cases in this chapter examine individual children who work alone and independently and not through cooperative or competitive play. In contrast, chapter 7 consists of two cases, both of which include individual children who engage in free play with other children, either cooperatively or competitively. In both chapters, we discuss the cognitive implications of each child's potential in the area of spatial, geometric, and architectural thinking. We close the volume with chapter 8 connecting what has been learned in the previous seven chapters with early childhood and childhood (i.e., elementary level) curriculum and pedagogical practice.

1

Spatial, Geometric, and Architectural Thinking: The Big Picture

> If two different authors use the words "red," "hard," or "disappointed," no one doubts that they mean approximately the same thing, because these words are connected with elementary experiences in a manner which is difficult to misinterpret. But in the case of words such as "place" or "space," whose relation with psychological experiences is less direct, there exists a far-reaching uncertainty of interpretation.
>
> Albert Einstein (1954, xii)

In order to accelerate and maximize discourse and practice in knowledge construction with regard to the spatial and, accordingly, geometric aspects of behavior, which is one of the ultimate goals of this book, we need to unpack the meanings and connotations of the words *space* and *geometry* and those of their derivatives (e.g., *spatial thinking*). Since a number of researchers in the related fields use terms interchangeably, it is necessary to classify commonly used definitions and terms. Moreover, researchers do not often define specific terms as they relate to our understanding of space and brain behavior. It is crucial, then, that discussions in this field are free of obfuscations with regard to terminology. What is meant by the terms *spatial thinking* or *spatial cognition*? In particular, what are the distinctions between certain aspects of space and geometry that have been commonly associated with the research in the various fields—psychology, geography, architecture, mathematics education—that are devoted to this broad subject area? Some of the most commonly used terms include spatial thinking, spatial cognition, spatial development, spatial perception, spatial representation, spatial relations (relationships), spatial sense, and spatial orientation. Liben argues that the confusion in discussing and analyzing past theories and research on knowledge about space has been caused by "a failure to recognize very fundamental differences in definitions and questions" (1981, 3).

The goal of this chapter is to examine these distinctions as a means of clarifying and defining young children's knowledge of space and geometry in the everyday context. We also examine the distinctions that both psychologists and researchers of other disciplines have made concerning the area of spatial and geometric knowledge. At the very basic level, we have the terms *space, geometry*, and their adjectival forms. One fascinating result when examining the purview of research in the field of spatial cognition has to do with the number of times researchers refer to *space* and *geometry* almost interchangeably. Ironically, these terms have very different meanings and very different origins.

WORD AND PHRASAL HISTORIES RELATING TO SPACE AND GEOMETRY

The English term *space* entered the lexicon some time after the Norman Conquest in 1066 and was shortened from the French version *espace*. Present-day scholars in numerous fields of inquiry refer to space and time as two symbiotically related yet differentiated concepts. In Middle English, the term *space*, however, referred to both time and duration (e.g., "in the space of an hour") on the one hand and area or extension (e.g., "the object occupies this space") on the other. *Space* in terms of the extent of solar systems and galaxies, as well as psychological and geographical content, did not develop until the seventeenth century.

The philosophical perspective of the term *space* today concerns the three-dimensional manifold in which physical objects are situated and how their mutual positions and distances are defined. In more general philosophical terms, DiSalle (1994) defines *space* as an extended manifold in numerous dimensions, and each dimension corresponds to a certain variable magnitude needed to identify a location in the manifold. We might be able to unpack DiSalle's definition by example. One transparent example is the so-called birthday present wrapping paper case. A manifold refers to a surface that, unless ripped or torn, cannot be altered. So, when we refer to the three-dimensional manifold in the everyday context, we can think of birthday present wrapping paper initially spread out on a table. Because of its lack of thickness, the wrapping paper is oftentimes considered in two-dimensional form—that is, its appearance is flat. But it does have thickness and therefore we conclude that everything in our environment is three-dimensional. This is further exemplified when we cover a birthday box with the wrapping paper—which at this point really appears as three-dimensional. A three-dimensional manifold, then, refers to the three-dimensional world in which we live. DiSalle extends this concept to generalize about space in multidimensional terms. We now turn to derivational terms having to do with space.

The *Spatial* in Spatial Thinking

If we were only to consider the adjective *spatial*, an entire system of diverse constellations of associations and meanings seems to surface. Witelson and Swallow (1988) offer a thorough explanation of how we might be able to classify the term. They insist that the term *spatial* seems to be used more often than not casually and at an intuitive level—as if the term were universal or absolute. Nevertheless, they offer three possible interpretations of *spatial* on an empirical or experimental level. First, researchers might use the term to refer to perception as it relates to visual or somesthetic (bodily or physiological sense perception) modalities (Landau, Spelke, and Gleitman 1984). A second way that researchers might refer to the term *spatial* is related to mental or physical manipulation of objects in Euclidean space—space having to do with the way humans see the world within their local environments (e.g., parallel lines, perpendicular lines, circular objects, rectilinear objects, and so forth). A large corpus of literature having to do with this meaning of *spatial* can be found in the literature on search, locative processes, and familiarity with one's environment (Acredolo 1982; Uttal 2000; Wellman, Somerville, and Haake 1979), which is also discussed below. Witelson and Swallow (1988) consider what *spatial* does not refer to and argue that some researchers use the term in a way which demonstrates stark contrast to one's linguistic actions. That is, spatial tasks or abilities are seen as a contrast to those which exhibit linguistic characteristics. Within this context, then, *spatial* has a great deal to do with the representation of symbolic information (Linn and Petersen 1985) and is further characterized by domain specificity (Baenninger and Newcombe 1989; Newcombe and Huttenlocher 2003).

Spatial thinking is an overarching, generalizable term that refers to a myriad of aspects having to do with space, undoubtedly because the terms *spatial* and *thinking* are psychologically indirect to interpretation. For example, *spatial thinking* can refer to the creation of codes or coding procedures for the individual to locate an object (Newcombe and Huttenlocher 2003). It can refer to activities involving search (Wellman 1985; Wellman and Somerville 1982). It is also important to consider what spatial thinking might not refer to. For example, it is not often associated with memory-based brain behavior. But again, this is only an observation from reviewing the research on humans' interaction with space; by no means should it be considered an inoperative factor in the process of spatial thinking.

Gleitman (1995) offers a more perspicuous and clearly organized psychologically-based definition of spatial thinking. He argues that the construct of spatial thinking is a subset of mental imagery, which can be identified in two ways: analogical imagery and symbolic imagery. Another definition is offered by Casati and Varzi (1999), who posit that spatial thinking has to do with the cognitive processes associated with spatial entities. They define spatial entities apart from spatial items (points, lines, planes, etc.) as objects or events that occupy, are located in, or take place in space. Casati and Varzi's definition of spatial thinking is provocative in that it forms a seemingly contrasting alternative to spatial development; the former deals with ephemeral situations involving objects or events in space whereas the latter is concerned primarily with process and stages of progression of spatial phenomena.

In helping early childhood educators define the term and identify the importance of spatial thinking, Clements (1999) argues that the fundamental components of spatial thinking are spatial abilities and spatial sense. But spatial sense, according to Clements, presupposes the development of one's spatial abilities. Two of the more important spatial abilities, Clements states, are spatial orientation, having to do with mapping and navigation skills, and spatial visualization and imagery. A great deal of what we know about the latter spatial ability—spatial visualization and imagery—is described below in our discussions of spatial perception and spatial relations, and to some extent, spatial representation. Spatial representation, however, can have a great deal to do with aspects involving navigation, direction, and location.

Spatial Perception

A one-month-old infant gazes at the numerous rungs of her crib, most likely unable to distinguish between one rung or more than one rung. A four-year-old looks at the sky before twilight and believes that the moon is closer to the earth than the clouds. While driving a car, an adult is deceived because the large pothole appeared black—as if it were filled with asphalt and repaired. One thing that these scenarios have in common is that all three individuals believe that their respective figment events are reality.

So, what implications might arise from these figment events that were perceived as reality? For one, spatial perception generally refers to one's extraction of the local environment on the one hand and one's self on the other. The former is often referred to by philosophers as exteroception and the latter as interoception. The source of spatial perception, as the empirical philosophers would have it, are the external senses. So, for example, sight delivers light, hearing delivers sound, and touch delivers physical makeup of objects. One of the difficulties with spatial perception is one's ability to distinguish between reality and fiction. Philosophers seem to dichotomize spatial perception into two fairly broad categories: fact perception and object perception. Fact perception, unlike object perception, considers the cognitive systems of the mind, such as conceptual understanding, procedural understanding, and memory, whereas object or event perception does not require us to remember the way we see, say, a large object in the road or the chalkboard in the classroom (Dretske 1971).

Spatial Representation

Spatial representation is not described as being a correlate or a subset of the larger domain known as mental representation (described above with spatial thinking). This term refers to the way in which one mentally organizes, describes, or constructs an image, depiction, or account of an object (or objects) in its given place.

Another aspect of higher mental functioning associated with spatial cognition is spatial representation. Hart and Moore (1973) refer to two types of spatial representation: internalized and external cognitive representations of space. Internalized cognitive representations of space, defined by numerous psychologists (Werners 1948; Shemyakin 1962; Piaget and Inhelder 1967; Laurendeau and Pinard 1970), refer to the ways individuals construct space through mental reproduction, that is, by reflecting on spatial attributes through thought without the aid of external objects or symbols. External cognitive representations of space, on the other hand, refer to the ways in which individuals construct models of space. Examples of external spatial (or geometric) representation may include children's drawings, a tenth-grader's written representation of a traversal intersecting two parallel lines, an architect's blueprint, or an experimental psychologist's map of psychophysical phenomena (Ekman, Lindman, and William-Olsson 1961). Liben defines external representations of space as those "in which at least some information about a spatial referent is carried via the spatial arrangement of the elements of the representation itself" (1999, 298).

Spatial Cognition

Like the term *spatial thinking*, *spatial cognition* has also been used in generalized contexts in cognitive and psychological research. As discussed in Kritchevsky (1988), spatial cognition refers to any behavior or activity of an organism that involves space or location with the premise that this behavior is mediated by cerebral functioning. In other words, spatial cognition deals with any characteristic of space—both visual and navigational—so long as the premise of any cognitive attribute of spatial features refer back to the neurological bases of behavior.

Each branch of research in these areas has its own position on the definition or description of an exhaustive or comprehensive concept of spatial
knowledge. In the crossroads of psychology and geography, Hart and
Moore (1973) have reviewed the literature on space by focusing on spatial
cognition as the all-encompassing domain. They define spatial cognition as
"the knowledge and internal or cognitive representation of the structure,
entities, and relations of space" or "the internalized reflection and reconstruction of space in thought" (248).

Further, Hart and Moore posit that spatial cognition encompasses all the
modes of an individual's knowledge of the subject of space—namely, perception, thinking, reasoning, and judgment. At the same time, however,
they argue that all these sub-areas interact with each other and may influence spatial cognition. Cognitive structures, according to Hart and Moore,
"influence perceptual selectivity which leads to a reconstruction of the
world through selected fields of attention" (1973, 250). Regarding the
reciprocating relationship between spatial perception and cognition, they
conclude, "Perception is thus both a subsystem of cognition and a function
of cognition" (250).

In addition, Hart and Moore (1973) suggest that spatial cognition
encompasses other modes of spatial knowledge as well. This assertion is
based on a connection they have made between Piaget's figurative and
operative distinction—two aspects of how individuals know the world. The
figurative form deals with percepts based on fleeting, perceptual configurations of pictures and images that individuals create upon direct contact,
whereas the operative concerns the ways in which individuals transform or
operate on two or more successive states into reconstructed patterns or
arrangements. Hart and Moore associate the figurative knowledge with spatial or visual perception, while operative knowledge is associated with
spatial cognition, or intelligence. In other words, they argue that spatial
cognition includes all the various attributes of spatial (or geometric)
knowledge—namely, perceiving (perception), thinking, imaging, reasoning, judging, remembering (memory), representing (representation), orienting (orientation), relating or associating (relations), and so forth.

Spatial Development

Spatial development is also a somewhat generic term often defined as the
process and unfolding of an individual's intellectual capabilities of space.
In the fields of psychology and education, we might generally refer to the
development of spatial thinking, the unfolding of biological and mental
processes connected with spatial thinking over time. In addition, when the
construct of *development* is included, we might infer the existence of periods,

or stages, of increasing (or, sometimes, decreasing) levels of ability over the course of a certain time period or duration.

We can appreciate the notion of spatial development through the work of Piaget and Inhelder (1956/1967) and their development of the topological primacy thesis, which will be discussed in much greater detail in the next chapter. Nevertheless, spatial development in Piagetian terms defines early spatial thinking of infants and young children as topological; that is, the way they construct spatial entities exhibits plasticity in the way they think about and describe the shape and disposition of objects in their immediate surroundings; that is, young children see geometric figures, whether two-dimensional or three-dimensional, as dynamic entities, not as static ideas that one finds in elementary and secondary school textbooks. So, for a three-year-old child, an object in the shape of a sphere has more in common with a brick than it does with a circular plate or Frisbee because the physical dispositions of three dimensions of the sphere and the brick are perceived differently from the two-dimensional characteristics of the latter two objects. It is not until the child reaches what Piaget refers to as concrete-operational thinking that she will identify spherical objects with circles or curvilinear and rectilinear objects with rectilinear figures.

There have been numerous critiques of Piaget's thesis to this day (discussed in detail in the next chapter). In the present text, we have found that young four- and five-year-old children do not necessarily provide topological explanations and descriptions of objects in the everyday context. Most of their verbal explanations seem to profoundly exhibit Euclidean qualities (see chapter 4).

Spatial Sense

Researchers in mathematics education talk about spatial sense. Such terminology seems to be associated with the idea of what children need to know in order to succeed in their spatial and geometric knowledge abilities. Clements (1999) argues that having spatial abilities (including spatial orientation and spatial visualization) presupposes spatial sense.

The term *spatial sense* can unfortunately be construed as a subjective term that cannot be identified or measured in any empirical or quantifiable manner. *Spatial sense* is often used with regard to what the common individual needs to know about space in order to function in everyday life. Due to this meaning of the term, a number of problems arise when using it. First, what does it really mean for one to have spatial sense? The very term implies a sense of cultural neutrality—that is, all individuals, irrespective of their cultural and social upbringing, should have a way of thinking about space that is not culturally bound. Second, by its semantic associations, *spatial sense* also can imply a way of experiencing the world in the same way that John

Locke argued for a philosophy of knowledge—that is, empirically, through the sense organs. If this were the case, then humans would have developed a sense for space in the same manner in which they possess senses for tactile, visual, olfactory, auditory, and taste behaviors. But *spatial sense* defined in this manner would be redundant if we use the same phenomena for spatial sense as we would for the visual sense.

This term is very much connected with the field of education; mathematics educators and early childhood researchers and practitioners use this term frequently, often without definition. In fact, one of the egregious problems in education today is the lack of definitive terminology in the discipline. We have a difficult enough time with psychologically indirect terms such as *spatial cognition*; the term *spatial sense* makes the field all the more obscure. But if we really consider the notion, why would anyone disagree with the idea that a child or student should have spatial sense?

The notion of reasoning about space and geometry has also been an important area of interest in research. It seems that for most researchers, particularly those involved in mathematics and mathematics-related subdisciplines, spatial thinking engenders geometric thinking because geometry deals with a certain understanding and awareness of space and spatial surroundings (Clements and Battista 1992; Clements 1999). The research of Clements and Battista in particular has focused not only on the relationship between these two domains, but also on how children develop reasoning skills and how these skills develop in school.

It is very important to distinguish between spatial *sense* as it relates to non-cognitive associations with brain behavior and spatial *thinking*, which is entirely dependent on the study of human cognitive abilities. The former seems to be very much connected with human memory, while the latter has more to do with cognitive ability and does not rely on memory alone.

Spatial Relations (or Relationships)

Spatial relations (or relationships) is yet another term used in the literature. Spatial relations cannot exist with one object alone; indeed, there must be a second object to which one can compare the first. Yakimanskaya defines spatial relations as the closeness "between objects in space or between the spatial attributes of these objects . . . [that] reflect such concepts as direction, distance, relative comparison, location, the dimensions of objects in space, and so forth" (1991, 17).

Spatial Orientation

Distinctions have also been made with the concept of spatial (and geometric) orientation and other forms of spatial knowledge. Spatial orientation is not as broad as spatial thinking or spatial cognition, as Hart and Moore (1973) suggest. More specifically, it refers to the manner in which location is determined within one's immediate environment. Clements defines *spatial orientation* as "understanding and operating on relationships between different positions in space, especially with respect to your own position" (1999, 72). Spatial orientation also involves navigational abilities as well. That is, when we orient ourselves from one place to another, we need to consider factors of location of place (topos) and direction from one location to another. This ability in orienteering, then, is very much related to the construct of spatial orientation.

As discussed by Shemyakin (1962), Howard and Templeton (1966), and Yakimanskaya (1991), spatial orientation presupposes the use of frames of reference and their relationship to the environment. Unlike the broad terms of spatial thinking or cognition, spatial (or geographic) orientation specifically calls for the individual's construction of either mental images or physical representations that are specifically related to his environment and that utilize frames of reference.

Geometry

The word *geometry* entered the English lexicon from Old French, which is derived from the Latin *geometria*. The Greek form of the word is *geometrein*, which means "to measure land." The root *geo* refers to "earth," and the affix *metron* means "measure." It is not too surprising, then, that the original goals of early geometers—people whose expertise is geometry—in classical Greek times was to identify, through calculation and scientific inquiry, the disposition and measurement of the earth's surface as well as other tellurian features.

Summary

Clearly, topics related to space abound and take many shapes and forms. As Liben (2002) suggests (and as we have suggested in the introduction to this text), it would be next to impossible to write a book or present a discussion on all aspects of space in terms of the ways in which we use it, live in it, and think it. Liben provides the following selection of additional topics related to space and thinking: neurological implications of spatial thinking; spatial thinking and vision; spatial illusions as they relate to the study of experimental psychology; the notions of horizontality, verticality, and diagonality; language and space; spatial thinking with regard to search skills; spatial thinking in terms of cultural boundedness; cognitive transfer and spatial development; and educational issues related to spatial thinking, which is this book's primary focus.

PHILOSOPHICAL FOUNDATIONS
OF SPATIAL DEVELOPMENT

Psychological investigations of any intellectual or behavioral domain emanate from philosophical inquiry. The debate on how humans deal with
space (and time) in their physical world has been discussed since early
Egypt and Greece.[1] Some of the key developments in spatial thought led to
the seminal ideas of the late eighteenth and early nineteenth century, which
spawned the key elements of spatial thinking as it relates to cognitive development.

The Classical Philosophers

It is difficult to pin down the earliest writings on the topic of space. A
good deal of twentieth-century writings focus on Greek origins; however,
this position has been hotly debated, due to the strong possibilities that
Greek primary sources emanated from other areas (possibly Africa or Per-
sia) and that some of the individuals like Pythagoras or Euclid may not
necessarily be of Greek origin. For example, there now seems to be strong
evidence that the coordinate system in the two-dimensional plane emanated from Egypt, well before the peak of Greek civilization in the tenth to
seventh centuries BC. It is evident from primary sources that nearly forty-
six hundred years ago (approximately 2550 BC), Egyptian civilization
developed towns and villages based on the grid system. Jammer (1954)
indicates that the Egyptians introduced the term *hesp* as a description of a
district based on a grid, or rectilinear pattern of thoroughfares. This form of
city planning, by its very nature, serves as a real-life version of the two-
dimensional coordinate system. Approximately two thousand years ago, a
planned grid pattern in Teotihuacán, Mexico, approximately forty kilometers northeast of Mexico City, was an example of a large-scale grid in the
Americas (Coe and Koontz 2002). But the coordinate system in two dimensions does not emerge in either Greek writings or oral histories. This might
have to do with the topographical conditions of cities and villages in Greece
and its neighboring, contiguous regions, and islands that were planned in
an irregular (non-grid) manner.

Pythagoras

The importance of space in our understanding of the world is evident in
one of the earliest examples of the association between mathematics and
how the world works—the pre-Socratic philosopher Pythagoras and his followers. Although shrouded in mystery, Pythagoras is one of the earliest
figures in the history of knowledge. He and his sect flourished circa 570 BC.

Pythagoras's central assertion about how and why the world operates is that there is an inextricable association between mathematics (along with harmony) and the world. Pythagoras and his followers placed a good deal of emphasis on the first four positive integers. In Greek, they are referred to as the Tetraktys: one, two, three, and four. One is a point; that is, the abstract character of the number one is the basis upon which there can be a point. The number two constitutes the basis upon which there can be a line. The Pythagoreans continue with three, and say that three constitutes the abstract primordium of the plane. Lastly, the number four constitutes the abstract foundation of the solid of the tetrahedron, which always had a special place in the teaching of Pythagoras. He emphasizes the importance of the number ten, which is the sum of the first four positive integers ($1 + 2 + 3 + 4 = 10$). So here is a very early example of space and geometry in the corpus of philosophical examination and introspection.

Pythagoras is perhaps best known for another important geometric discovery, namely the famous theorem which is named after him: $a^2 + b^2 = c^2$ (or, a-squared plus b-squared equals c-squared). When we are told that a right angle triangle contains 180 degrees (like all triangles) and one of those angles is 90 degrees, how do we know that? To begin with, one might take out some sort of measuring instrument, draw a right angle triangle with it, and make certain that there are two acute angles and that one angle is 90 degrees. The problem is that one can never achieve this task. The individual might be fooled into thinking that it can be done, but if the measuring instruments are crude enough, one will be satisfied that the right angle triangle is completed. However, the more precise the measuring instrument, the more obvious it becomes that there is not a 90 degree angle. The point that Pythagoras shows us here is that there always was, always is, and always will be right angle triangles in the abstract sense, but we can never achieve them in the practical sense through the use of measuring and writing instruments or any form of technology. This is evidence of space as an a priori phenomenon—space, as it relates to mathematics, defines our world, lives our world, and will be around after the world. So, Immanuel Kant's contention of space as an a priori phenomenon (discussed below) certainly has its precedents in the ideas of Pythagoras.

Plato

Plato's conception of space appears in the dialogue *Timaeus*, in which he elucidates on the spatial and geometric "dispositions" of the so-called four elements and expands on prior discussions that took place in the pre-Socratic Pythagorean school. For earth, Plato assigns the spatial structure of a cube. Plato assigns a pyramid to fire, an octahedron to air, and an icosahedron to water. For Plato, it seems that ideas about space and geometry were intimately related to physical properties.

Aristotle

Aristotle's conception of space, in contrast to his predecessor's, does not associate geometric figures with the four elements. To begin with, Aristotle does not think of space as an empty region. Rather, space is considered in direct relationship to objects. That is, objects have positions or places (topoi) in a spatial region. This point is elaborated to a great extent in his *Physics*, where he consistently refers to place as the definitive characteristic of spatial structure. Aristotle discusses his views on space in one additional book, *Categories*, in which he refers to space as a quantity. The construct of quantity, Aristotle says, is made up of two types: continuous quantity and discrete quantity. The notion of space is within the domain of continuous quantity. In reference to Aristotle's definition, "'Space' here is conceived as the sum total of all places occupied by bodies, and 'place' (topos), conversely, is conceived as that part of space whose limits coincide with the limits of the occupying body" (See Jammer 1954, 17). Space, then, refers to the boundary of an object, which is defined in terms of place. In sum, space for Aristotle was not synonymous with a void, a vacuum, or emptiness. Aristotle's philosophy of knowledge in terms of space fell into question, however, as physical characteristics of elements and related phenomena needed to be redefined.

Renaissance and Post-Renaissance Philosophers

The problem or definition of spatial cognition and geometrical thinking has been a preoccupation for several centuries. One of the predominant controversies had to do with whether the concept of space was based on innate, universal characteristics or on an individual's experience and learning. Rene Descartes argues that the construct of space is an ideal that is "given" innately to the child without prior experience. George Berkeley, on the other hand, takes the empiricist stance and argues that space is not an ideal but a concept experienced in reality through sensation. In short, the question was whether space is an ideal, an innate feature inherent in all human beings, or based on the child's experiences and sensations of reality.

John Locke

Locke's version of space runs counter to both Descartes' and Berkeley's positions. Perhaps the most illustrative account of Locke's position on spatial thinking was his correspondence with the Irish scientist and lawyer, William Molyneaux. In fact, Locke inserts Molyneaux's well-known question in the text of his *Essay Concerning Human Understanding* (1694). Molyneaux's question, cited verbatim by Locke, states:

Suppose a Man born blind, and now adult, and taught by his touch to distinguish a Cube, and a Sphere of the same metal, and nighly of the same bigness, so as to tell, when he felt one and t'other, which is the Cube, which the Sphere. Suppose then the Cube and Sphere placed on a Table, and the Blind Man to be made to see. Quære, Whether by his sight, before he touch'd them, he could now distinguish, and tell, which is the Globe, which the Cube (144).

As illustrated in Locke's account of the problem, Molyneaux is asking whether a person who was born blind and subsequently acquired sight would be able to recognize visually what he had long learned how to recognize tactually. For example, a blind person who can feel around the edges of objects and always be able to recognize it as a square, rectangle, or circle now has some cataract removed that was present at birth. Would this person be able to *look* at objects in the external world and identify them as squares, triangles, and the like? To answer this question, Locke uses the notion of color instead of geometric figures and argues that the individual would have no ability to distinguish one color from another. If we extend this contention, Locke would argue that the once blind person would be unable to distinguish between shapes.

Locke is clearly investigating the human mind analogous to the way that Newton looked at science. Newton, with the influence of Sir Francis Bacon's *Novum Organum*, developed a corpuscular and atomistic view of science that was virtually incomparable to this point in world history. Locke essentially committed himself to a Newtonian approach to the study of mind: he studied human knowledge by focusing on the most elementary units of mental life—sensations. For Locke, knowing anything is based entirely on sensation. Our understanding of objects in the real world is based on mere copies of those objects. That is, our interaction with the world is based entirely on how our senses interact with those objects. Locke's position on the mind and knowledge influenced numerous thinkers after him, especially the eighteenth-century philosopher David Hume.

David Hume

Well known for his skeptical view of the way in which humans act and behave in the external world, Hume was primarily influential with his debate concerning causation. Hume only tangentially discusses space as a subject of knowledge and intellect in reference to the concept of causation as simply the constant conjunction of two things or events in terms of space or time. His treatises place a great deal of emphasis on one's knowledge or understanding of objects or things in the external world. For Hume, an external object that one can see, touch, smell, or hear is only a copy of the actual disposition of the substance or substances that the object is made of. Essentially, the mind makes copies of images perceived from the senses. In sum, Hume's treatises expand on the empiricist traditions of Locke and include problems of causation. We briefly allude to Hume's treatises because they incited the interest of Thomas Reid, whose philosophical arguments included the human's conception of space as a direct subject of the intellect.

Thomas Reid

That Locke and his successors identified human knowledge of objects in the external world as copies of the real entities is no digression in the discussion on the manner in which humans think about space. The reason has to do with a fairly obscure critique of Hume's skeptical argument on causation: Thomas Reid's *An Inquiry into the Human Mind*, originally published in 1764. A Presbyterian minister from Scotland, Thomas Reid not only critiqued the empiricist position on knowledge—Lockean and Humean perspectives on the human mind—but also was the first individual to identify some of the basic tenets of non-Euclidean geometry almost a century before Georg Friedrich Bernhard Riemann. One part of Reid's *An Inquiry into the Human Mind* in particular, the "Geometry of Visibles," sheds light on this most impressive contribution to human knowledge about space and spatial thinking. In Principle No. 1 of the "Geometry of Visibles," Reid states:

> Supposing the eye placed in the center of a sphere, every great circle of the sphere will have the same appearance to the eye as if it was a straight line. For the curvature of the circle being turned directly toward the eye, is not perceived by it. And for the same reason, any line which is drawn in the plane of a great circle of the sphere, whether it be in reality straight or curve, will appear straight to the eye (103).

Reid provides a clear-cut example of how the external world impresses itself on the senses. As the bottom of the eye is itself curved, then any projection from the external world is going to take on that curvature except in the very small portion of the eye. If it is so small, there will be very little discrepancy between a curved triangle and a rectilinear triangle. Now suppose a right-angle triangle is drawn on a piece of paper. What is it that you see? Instead of seeing it as the curvilinear projection that would take place optically, you see the triangle as a tangible triangle, a rectilinear triangle. It has none of the spherical geometric projective properties that one would expect if the mind were simply making a copy of whatever is taking place at the bottom of the eye (see figures 1.1 and 1.2).

Reid argues that when the external world impinges on the sense organs, it sets up an activity. This physiological activity constitutes a kind of natural sign system. The external world creates natural consequences in our sensory

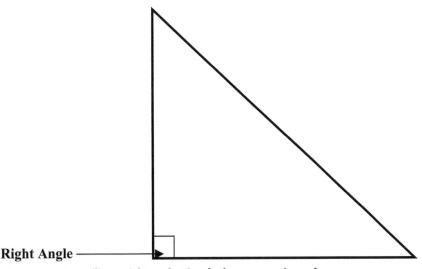

Figure 1.1. A rectilinear right-angle triangle drawn on a piece of paper

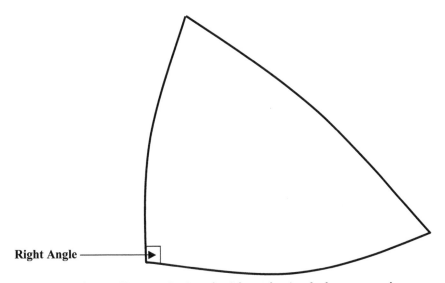

Figure 1.2. The curvilinear projection of a right-angle triangle drawn on a sphere

biology. According to Reid, the mind, "by a way we do not understand," is able to go from these physiological signs to the things signified. He came too early to know that the physiological events envisioned are initially biochemical—that is, first, there are changes in the pigment chemistry of the retinal receptors; as a result of these biochemical changes, patterns of electrical activity are set up in the optical nerve fibers; these signals are then sent back into the brain, so that the whole set of events is played out at the level of neuro-electric processing. Of course, we see trains, buses, and buildings, but we do not see neuro-electric events. In other words, we skip over them; we move from the physiological sign of events in the external world—the right-angle triangle that we might draw—to what is signified by those signs—the right-angle triangle in our mind.

Reid posits that whatever it is that one is talking about, there is a perfect fitness and aptness between the constitutive principles of our biology and the demands the external world places on us. If we only knew what the mind is possessed of when it makes copies of what is in the sense organs, we could not get from point A to point B. We would be doubtful about there even being an external world. Reid argues that there is an external world and our senses do not merely make copies of objects that we then generate when we think about anything.

So, Reid rejects Hume's (and others') so-called copy theory—that the mind somehow makes copies of what is taking place with regard to images. The only sense modality in which one can discuss these copies is the modality of vision. No one can make a copy of an odor, a sound, a taste, or a texture. Thus, if the "Geometry of Visibles" demonstrates that the ideal theory does not work in vision, it certainly cannot work with the other senses. As stated above, Reid not only paves the way for our increased understanding of the spatial characteristics of our world, but he also re-examines the way we think of abstract geometry through his critique of Hume's "An Enquiry Concerning Human Understanding," particularly regarding the role that the senses play in our understanding of the world.

Kant and Nineteenth-Century Positions of the Kantian Perspective

Unlike earlier and contemporary philosophical arguments, Immanuel Kant feels that the concept of space is neither innate for the individual nor is it a concept developed empirically through sensation. Instead, Kant believes that space is constructed by human beings through experience and exposure to phenomena surrounding them. For Kant, phenomena are based on experience; yet at the same time, he considers the form or origin of these phenomena as a priori foundations of sensory perceptions. For Kant, these foundations are space and time. In Kant's words,

> it follows that, with respect to space, an intuition a priori, which is not empirical, must form the foundation of all conceptions of space. In the same manner all geometric principles . . . are never to be derived from the general concepts of side and triangle, but from an intuition, and that a priori, with apodictic certainty. (1781/1902, 40)

Space, then, is a self-evident truth, based on pure intuition, forming the foundation of external intuitions. Examples of external intuitions, according to Kant, are principles of geometry, which can only be derived from space. As Kant argues, if space were an intuition that was determined a posteriori, the initial principles of geometry, or mathematics in general, would be based almost entirely on one's perceptions rather than definitions. Using Kant's example of the definition of a line, two points being the determining elements of a line would no longer be a necessity but only something taught in each case by experience. Kant's philosophical approach, then, differs radically from Hume's in that the latter emphasizes the laws of association as a sine qua non in any psychological state and either outright rejects or ignores the necessary conditions of space and time as functions of human understanding.

Ernst Cassirer (1944, 1953–1957), a dedicated follower of Kantian philosophy, identifies three forms of spatial experiences: organic-active or sensorimotor space, perceptual space, and abstract-symbolic-contemplative space. These forms of spatial experience are characteristic of both the animal and human kingdoms. Organic-active or sensorimotor space is the form that ranks lowest in order. According to Cassirer, it is characteristic of the animal kingdom as well as human infants and deals with space concretely, bereft of abstraction or differentiation. Perceptual space, the next spatial form in Cassirer's hierarchical classification, has to do with the ways in which the visual, auditory, tactile, vestibular, and kinesthetic senses are used as a means of interpreting or thinking about space of objects. It nevertheless still requires the need for a concrete referent. According to Cassirer, and Werner who followed him, abstract-symbolic-contemplative space, the third and highest form, is the level of spatial thought that differentiates humans from animals. It is the ability that only humans possess to think of space in an abstract manner, without a concrete referent and from multiple perspectives.

Perhaps the most vehement critic of the Kantian and the so-called rationalist approach to both intuitive and physical space was the physiologist and physicist Hermann von Helmholtz, whose work earned him great acclaim in the early years of psychology.[2] Helmholtz argues that human knowledge of three-dimensional space and geometrical structures is not associated with innate physiological systems. Rather, Helmholtz posits, human knowledge of space is based almost exclusively on inferential grounds and the accumulation of experience. Helmholtz further derides Kant's argument that Euclidean geometry is exclusively based on a priori precepts of intuition by asserting the proposition that one can have visually experiential knowledge of non-Euclidean space. Helmholtz's argument serves as a springboard for arguments in mathematics (e.g., Jules Henri

Poincaré) and the implementation of non-Euclidean geometries in physics (e.g., Albert Einstein).

Contemporary Philosophical Discussions of Space

Most current philosophical perspectives on spatial notions of the world emanate from the literature in psychology, perhaps because psychology itself offers a vast repertoire of knowledge that is connected with philosophy and closely associated with the subject of knowledge—that is, how we get to know anything.

Possibly one of the most exhaustive accounts of space as apart from other physical and intellectual concepts—such as time and existence—is Casati and Varzi's philosophical position (1999) on the structures of spatial representations. We introduce their work to elaborate on contemporary philosophical perspectives of space and spatial structures. We do not, however, discuss their theoretical position in detail because it requires a large technical lexicon that is well beyond the scope of this book.

For Casati and Varzi, the subject of space is intrinsically associated with two areas of study: topology and mereology. Topology is traditionally a subdiscipline of mathematics, particularly the areas of geometry and analysis; like most mathematical subdisciplines, it is difficult to define briefly. Casati and Varzi refer to topology as the study of spatial continuity and compactness. But in a more general sense, topological properties are determined by comparing two (or more) figures. For example, one might say that a cube, disk, and a sphere are topologically related because each geometric figure is not cut or torn; in other words, there are no holes in these figures. On the other hand, these figures are topologically different from a torus—in everyday terms, a figure in the shape of a doughnut. We can also show topological relationships in a way that follows Alfred North Whitehead's model (1919): We say that two entities A and B are connected to each other if there is a third entity, C, which lies entirely within A and B. If C does not lie entirely within A and B, then A and B are not connected. Of course, C itself must be self-connected (see figure 1.3). Connectivity, then, is an important feature of topology because it involves continuity—that is, A and B are continuous if there is an entity, C, which lies entirely within A and B and is therefore connected.

Mereology, Casati and Varzi state, is the study of part-whole relations. Using a concrete example, we can provide the following statements:

- The living room is part of the house. The space taken up by the living room makes up part of the space taken up by the house.
- The rug covers the floor of the living room, and the living room is part of the house. We can then say that the rug is in the house.

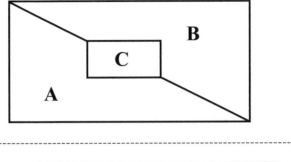

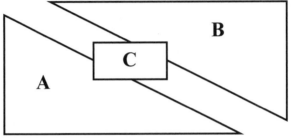

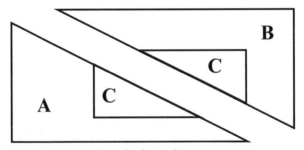

Figure 1.3. Connectivity and topological relationship

- Only part of the rug is in the living room, and it follows that the rug is partly in the living room (and partly somewhere else, possibly the dining room). The rug, however, is entirely within the house. (1999, 9–10)

Casati and Varzi argue that spatial entities in general are organized in a mereological manner. If two regions overlap or there is some kind of spatial intersection, then we say that the regions share parts. In other words, there is a part (or parts) in common with two or more regions. In figure 1.3, if regions A and B shared region C, then we can argue that region C is the region in common with both A and B. As Casati and Varzi posit, "to uncover the spatial structure of an object (or at least a good approximation of it), look at its mereological structure. More generally, use the concepts and principles of mereology as concepts and principles for the theory of spatial representation" (1999, 10).

The two areas of mereology and topology seem symbiotically related. Casati and Varzi refer to the interrelationships between these areas as a *mereotopology*. Their basic argument is that in order to study spatial structures and relationships between objects, it is necessary to analyze the interplay between part-whole relations (mereology) and spatial continuity (topology). This mereotopological approach is the basis of their theory of the representation of spatial entities. From this framework, one can study the differences between spatial entities in the form of material objects versus events or even ideas and concepts. From a philosophical standpoint, mereotopology seems to be an essential and foundational centerpiece concerning the study of space and geometry.

PSYCHOLOGICAL DEFINITIONS IN THE EXPERIMENTAL AND COGNITIVE DOMAINS

The fields of experimental and social psychology have also dealt a great deal with the issues of spatial and geometric abilities. The Russian psychologist Yakimanskaya (1991) refers to the term *space* as having two meanings: actual space, or space that can be "seen" in the sense of usable space, and abstract, mathematical space, or the space created from an individual's mental constructs. Other psychologists have expanded on this definition.

Miller (1998) also distinguishes between two types of space: perceptual space and conceptual space. Perceptual space, according to Miller, has to do with the mental schemata associated with an individual's senses—visual, auditory, olfactory, and tactile. It concerns our everyday manipulation of objects and all our movements. Conceptual space, on the other hand, deals with our understanding of the existence of spatial phenomena beyond our senses. So, as Miller contends, the individual knows that on the other side of a wall there are familiar objects that cannot be seen or touched. Similarly, we are familiar with the city in which we live, which we know is situated somewhere on a continent. Conceptual space involves the individual's interpretation of spatial ideas that cannot be seen or felt (as in perceptual space). These spatial ideas are interpreted through particular representations, such as maps, pictures, or even ideas or mental constructions that may not necessarily be translated into symbolic form.

One of the loci classici on perception is Hochberg's book (1964) on the subject. As it relates to the present study, Hochberg demonstrates how perception, through visual stimuli, develops in terms of an individual's spatial and geometric cognition. For Hochberg, the perception of shape is more than merely observed shapes that an individual has experienced or learned. Instead, Hochberg posits that a shape is simply "the sum of the sensations of points of color and shade at a particular set of positions" (1964, 58). This position seems to run counter to developmental theory, which suggests that the development of spatial perception and shape is based on recognition of shape due to past experience.

In another study, Hochberg (1995) examined the meaning of two-dimensional pictures and their relationship to shape. His argument is as follows: The perception of objects that exist in the real world does not necessarily derive from one's perception of their three-dimensional form. At the same time, depth cues, which are pictorial pieces of information about depth, are not necessary for one's recognition of three-dimensional objects in two-dimensional pictures. Hochberg uses an analogy of perception with language to describe the act of recognition of shape:

> To discuss pictures in terms of their stimulus properties alone, or in terms of naming responses, is like an attempt to account for reading in terms only of what word is specified in some dictionary by some set of letters. Because where one looks and what one takes into account is both elective and selective, and depends on what one seeks from that glance, no useful account of perception can be offered in terms of stimulus characteristics alone. (1995, 134–35)

This passage ties back to Hochberg's earlier argument—namely, that one does not need training or depth information in order to recognize two-dimensional representations.

The idea of depth cues, then, is not a critical factor when one perceives objects either as pictures or as real-world phenomena. As an example, a child does not need any pictorial training for recognizing any two-dimensional representation of an object or shape (e.g., car, shoe, keys). In sum, Hochberg's dicta seem to support the notion that shape recognition or identification is not a learned phenomenon, but one merely related to sensation of points of color and shade as well as its positioning. Again, this view seems to counter the Piagetian topological primacy thesis, which maintains that humans, who construct perceptual space as early as infancy through direct contact with objects, develop meanings of shape and size through experience and learning (Hochberg 1988, 1994).

Some psychologists make the distinction between psychological space and physical space. O'Keefe and Nadel (1978) argue that for the psychologist and physiologist, psychological space is the subject of interest, while for the physicist, physical space is the subject of interest. They define psychological space as "any space which is attributed to the mind . . . and which would not exist if mind did not exist. . . . In contrast, physical space is any space attributed to the external world independent of the existence of minds" (1978, 6–7).

Liben (1981), however, argues that the distinction between physical and psychological space should be made with caution. For Liben, the two types of space form a symbiotic relationship. On the one hand, physical space is important for psychologists who believe that an individual's psychological space is learned directly from physical space. Yet, at the same time, physical space cannot be learned or measured independent of one's mental construction of it.

Some distinctions concerning the definitions of particular areas of spatial and geometric knowledge have been considered. As it stands, few researchers or theorists have attempted to define or categorize these areas in any great depth. Werner (1948) and his colleagues (Wapner and Werner 1957) posit that spatial perception is subordinate to spatial cognition, yet at the same time, it is one of its functions, so both are reciprocating processes. Piaget and Inhelder's (1956/1967) position on this issue is similar to that of Werner. They argue that spatial perception is figurative in that it refers to the images created upon direct contact with the world, while spatial cognition is based on the operative mode, referring to the individual's transformation of the world into specific patterns or schemas.

Crossroads of Psychology and Anthropology

The field of anthropology, too, is by no means lacking of research on spatial or geometric thinking. Pinxten, an anthropologist whose work is greatly influenced by research in cognition and developmental psychology, has written extensively on the subject of spatial perception and representation and its role in the field of education. In contrast to the description of spatial structures by many psychologists, he considers varying frames of reference (Pinxten, van Dooren, and Harvey 1983). In his Universal Frames of Reference (UFOR) model, Pinxten identifies three types of space in semantic representation: physical space; socio-geographical space; and cosmological space.

Physical space deals with all the characteristics of spatial phenomena that confront individuals in their immediate environment. This type of space also concerns objects within the child's immediate environment that can be manipulated in some way. A child, for example, manipulating wooden play blocks would clearly fall in the domain of physical space.

In contrast, socio-geographical space has to do with specific characteristics relating to the human's interaction with objects or aspects of space that are larger in magnitude than the objects found in physical space. Individuals cannot manipulate these objects; instead, they confront or enter this space. Socio-geographic space is locative in form, involving one's relative position, as in entering another room of a house or crossing the border of two states or countries.

The components of cosmological space—Pinxten's third type—are even larger than the second spatial form. Phenomena in cosmological space include celestial bodies, such as the sun, moon, planets, and stars. Human "contact" with this type only includes observation at a distance.

Cultural Differences in Spatial and Geometric Thinking

Studies on cultural differences in spatial (and geometric, to some extent) thinking are not new. In fact, Werner (1948) describes Sir Francis Galton's amazement in learning of an Eskimo who, after traveling on a single occasion nearly sixty-five hundred miles on kayak along a shoreline, was able to produce a map that was in virtual agreement with an admiralty chart printed in 1870. Studies on cultural variation of intelligence flourished in the early and middle twentieth century, particularly in the fields of anthropology and psychology. Berry (1971) contends that certain cultures, particularly those whose members survive through hunting and gathering, are much more adept at spatial reasoning than other groups, like agricultural societies, and outperform other groups on visual-spatial tests. In studying the abilities of native North Americans, the Inuit in particular, McShane and Berry (1988) claim that the spatial intelligence of the Inuit is especially strong due to the nature of their lifestyle—namely, they must travel long distances for the purposes of hunting and gathering and must remember specific landmarks as a means of keeping track of their direction. A related study conducted by Norman (1980) shows that, with the administration of a Piagetian map-drawing task, Appalachian children scored higher than urban and suburban children in three out of four tests on spatial concepts.

Mitchelmore (1976, 1980) concurs with Berry, arguing that most native North Americans are more, or at least equally as, adept in spatial reasoning when compared to Europeans of the same age and surpass nearly all school-attending individuals of most African societies in spatial reasoning abilities. In his discussion, Mitchelmore attributes a particular culture's superiority or inferiority in spatial reasoning to social, cultural, and environmental factors.

When examining the works of cross-cultural psychologists or anthropologists who study spatial abilities of individuals belonging to non-Western societies, it is important to consider the gauge in which they measure spatial "superiority" or "inferiority." Like most standardized testing procedures, those used to measure spatial abilities of members of cultures may fail to capture accurate cognitive behaviors or understanding of particular concepts. Furthermore, Pinxten, van Dooren, and Harvey (1983) argue that the fundamental problem with nearly all cross-cultural studies on spatial thinking is that they fail to consider culturally specific notions and philosophies regarding space. As mentioned earlier, Pinxten posits that the Western conception of space may not adequately serve the purposes of non-Western societies. Thus, it would be in the best interest of the culture to identify the relevance of spatial thinking and how it is used in that very culture as a means of improving the education (and living conditions) of its members.

A related yet contrasting point of view on the development of the history of geometric and spatial thinking concerns the research conducted by Gerdes (1995, 1999), an anthropologist and mathematician. For Gerdes, geometric constructions, like any mathematical construction, are culturally bound phenomena. More specifically, he discusses how an understanding of the so-called Pythagorean theorem had been prevalent in Mozambican society prior to colonization. Gerdes provides a method in which he and his colleagues uncover unique geometric and spatial insight of individual Mozambican artisans and merchants. This method requires intensive observation of the participants involved and is one perspective useful for interpreting the constructions produced by preschool children during free play. As Gerdes describes it

> We looked to the geometric forms and patterns of traditional objects like baskets, mats, pots, houses, fish traps, etc. and posed the question: Why do these material products possess the form they have? In order to answer this question, we learned the usual production techniques and tried to vary the forms. It came out that the form of these objects is almost never arbitrary, but generally represents many practical advantages and is, quite a lot of times, the only possible or optimal solution of a production problem. The traditional form reflects accumulated experience and wisdom. It constitutes . . . mathematical knowledge, knowledge about the properties and relations of circles, angles, rectangles, squares, regular pentagons and hexagons, cones, pyramids, cylinders, etc. (1995, 34).

The important idea here is how Gerdes and his colleagues have broadened the meaning of mathematical knowledge. As D'Ambrosio (1984, 1985) would argue, in order to understand how a culture uses mathematics, it is necessary that we, the individuals studying mathematical knowledge, broaden our conception of the meaning of mathematics.

Brain Functioning and Spatial Thinking

From the mid-nineteenth to the mid-twentieth century, research on hemisphericity concluded that the loss of the left hemisphere was more damaging with regard to intellectual development than loss of the right hemisphere. Researchers at the time believed that the left hemisphere controlled one's verbal ability and that losing access to the right hemisphere was not as crucial. It was not until the late 1960s and early 1970s that research shed light on the importance of the right hemisphere, especially in terms of its significance in one's spatial and geometric competencies. Based on much of the research of psychologists like Luria (1966, 1970) and Milner (1974), evidence seemed to mount showing that damage to the right hemisphere contributed to deficits in one's ability to discern various spatial relationships. During the 1970s, it became ever-increasingly clear that the left hemisphere controlled verbal behavior while the right controlled one's spatial abilities.

Mapping and Searching

Research on mapping and searching from the perspective of location and direction represents another field that has been examined in the space and geometry literature. We know a great deal about the role of navigation and location in the intellectual development of the young child (Blaut and Stea 1974; Downs 1981; Liben 2001). Blaut and Stea's results (1974) indicate that children as young as three are capable of producing maps when given miniature trees, houses, and cars. Huttenlocher and Newcombe (1984), however, argue that although young children are capable of having some knowledge about maps, they will make mistakes if maps lack specific landmarks.

Research on spatial cognition also has addressed issues relating to young children's understanding of maps and their local environments as well (Cohen and Schuepfer 1980; Downs 1981; Downs and Liben 1987; Downs and Stea 1973; Hart 1981; Liben 1981, 1988; Liben and Downs 1989, 1991, 2001; Presson 1982a, 1982b). In agreement with Blaut and Stea, Liben and Downs (2001) conclude that "most preschool children have at least some understanding of the general representational nature of maps" and that "representational insight is established by three years" (240). It takes a good deal of time from birth and into childhood for children to identify with what maps not only represent but what they are for (Liben 2001).

Clements (1999) argues that the ability of orienting one's self—knowledge or understanding of mental or physical maps—is essential in improving spatial abilities. He cautions, however, that children who process mathematical information visually or graphically do not necessarily perform better in geometric or geographic skills than those who process this information through verbal-logical means.

RESEARCH ON SPECIFIED SPATIAL
AND GEOMETRIC CONCEPTS

Mathematicians and mathematics educators over the years have argued that spatial abilities are essential in one's ability to think mathematically (Lean and Clements 1981; Wheatley 1990). Yet, very little research on children's thinking has been devoted to specific spatial and geometric concepts. This section describes actual studies that examine young children's thinking with regard to specific spatial or geometric concepts.

Symmetric Relations

All individuals in all contexts encounter symmetry in some form or another. Furthermore, the ability to detect symmetric relations is a cognitive process that is encountered by nearly all individuals (Rosen 1998; Weyl 1980). Few researchers, however, have examined the role of symmetry in young children's geometric thinking. Genkins (1971, 1975) studied how the concept of symmetry is learned among kindergarten and second-grade children. Through paper folding exercises, her results show that young children are able to classify point-symmetric figures and asymmetric figures as nonbilaterally symmetric figures.

In similar investigations led by Gerdes and his colleagues, Mapapá (1994) examined symmetries in the everyday context of merchants and artisans in Maputo, Mozambique. He found that these skilled workers, particularly metal grate workers, have an adept sense of symmetric relations, a necessary skill for their source of revenue.

One of the few studies that seems to take into account young children's activities involving symmetry in the everyday context is Zvonkin's article (1991) on children's informal mathematical thinking. Zvonkin describes his use of a 15 x 15 pegged square field with mosaics (see figure 1.4). The participants included his son and three other boys from their neighborhood. The task asked for the boys (taking turns) to produce the same figure in symmetric fashion that the author had produced on the other side of the axis (or the "looking glass") that the author created. His results demonstrated that the boys continually produced symmetric figures to the original—that is, the boys created figures that appeared as mirror images of those produced by Zvonkin himself.

Direction/Location

A fair amount of research exists on children's acquisition of notions concerning direction or location. Harris and Strommen (1972) posit that children acquire knowledge of the front-back-side concept by age five; however,

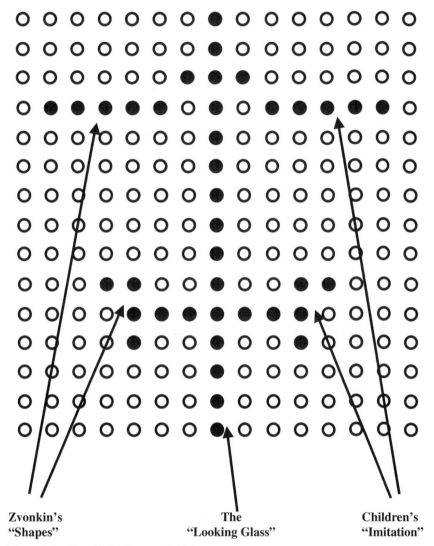

Figure 1.4. Zvonkin's "Square Field"

they do not inquire how and when children acquire each concept. Kuczaj and Maratsos (1975) find that children seem to encounter the notions of *front* and *back* as opposites before they actually learn the meaning of each term. Children learn the meanings of these terms when they first apply each word to themselves before associating *front* and *back* to other objects. Further, they maintain that the notion of *side* appears last. According to Teller (1969) and Clark (1973), children's (and adults') notion of *front* is the

most prominent side of almost all objects and living things. Certain characteristics of objects tend to represent notions of *front*: with moving objects,
front is generally associated with the part of the object or being that is at the
most forward point, such as the head of a dog or the headlights of a car; for
stationery objects, *front* generally concerns the parts of the objects that are
manipulated in some way, like the door of a refrigerator. Characteristics of
back include the tails of animals, trunks of cars, and the like. The main
point is that children generally do not learn *front* and *back* in any particular
order because they are usually learned simultaneously. In terms of older
children (between 7 and 13 years), Anooshian and Young (1981) found
that the accuracy in which individuals can identify particular landmarks in
a housing development by pointing to those landmarks from different van-
tage points markedly increases with age. This finding suggests that the older
children get, the more likely they will parse a neighborhood into smaller
components for accurate identification of particular locations of landmarks.

Research on the Comparison between Spatial Concepts and Number Concepts

   The literature on the connection between spatial thinking with arithmetic
or quantitative thinking is minimal. Mix, Huttenlocher, and Levine (2002)
develop this issue to a great extent by arguing that the development of space
and number concepts are not as distant as many people might think. Their
term "spatial quantification," in fact, refers to the thinking strategies of
infants and young children when confronted with tasks involving number.
The rationale here seems to reflect the Aristotelian view that number of
objects and the amount of a substance are two forms of quantity. Wynn
(1995) found through experimentation that recognition of number was
evident with infants even a few days old. Mix and her colleagues, however,
note that there is a growing body of research showing that infants recognize
quantity more in terms of amount than of quantity. Studies concerning
developmental achievements and deficits show that the development of
spatial thinking seems to run parallel to the development of number from
infancy and early childhood. For example, children with poor number
skills seem to perform more poorly on spatial skills than children who are
adept in both skills (McLean and Hitch 1999). Other studies seem to corroborate this evidence (Morris and Mervis 1999; Semrud-Clikeman and
Hynd 1990; Spiers 1987; Tranel et al. 1987).

CROSS-NATIONAL DIFFERENCES IN SPATIAL AND GEOMETRIC THINKING

Cross-national studies on the cognitive processes of space and geometry are
very limited in number. One tangentially related study is that of Lesser,

Fifer, and Clark (1965), who attempt to compare intellectual competencies of immigrant children of four ethnic groups living in New York City. One area in which the children were tested involved spatial thinking, in which the Chinese children scored roughly the same as the Jewish children, and significantly better than African American and Latino children. Lesser, Fifer, and Clark's study, however, employs only standardized methods of assessment and does not provide sufficiently rich or accurate information concerning what children of varying ethnic backgrounds really know about spatial relationships or other areas of knowledge. A more recent study is that of Case and his colleagues (see Okamoto et al. 1996), who compare the differences of spatial structures and drawings of 210 four-, six-, eight-, and ten-year-old children from Canada and mainland China. Their results, mostly descriptive, show that the drawings of the Chinese children tended to be more complete with more attention given to line precision than their Canadian peers.

Using the method of naturalistic observation, Lin and Ness (2000) and Ginsburg, Lin, Ness, and Seo (2003) compare Chinese and American children aged four to six years in terms of the amount of time each group engaged in mathematical activity as well as the types of mathematical activity that were involved. Their results indicate that the Chinese children engaged in more mathematical activity that involved spatial and geometric relations than did their American peers. Surprisingly, although much cross-national research emphasizes East Asian children's adeptness in the use of number, there is no significant difference in terms of each group's engagement in enumeration activity. However, with the exception of this investigation, cross-national research is bereft of studies investigating comparisons of spatial and geometric thinking in the everyday context.

CONCLUSION

As we have indicated in the introduction to this book, it is virtually impossible to cover every aspect associated with the study of space and the psychological domain of spatial and geometric thinking in one text. Nevertheless, the research corpus in contemporary studies of psychological and educational inquiry regarding the broad areas of space and geometry is growing. Indeed, most journals in developmental (e.g., *Child Development; Developmental Psychology*) and cognitive psychology (e.g., *Cognitive Development; Spatial Cognition and Computation*) demonstrate this growing body of research. The cognitive domain of spatial thinking has not, however, been studied through the lens of socioeconomic class, nor has it been investigated in terms of age and gender relationships in the everyday free play setting. Before examining these important areas in relationship to spatial cognition and development, we provide an overview of theoretical frameworks on children's conceptions of space and geometry in the next chapter. At the end of the second chapter, we present our everyday model, and in chapter 3, we discuss the close connections between emergent spatial thinking with principles in architecture and engineering.

CHAPTER TOPICS FOR DISCUSSION

1. Explain the relationships between spatial perception, spatial representation, and spatial orientation. Is one of any of these precepts prerequisite knowledge for the other two? Explain your answer using examples.

2. Compare and contrast the content of the philosophical treatises on space by Rene Descartes, George Berkeley, and Immanuel Kant with the research studies conducted by the twentieth-century psychologists George Armitage Miller, Julian Hochberg, and Roger Hart and Gary Moore. Discuss some of the major contributions of Descartes, Berkeley, and Kant on twentieth-century thought and research on spatial thinking. Also consider the fundamental differences that contributed to change our understanding of space from the seventeenth and eighteenth century to today.

3. Thomas Reid was one of the first thinkers to identify the relationships between human understanding and thinking with the way we investigate ideas associated with geometry. His discussion entitled "Geometry of Visibles" from his treatise, *An Inquiry into the Human Mind*, indirectly challenges Euclidean geometry—the geometry, based on the postulates and definitions of Euclid (400 BC), that has been the staple of geometry curriculum in formal elementary and secondary education. Based on your knowledge of Reid's "Geometry of Visibles," think of at least three ways in which his approach to abstract knowledge can be used in the teaching and learning of geometric ideas in today's classroom. Reid uses the triangle in his first principle from "Geometry of Visibles." Use the example of a circle to show how the shape, when projected onto a sphere, would appear to the human eye. How does this appearance of a circle projected onto a sphere compare or contrast with the way we learn about circles in the typical formal lesson of circles in schools today?

4. Plato's dialogue "Meno" presents an early account of the intuitive knowledge of geometric concepts. In his dialogue with Meno, Socrates argues that the so-called Pythagorean theorem represents a universal or absolute idea that need not be learned in a formal setting. Through probing questions and gentle guidance by Socrates, an "uneducated" young servant knows that the area of a square is uniquely determined

by the length of the diagonal drawn through it. In a sense, the boy knows the Pythagorean theorem, though he never studied such subjects, nor did Socrates give him the answer. Socrates believed that the young boy knew these geometric relationships, not from experience or habituation, but solely based on universals. Compare and contrast this seemingly Western account of the Pythagorean theorem with that of the merchants and artisans in Mozambique as discussed by Paulus Gerdes. Based on the discussion in the text, do you believe that the two examples of the Pythagorean theorem, both based on oral traditions—one from Greece and the other from Mozambique—were discovered (or developed) in a mutually exclusive manner? Explain.

5. Based on the sample of academic journals mentioned earlier, identify the main ideas of five articles from each of two or more different journals (e.g., 5 from *Child Development* and 5 from *Spatial Cognition and Computation*). Does the sample of articles from one journal differ somewhat or substantially from the sample from the other journal? If so, explain the main differences between each group. For example, how are the journals you selected similar (or different) with regard to spatial development? Or with regard to spatial orientation and mapping concepts? Think of other examples to compare.

6. Although difficult to define in a mere sentence, mereology is the study of part-whole relationships, and topology is the study of spatial continuity and compactness. How can Casati and Varzi's philosophical approach (in the form of mereotopology) be applied to the study of children playing in the Lego or block area of a preschool? Can Casati and Varzi's ideas inform us of young children's spatial and geometric thinking processes? Provide an explanation.

NOTES

1. See Max Jammer's (1954) primer or O'Keefe and Nadel's (1978) text for a thorough discussion of the development of space and time in relationship to the physical world and of the debates and discoveries of early thinkers of antiquity.

2. Most psychology textbooks, however, usually attribute the origins of psychology as a discipline to Wilhelm Wundt, eleven years Helmoltz's junior, who opened the first psychology laboratory in 1879.

2

Developmental Perspectives on Spatial and Geometric Thinking

> [R]ather than envisaging human knowledge as a pyramid or building of some sort, we should speak of it as a spiral the radius of whose turns increases as the spiral rises.
>
> Jean Piaget (1968, 34)

Parents often look to professionals who work with young children for guidance regarding their children's overall development. Teachers and students of human development need to enhance their understanding of the theoretical perspectives of spatial, geometric, and scientific thinking in order to gain perspectives on children's overall cognitive functioning. The knowledge gained from the theoretical perspectives provides the fertile ground on which to place one's observations of young children's play. Further, for all the readers who work with children, the theoretical perspectives provide a framework to make evaluations of young children's cognitive behaviors.

In this chapter, we outline and examine four theoretical frameworks and perspectives on the nature of spatial and geometric thinking and development that have shaped our understanding of cognitive and intellectual development as it relates to humans and their interaction with space in different contexts. In the previous chapter, we provided an overview of space in terms of its semantic derivations and also in terms of its use in both philosophical and general psychological contexts.

One of the more recent reviews of theoretical perspectives on spatial development is put forth by Newcombe and Huttenlocher (2003). In their book, *Making Space*, Newcombe and Huttenlocher delineate three overarching perspectives on the development of spatial sense: Piagetianism, nativism, and Vygotskyanism. In this chapter, we review Newcombe and Huttenlocher's examination of frameworks associated with spatial development—namely, those posited by Piaget, the nativists, and Vygotsky and his colleagues. Among these three perspectives, we emphasize Piagetianism to a greater degree because Piaget and his colleagues wrote extensively and explicitly on the study of the child's conception of space. We then discuss the psycho-social environmental perspective that was embraced by Vygotsky. This is followed by a discussion on researchers and theorists who espouse the innateness argument with regard to spatial thinking in particular and cognitive domains in general. Newcombe and Huttenlocher's own framework, which they call the "interactionist" approach, is also discussed.

We support each of the perspectives on spatial cognition with the works of both past and contemporary researchers. For example, Pinxten's a posteriori universalism is discussed in context to the psycho-social Vygotskyan perspective. Under the Piagetian perspective, we identify the works of Werner, one of Piaget's contemporaries, as well as the Van Hiele model of geometric levels of development. We then propose a framework which not only applies to the ways in which spatial development emerges but also to the ways in which spatial development can be recorded in the context of everyday, spontaneous free play. We elaborate on our empirical investigations and case studies in chapters 6 and 7 and our protocognitive model (protomathematical and protoscientific everyday behaviors of young children) in chapter 8.

PIAGETIAN PERSPECTIVE

It was not until the 1940s and 1950s that intensive empirical research devoted to cognitive processes of space and geometry had taken place. Much of this work had been conducted by Werner and his Clark University colleagues in the 1940s and by Piaget and a number of his Genevan colleagues in the late 1940s and early 1950s. The next two sections of the present chapter examine Werner's contribution to theory and research on the development of spatial thinking and the topological primacy thesis of Piaget.

Werner's Organismic Theory of Spatial Thinking and Development

What is Heinz Werner's position on the development of spatial thinking in young children? Although Werner was perhaps the first psychologist to develop a theoretical framework of spatial thinking, its origins, and development solely on empirical grounds, his work has clearly been overshadowed by Piaget's developmental theory of spatial conception of the child. Nevertheless, Werner's monumental work in this area deserves discussion.

Werner was born in Vienna, Austria, in 1890. With an initial penchant for music and history, Werner quickly turned to psychology and philosophy and completed a doctoral thesis at the University of Vienna on the psychology of aesthetic enjoyment (Crain 1992). Like Piaget, Werner followed in the tradition of Rousseau, Kant, and Cassirer in the ways in which he studied the concept of space. With the possible exception of Wilhelm Wundt, he was perhaps the first psychologist to study the development of mental life as a whole from a comparative perspective in terms of social, cultural, and even animal-human characteristics.

Orthogenetic Principle

For Werner, the notion of development was not one merely of temporal characteristics, nor was it one of increases in size. As defined by the orthogenetic principle (1948), development is a change in structure. Werner and Kaplan state: "Whenever development occurs, it proceeds from a state of relative lack of differentiation to a state of increasing differentiation and hierarchic integration" (1956, 866). In his first book, *Comparative Psychology of Mental Development*, Werner (1948) cites the German playwright, Goethe, who believed that the "perfect creature" was one whose parts were dissimilar yet subordinated to the whole. Werner writes

> Indeed it does appear that the development of biological forms is expressed in an increasing differentiation of parts and an increasing subordination, or hierarchization. Such a process of hierarchization means for any organic structure the organization of the differentiated parts for a closed totality, an ordering and grouping of parts in terms of the whole organism. (1948, 41)

Clearly, then, two forces—differentiation and hierarchic integration—impose themselves on the animal or human as a means of promoting development.

As an example, a child may enter a first-grade classroom without a firm background of the four arithmetic operations. He may have a vague or global impression of what addition, subtraction, multiplication, or division means. In due time, however, the child's picture of the arithmetic operations (at least addition and subtraction by the beginning of second grade) becomes more differentiated; he knows that the process of adding requires the combining of two (or more) sets of objects into one and subtracting means the taking of a certain number of objects away from a larger set. But, while differentiation occurs, the child may not yet appreciate the interrelation between addition and subtraction. Only later, say, by the end of the third grade (or later), does the child hierarchically integrate the four arithmetic operations into a coherent whole. A teacher can observe this principle in action when a child recognizes number families so that he is now able to identify the inverse relationship between addition and subtraction or appreciate the idea that a powerful aspect of multiplication can be repeated addition.

Development, then, as defined by the orthogenetic principle, begins with ideas or events that are fused with emotion or sensation. Ideas or events begin in disarray. Subsequently, they become differentiated as soon as there is knowledge of the disparate parts of a whole. The realization of how these parts function as (or in) a whole has to do with hierarchical integration, the final state of the developmental process, which involves behaviors as subsidiaries or subordinate parts of higher regulatory centers. We have organized Werner's orthogenetic principle through a hierarchical model shown in figure 2.1.

Werner's Theoretical Position on Space

How, then, does Werner's theory of organismic-comparative development relate to space and the development of spatial thinking? Werner wrote extensively on the subject of space and spatial cognition and the ways in which these ideas fit within his framework (1948, 1957; Werner and Kaplan 1956). To begin with, based on his organismic developmental theory, Werner's notion of space and spatial cognition deals with a developmental sequence of events—namely, action-in-space to perception-of-space to conceptions-about-space—and in this sequence, the orthogenetic principle, increasing levels of differentiation leading to hierarchical integration, plays a primary role. Werner, however, was mostly interested in space involving action on the one hand and that of conception, representation, or contemplation on the other—the two endpoints of this continuum (cf. Hart and Moore 1973).

Werner's theoretical framework on spatial thinking did not really differ to a great extent from Piaget's theory of the child's conception of space. One major difference between the two, however, was that Werner's generalizations did not seem to be based as much on intensive observation of young children within distinct age groups as was Piaget's. Werner did, however, base much of his theory on his studies of young children with mental illness. Essentially, Werner believed that an infant's space is at first undifferentiated from his own body and begins with a proprioceptive space in which space is passive; that is, the infant's spatial environment is based on sensation, or stimuli acting upon sensory nerve endings, providing him with a sense of position of his body. As time progresses, after a few weeks or so,

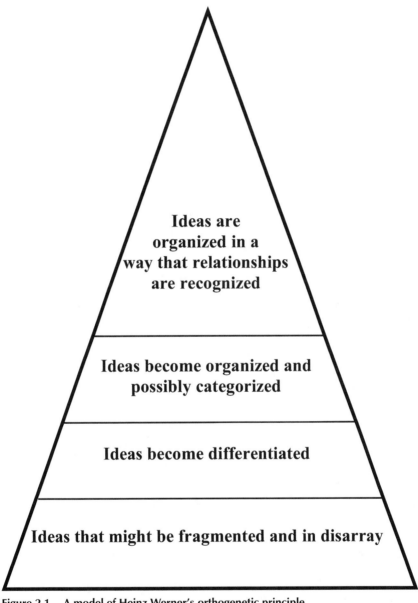

Figure 2.1.   A model of Heinz Werner's orthogenetic principle

his body begins to react to external stimuli, what Werner refers to as "far-space." In Werner's words

> For the infant, surrounding space and private, corporeally centered space are one, and together constitute an *Ur-raum*, [our italics] i.e. a "primordial space." The mouth is the primitive means of knowing objects, that is, in the literal sense, through the grasping of objects. . . . Out of this "primordial space" there gradually arises, in the course of a few weeks, a space-of-nearness, of propinquity, in which the space surrounding the body becomes differentiated from body proper. (1974, 172–73)

For the first six or seven years of life, the child's notion of space becomes increasingly active. At first, it is undifferentiated with a lack of interrelation between parts of a whole. Only at age eight or nine does the child begin to lose syncretism, or the act of combining unrelated objects into a whole. Space, then, progresses from being bound to the child's body or immediate environment (egocentrism) to one of perspective in which the child bases spatial phenomena on a more abstract coordinated system, what Werner refers to as perspectivism.

Werner's and Piaget's theoretical perspectives on the development of spatial thinking appear to be the result of each theorist's experiences. The next section discusses Piaget's topological primacy thesis and the topological-projective-Euclidean chronology.

Jean Piaget

Perhaps the most extensive theoretical framework on the child's conception of space to date, and on human development in general, is that of the Genevan genetic epistemologist and psychologist, Jean Piaget (1954; Piaget and Inhelder 1956/1967; Piaget, Inhelder, and Szeminska, 1960). Like Werner, Piaget's interests clearly extended beyond solely the child's conception of space and the development of spatial thinking; indeed, his research agenda and program was devoted to the epistemological underpinnings of human thought in general. Nevertheless, his contributions to research on children's conception of space and geometry are quite extensive.

What is the importance of Piaget's perspective on the development of spatial thinking? It would seem difficult for any researcher on spatial or geometric thinking or cognition to ignore Jean Piaget's contributions to the subject. Piaget (1954) and Inhelder (Piaget and Inhelder 1956/1967) advanced a general theory of spatial and geometrical development (Piaget, Inhelder, and Szeminska 1960)—particularly the theoretical underpinnings of the topological primacy thesis—by intensively observing and interviewing approximately 140 children between the ages of two-and-a-half and

Substage	Approximate Ages	Model 4 (Circle)	Model 6 (Triangle)	Model 21 (X-shaped cross)
0	(Birth) to 2 years, 6 months	Scribble-like	Scribble-like	Scribble-like
IA	2 years, 6 months to 3 years, 6 months			
IB	3 years, 6 months to 4 years			
Transition (IB and IIA)	4 years to 4 years, 6 months			
IIA	4 years, 6 months to 5 years	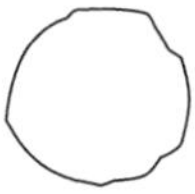		
IIB	5 years to 5 years, 6 months	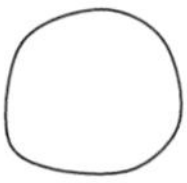		

Figure adapted from Piaget, J., & B. Inhelder. (1956/1967).

Figure 2.2. Simulations of a child's representations of Piaget's models 4, 6, and 21 when engaged in haptic perception tasks

seven years in a task he refers to as haptic perception, or a child's representation (drawing) of an object (not in sight) after touching it (1967). Figure 2.2 shows simulations of children's representations of a circle, triangle, and cross (models 4, 6, and 21 respectively) when engaged in haptic perception tasks. Instead of using standardized methods of assessment, Piaget employed the clinical method, which he had developed in the early to mid-1920s. What follows is a discussion of Piaget's theory, based on the topological-projective-Euclidean chronology and the arguments for and against Piaget's theory of spatial and geometric development. A critique of these arguments is then discussed.

The Topological-Projective-Euclidean Chronology

What do we mean by topological space? What is projective space? Or Euclidean space? It is important to keep in mind that these mathematical terms are defined by Piaget and may not necessarily overlap in meaning with their prospective mathematical definitions. In addition, at the expense of avoiding sweeping generalizations, we will attempt to define these terms—as Piaget referred to them—without distortion or oversimplification of their meanings in this short introduction. We provide more detail of these terms in the sections that follow. Also, keep in mind that Piaget's reference to age limits are not set in stone, as with any other area of conceptual development, and vary dramatically depending on the individual child.

First, *topological space* refers to the conception of space from birth to approximately six or seven years of age. Children at this level view objects in space in a somewhat plastic or re-forming way. That is, the shape of objects are not considered in terms of their association to polygons (e.g., a bowl is like a circle) but rather in terms of their physical appearance in relation to other objects (e.g., a bowl is like a dish, whereas a coffee mug is like a doughnut because they both have holes). In addition, spatial development at this early level is closely connected with how close objects are (proximity); how two or more objects are distinguishable (separation); how and when two or more objects appear (order); the location of a middle object (enclosure); and sequences of objects (continuity).

Second, *projective space* refers to the child's conception of objects that are associated with their polygon equivalents. But, in order for the child to represent an object through drawing, she will need a frame of reference to complete the figure. For example, if a child is asked to draw a triangle, one of the edges of the triangle will be parallel with the edge of the table. Children exhibiting concepts of space from a projective standpoint are often between the ages of approximately four or five years to nine or ten (and possibly eleven or twelve) years of age. Children's drawings, especially during the early part of the projective period, will often fail to treat an object as a three-dimensional entity and will represent it as a two-dimensional figure.

Finally, *Euclidean space*, which is based on precepts of Euclidean geometry, refers to a child's ability to represent objects in a way that closely conforms to their appearance. These children will exhibit knowledge of parallel or perpendicular lines with respect to rectilinear objects (e.g., drawing a window or a house) and will not depend on frames of reference (e.g., table edges). Children who exhibit Euclidean tendencies are generally older than seven or eight years of age.

Given that the present volume focuses on the development of spatial and geometric thinking of four- and five-year-old children, more attention will be devoted to Piaget and Inhelder's (1956/1967) topological primacy thesis. Less attention is given to projective and Euclidean geometry, since the transition to projective and Euclidean thinking occurs later in the child's life. A more exhaustive description of post-topological thinking can be found in the work of Clements and Battista (1992).

Topological Primacy Thesis

Like Werner, Piaget's clinically and empirically based theory of the child's conception of space developed out of the tradition of the epistemological problems that philosophers such as Descartes, Berkeley, Rousseau, Kant, and Cassirer faced when dealing with the fundamental concepts of space. According to Piaget's theory (1954), spatial thinking begins from infancy. From approximately the end of the first month of life, the infant begins to construct perceptual space, which refers to an individual's direct contact with an object or group of objects and their surroundings. As Piaget and Inhelder state

> perception (such as the sight of a feeding bottle turned wrong way round) is a system of relationships organized in an immediate whole. But the equilibrium of this whole depends not only upon real (i.e. actually perceived) relations but also, like a mechanical equilibrium, upon virtual relations which refer to earlier or contingent perceptions (for instance, anticipation of the result of semi-rotation of the feeding bottle). (1967, 14)

Unlike older children and adults, infants are unable to conceive of objects as having a "life" of their own. Infants, then, are unable to consider objects beyond their immediate perception. Like representational space, which comes much later, perceptual space is not acquired passively; individuals develop perceptual space from experience and active engagement with objects or other individuals in their environment or immediate surroundings. And, as Piaget claims, these experiences begin with the infant's use of reflexes and the subsequent development of primary circular reactions in the second stage of the sensorimotor period. The first and second stages in the sensorimotor period form the first of three periods in the development of perceptual space.

It is in this first period, according to Piaget, that infants develop five elementary spatial relations: proximity, separation, order, enclosure, and continuity. Proximity deals with the nearness or "neighborhood" of objects within the infant's perceptual field. Piaget posits that young infants initially resort to this spatial relation before identifying with others, so proximity is considered the first elementary spatial relation.

In recalling Werner's (1948) organismic theory as it relates to spatial thinking, he also alludes to the idea of proximity as an early outcome of the newborn's "premordial space." As Werner suggests, a few weeks after birth, "there gradually arises . . . a space-of-nearness," (1948, 172–73) or what Piaget refers to as "proximity." (Unlike Piaget, however, Werner's notion of nearness, or proximity, does not seem to refer to the self and the object dyad, but the distinction between self and non-self in general.)

Separation refers to the infant's ability to distinguish between, for example, two objects that seem blurred or extremely close in proximity. Of course, as the infant becomes more analytical toward her perceptual space, she is able to separate objects that may have originally seemed blurred. One can possibly conceive of separation as the primordial indication of an infant's abilities in the human trait of classification. That is, separation of objects or people seems to be an indicator of one's ability to distinguish between two or more entities solely on the differences between and among them.

The next spatial relation, order, is more complex and appears when the infant is able to distinguish between two or more elements in which one element appears or is seen before a second related or identical one. Piaget provides the well-known example of repeated ornaments on the infant's crib (1956/1967, 7). An infant noticing the door opening, an adult appearing, and food coming demonstrates order through both spatial and temporal means.

Enclosure, the fourth spatial relation of the first period of the sensorimotor stage, is initially conceived of as a one-dimensional idea in which an object is seen as the middle of two outer objects—of three objects, A, B, and C, B is the middle one. Later on, infants conceive of the notion of enclosure in three dimensions as a situation in which an object is "lost" or loses its entity once it "disappears" inside a box or an enclosed area. Finally, the spatial relationship of continuity refers to the perception of connected elements that form a line or a surface.

In terms of the period of topological primacy (birth through age seven), Piaget designates the period from birth through two-and-a-half years as Stage 0 because the young child overwhelmingly exhibits evidence of perceptual space in which objects, whose permanence is unstable, appear as fleeting, ephemeral images; there is little or no evidence of representational space in this earliest stage.

Continuing through the stages of spatial and geometric development, Piaget distinguishes between two substages of Stage I. Substage IA describes a child whose age is between two-and-a-half and three-and-a-half years. According to Piaget, the Substage IA child is still unable to differentiate between shapes. However, she is now able to distinguish, through both tactile and visual exploration, between familiar objects based on their differentiating contours. (These objects included a ball, key, scissors, spoon, and a pencil.) Whereas Substage IA children find it difficult to differentiate between different shapes, Substage IB children, ages three-and-a-half to five years, are able to differentiate between shapes topologically and not in Euclidean form. That is, Substage IB children do not seem able to differentiate between circles and rectangles, for both are closed figures; they are, however, able to distinguish between figures that are closed (e.g. circle, square, triangle) from those that are open (e.g. a U-shaped figure, an open "circular-shaped" figure).

Like the previous stages, Stage II is divided into two substages. According to Piaget, although children between Substages IB and IIA demonstrate a crude recognition between rectilinear shapes (e.g. squares and rectangles) and curvilinear ones (e.g. circles and ellipses), they are unable to differentiate between the shapes themselves. As Piaget describes, representation by drawing is possible for some children but lags behind recognition of shape or object. This transitory period occurs between the ages of four and four-and-a-half years. In the heart of Substage IIA—ages four-and-a-half to five years—children seem able to differentiate between shape by angle and sometimes dimension. For example, these children can distinguish between a square and a triangle and between a square and a circle. In Substage IIB, which usually commences at five and ends at five-and-a-half years, children progress to the level of differentiating between similar shapes. Piaget uses the example of Substage IIB children who are able to distinguish between the rhombus and the trapezoid—both quadrilaterals but possessing different properties in terms of parallelism.

Stage III, which begins at approximately six-and-a-half years of age, is the final stage in the "topological primacy" period. Although children in Substage IIB are able to differentiate between shapes through active exploration, they are not always systematic. By Stage III, children are able to synthesize and organize complex forms of shapes without hesitation. According to Piaget, Stage III of this period forms the beginning of the transition from topological thinking to projective thinking.

Transition from Topological Thinking to Projective and
Euclidean Geometry

To recount the topological primacy thesis, Piaget argues that the young child progresses from a generally passive individual (from birth to three-and-a-half years) who develops her spatial thinking through an acquaintance with objects visually and then through tactile means to one who actively engages in activities that broaden her spatial and geometric knowledge. Spatial and geometric thinking, then, is not passive in the sense that knowledge is brought or given to the child by external means. Rather, the passivity of the child's engagement with her surroundings is temporary, and over time and through manipulation of objects, the child becomes an active participant in her own spatial and geometric thinking. Only through active engagement does the child progress to using more systematic methods and developing more complex spatial and geometric structures.

However, Piaget (Piaget and Inhelder 1956/1967) believes that children do not "automatically" develop into Euclidean thinkers from thinking topologically at first. That is, in the course of development, children do not necessarily progress from differentiating between curvilinear and rectilinear shapes to being able to understand, for example, the properties of parallelism. Instead, Piaget believes that there exists an intermediary period—a transition occurs from topological thinking to projective thinking. Unlike topological space, which deals with individual objects viewed in isolation from others, in projective space, the child is able to coordinate numerous objects and shapes and identify the relationships among them. For Piaget, then,

> Projective space . . . begins psychologically at the point when the object or pattern is no longer viewed in isolation, but begins to be considered in relation to a "point of view." This is either the viewpoint of the subject, in which case a perspective relationship is involved, or else that of other objects on which the first is projected. Thus, from the outset, projective relationships presume the inter-coordination of objects separated in space, as opposed to the internal analysis of isolated objects by means of topological relationships. (1956/1967, 153–54)

An illustrative example of the development of projective space concerns how children develop an understanding of the straight line. At first, the line, in a topological sense, is not straight at all and occurs without perspective (Stage 0 and Stage 1). The child is unable to draw a straight line or form one from the edge of a table. In Stage II, the child does develop a perspective and is capable of producing a line parallel to the edge of a table. However, he is unable to form an abstract line—that is, to produce a line at an angle to the edge of a table. In Stage III, a straight line is produced anywhere on a table; the edge of a table is no longer necessary as a perspective or model of a straight line.

It is only after children develop an ability to coordinate perspectives and demonstrate the ability to rotate surfaces that the transition from projective to Euclidean thinking occurs. One's development of the straight line, or any other concept, as it is seen throughout the topological-projective-Euclidean continuum, occurs at different rates from one individual to another—a situation that Piaget refers to as *décalage*. The temporal *décalage* occurring during projective and Euclidean operations is considerably greater in comparison to that of topological operations.

Post-Piagetian Studies on the Development of Spatial Thinking

There have been numerous follow-up studies based on Piaget's topological primacy thesis, as well as the topological-projective-Euclidean stages of spatial conception for the child. These follow-up studies are in the forms of both replicative research and polemic.

In terms of the former, Page (1959) replicates Piaget and Inhelder's experiments and attempts to examine young children's haptic perception. Each child is placed before a screen and asked to determine shapes by touching objects without seeing them. Again, haptic perception deals with the individual child's active touch—a sensory mechanism—and does not include symbolic representation. Page's results seem to confirm Piaget's topological primacy thesis in the sense that Euclidean forms stem from topological ones.

Peel's (1959) study is essentially a meta-analysis that describes several studies on the mental development of children, two of which are based on the child's haptic perception. Although his study confirms Piaget's findings, Peel leaves open the idea of whether children's spatial perceptions are based on maturation and physical development or on experience and learning.

Lovell (1959), too, replicates Piaget and Inhelder's work and finds that his results both confirm and diverge from theirs. Lovell was perhaps the first researcher to question the socioeconomic factors of the children in Piaget's sample. Lovell states, "One suspects there were often only a very few children attempting some of their experiments and these may have come from superior backgrounds" (1959, 105). One problem with this allegation, however, is that Lovell offers no evidence to support his assertion; Piaget did in fact study children of low socioeconomic status (1965). Lovell also argues that the precise phrasing or line of questioning that Piaget used in his interviews with children were unclear.

One of the most extensive follow-up studies of Piaget's work on the development of spatial thinking is that of Laurendeau and Pinard (1970). Laurendeau and Pinard critically examine five of the many tests designed by Piaget. These five tests deal with the following: stereognostic recognition of objects and shapes; construction of a projective straight line; localization of topological positions; concepts of left and right; and coordination of perspectives. A great deal of Laurendeau and Pinard's work is replicative. Yet, one of their major criticisms of the Piagetian theoretical framework is that

Piaget and Inhelder's conclusions are not based on extensive experimental data. In fact, while Piaget's sample size was one hundred forty subjects, Laurendeau and Pinard's replicative study of five Piagetian tests included the participation of five hundred fifty subjects—fifty subjects at all age levels from two to twelve years. As Laurendeau and Pinard assert,

> Piaget and Inhelder's general conclusions on the development of space still await experimental confirmation. They depend too often on experimental facts which do not satisfy some of the scientific standards of uniformity of the testing methods, the size and qualities of the samples, the equivalence of the groups selected to represent each age level, etc. The uneasiness caused by the lack of precision in these different methodological aspects of Piaget and Inhelder's research demands replication of at least a sample of these experiments in better-defined and more rigorous methodological frameworks. (1970, 20)

In short, Laurendeau and Pinard's replicative study is an intensive analysis of a selection of five tests on the elementary spatial relations of the sensorimotor stage devised by Piaget himself. Their study essentially corroborates Piaget and Inhelder's theory of topological primacy. For example, unlike Lovell (1959) and Page (1959), who conclude that contrary to Piaget's topological primacy thesis, children under three years are able to distinguish between curvilinear and rectilinear shapes, Laurendeau and Pinard's results support Piaget's findings which demonstrate young children's inability to distinguish between them.

Another replicative study of Piaget and Inhelder's theoretical framework was that of Cousins and Abravanel (1971), who used a comparative similarity task as a means of validating the topological primacy thesis. In their study, subjects between the ages of three-and-a-half and five years, five months were asked to determine which of two figures—one topological and the other Euclidean—"looked most like" the figure in question. Their results, which do not support the topological primacy thesis, show that nearly all the children's selections regarding similarity between figures favor Euclidean features.

A Re-consideration of Criticisms of the Topological Primacy Theory

Despite its overwhelming presence in the literature of spatial development, Piaget's topological primacy thesis has been subject to a great deal of scrutiny. What follows is a brief overview of the work that critiques Piaget and Inhelder's topological primacy thesis. Subsequently, we show the relationships between Piaget's theory and spatial thinking in the everyday context.

There have been a number of polemics against Piaget's thesis of topological primacy; the most faultfinding of the topological primacy thesis seem to have been written by mathematics and mathematics education researchers (cf. Kapadia 1974; Martin 1976; Darke 1982). Martin (1976), for instance, makes several arguments—perhaps most serious is the one in which he criticizes Piaget for using mathematical terms too loosely. In particular, he challenges the dichotomy Piaget seems to make between topological properties and projective and Euclidean ones, arguing that all Euclidean properties are also topological in form and structure. A second criticism concerns Piaget's method during his experimentation of haptic perception. According to Martin, Piaget presented each child with a subcollection of objects to choose from and not the total collection of shapes (cf. Laurendeau and Pinard 1970). "If this were true," Martin adds, "one would need to know what figures were in those subcollections before attempting to characterize behavior" (1976, 11). Another problem with the thesis, according to Martin, is that Piaget ignores the possibility of a child selecting topologically equivalent objects simply by chance.

There are some concerns, however, regarding the nature of the critiques and polemics against Piaget's topological primacy thesis. First, while Piaget and other psychologists have attempted to broaden the knowledge base regarding the development and cognition of spatial and geometrical understanding, the critics of Piaget's thesis argue that the definitions used by developmental and cognitive psychologists in general have obfuscated the meanings of mathematical ideas and definitions.

The problem with this accusation arises when critiquing the dichotomous relationship between topological primacy and Euclidean geometry. Indeed, all topological relations are Euclidean, as Martin and others assert, but as Piaget's thesis shows, there are numerous Euclidean relationships, such as the definition of "parallel lines," which are not manifest in young children's mathematical thinking.

Another common criticism of Piaget's topological primacy thesis and perhaps the most widespread in the research concerns the possible lack of validity when analyzing subjects of other cultures (Pinxten, van Dooren, and Harvey 1983) or of other socioeconomic status (Lovell 1959). Yet even with these arguments posed, ambiguities arise when consulting research that has shown the validity of Piagetian theory of intellectual development across culture and socioeconomic status (Dasen 1972; Opper 1979).

Baillargeon has conducted a number of studies to tap whether infants may have much more by way of a cognitive appreciation of the physical world and reality than Piaget would have contended, based on his writing on the sensorimotor stage. One study (Baillargeon 1993) that illustrates Baillargeon's approach is presented in the following set of scenarios:

An infant is able to look at a platform that has a box on it. And there are several scenes presented. In one scene, the box is quite firmly sitting on the middle of the platform. In the next scene, the box has been moved very close to the edge of the platform. In the third scene, the box has been moved right off the platform.

The technique used by Baillargeon and many other infant development specialists, like Wynn (1995) with number cognition, is known as inspection time—the amount of time a child actually looks at something as evidence of recognition or interest. An infant of three months old will spend very little time looking at the depiction of the box on a platform. The infant will spend a little bit more time but not a significantly greater time looking at a box that is at the edge of the platform. The movement of a box from the center of the platform to the edge of the platform is referred to as the *habituation event*. Now, the box is off the platform suspended in midair without any supports whatsoever, the three-month-old infant veritably gapes at the scene. The evidence of manifest dubiety ("What is going on here?") is clear when observing videotaped excerpts of infants subject to these and similar scenarios. Any adult looking at the scenes of the box would say: "This box is suspended in thin air, and there is absolutely nothing holding it" (see figure 2.3). Baillargeon's findings suggest that the infant already has a conception of how objects in the external world are supposed to behave. And when a depicted object in the external world violates the laws of physics as understood within the experiential context of infant life, we need to reconsider when cognition and spatial sense really begin.

Baillargeon (1993) then takes infants who are six-and-a-half months old, which is a long time in development from 3 months. Now the box is either in the middle of the platform or at the edge of the platform—half on and half off or a little bit more than half off the platform. This arrests the attention of the six-and-a-half month old because this young child is having one of those "surprise" perceptions: "This object is very close to be going off the edge."

Research of this kind is part of a large realm of findings challenging Piagetian stage theory. The more we learn about infants, the more we learn that they are more intelligent than we ever thought. They are able to do things at much earlier points than Piagetian theory would suggest. It is not even quite clear whether the stage concept is the most valid concept. Different infants differ in abilities related to perception of spatial structures. Some have argued that cognitive development is a kind of undulatory ebb and flow of varying abilities.

Related Post-Piagetian Research

The work of Clements provides insight into aspects of geometric and spatial thinking, such as the connection between spatial and geometric con-

Habituation Event

Possible Event

Impossible Event

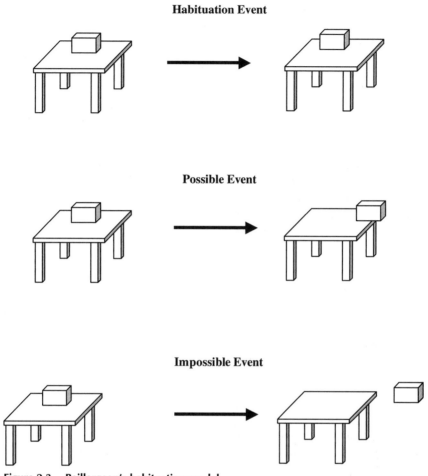

Figure 2.3.   Baillargeon's habituation model

cepts and technology (Clements and Battista 1989) and understanding maps and location (Clements 1999), two areas that, with the exception of Liben (1981; Liben and Downs 2001) and Presson (1982a), have been otherwise missing from psychology and mathematics education literature.

Clements and his colleagues' work has been seminal in terms of their research on the strengths of the Logo programming language and its impact in the conceptual understanding of geometry. Battista and Clements (1988) argue that since children's understanding of space and geometry develops through action, Logo programming brings abstract geometric concepts to children in an explicit way. Here, the link between motor action and abstract concept learning is important to cognitive development. We emphasize a similar finding with young children engaged in block play and the development of cognitive abilities related to spatial, geometric, and scientific thinking.

Clements and Battista (Battista et al. 1998) suggest the notion of spatial structures, which are defined as the mental operations of constructing a system which determines the form of an object. As Battista et al. claim, "Spatially structuring an object determines its nature or shape by identifying its components, combining components into spatial composites, and establishing interrelationships between and among components and composites" (1998, 503–4). For Clements and Battista, spatial structuring is an abstraction and requires mental representation to take place. Again, like other post-Piagetian studies on the subject, spatial structuring developed from the idea that from infancy (Acredolo 1981), the child develops mental spatial abilities through actively and repetitively putting an object or objects in relation with surrounding objects (Piaget and Inhelder 1956/1967).

Van Hiele Model

What are the advantages of the Van Hiele model in understanding the development of geometric thinking? The Van Hieles developed a theoretical perspective based on students' levels of geometric thinking and cognition. Both Piaget's topological-projective-Euclidean chronology and Van Hiele's model are chronological in that progress from one stage (as in Piaget) or level (as in Van Hiele) to the next is a gradual process that happens over time. Like Piaget's framework, the transition from one Van Hiele level of geometric thinking to another is not age dependent as far as individual comparisons are concerned. For example, a five-year-old may begin to exhibit Level 2 characteristics of geometric thinking, while a twenty-one-year-old adult may still possess signs of Level 1 thinking. In addition to chronology, there are a number of other features of Van Hiele's theoretical framework that seem to make it an attractive theoretical model for consideration in both research and practice.

First, the Van Hiele model is based on a constructivist approach in two ways: 1) an individual's success in a later level is dependent on prior knowledge, experience with, and mastery of geometric knowledge in earlier levels; and 2) individuals do not merely engage in geometric activity in a passive way; instead, they actively manipulate, transform, and build upon notions of shape and measure. Moreover, the chronological features of the Van Hiele levels are supported more on a student's experience in school—for example, level of instruction, understanding of the material, and so forth—than by age or biological maturation (Fuys, Geddes, and Tischler 1984; Van Hiele 1986). Second, a student's success in any one Van Hiele level is not based on rote memorization. Although this process may enhance other mathematical areas, like procedural knowledge in arithmetic, it is not a helpful mechanism for success in geometric thinking.

In most of their writings, the Van Hieles discuss their indebtedness to Piaget and his colleagues' research on, and contributions to, the development of spatial and geometric thinking. But, as they have pointed out, Piaget's framework did not necessarily address ways in which educators and psychologists can measure students' in-school geometric understanding.

A standard procedure for numbering the Van Hiele levels does not seem to exist. Some researchers refer to the first level as Level 0, while others refer to it as Level 1. In this chapter, the Van Hiele levels will be labeled as Levels 1 through 5. The five Van Hiele levels of geometric thinking, then, are the following: Level 1—Visualization; Level 2—Descriptive/Analytic; Level 3—Abstract/Relational; Level 4—Formal Deduction; and Level 5—Rigor/Metamathematical. A description and analysis, along with pertinent research on the subject of the Van Hiele levels follow. See table 2.1 for additional information on the five Van Hiele levels and the types of cognitive processes associated with each.

Level 1—Visualization

According to Van Hiele's hierarchical model, visualization, the first level of geometric thinking, involves the individual's understanding of geometric properties by appearance alone. Specified shapes are generally attributed to real-world objects based on their physical form or gestalt. So, a child might

Table 2.1. Van Hiele levels and examples

Level	Name	Example of Individual in Level
5	Rigor/Metamathematical	Victoria challenges the well-known Euclidean concept that two straight lines never meet by introducing straight lines on the surface of a sphere.
4	Formal Deduction	Raul realizes that two triangular figures are similar because the measure of the angles of one triangle is equal to the measure of the respective angles of the second triangle.
3	Abstract/Relational	Tina is aware of the properties of various geometric figures because she can explain that triangles with equal sides are differentiated from other types of triangles.
2	Descriptive/Analytic	Alejandro sorts various blocks by geometric shape because he is aware of the classification of shapes.
1	Visualization	Samantha refers to a rectangular block arrangement on the floor as a ''big square.''

associate a circle to a Frisbee or clock face or a rectangle to a door or window simply because these objects look like the shapes that represent them: "That shape is a triangle because it looks like an ice cream cone." In short, the understanding of shapes or geometric figures at this level is based almost entirely on perception. Because this level of thinking is almost exclusively perceptual, Level 1 individuals do not attend to, and are not concerned with, specific properties or characteristics of shapes.

The transition from Level 1 to Level 2 requires that the individual is able to relate many types of different objects to the same shape. Attainment of the second level occurs when, for example, a student can conceptualize a rectangle by relating it to several objects (e.g., door, window) and is able to identify the defining characteristics and properties common to all of them.

Level 2—Analysis

Unlike Level 1 (visualization), the subsequent levels of Van Hiele's theoretical model of geometric thinking have been given more than one descriptor. Some researchers have identified Level 2 individuals as descriptive/ analytic (Clements and Battista 1992), while others, including the Van Hieles, have labeled this level as simply the analysis or analytic level (Hoffer 1983; Fuys, Geddes, and Tischler 1984; Van de Walle 1998; Van Hiele 1999).

At this level, the individual no longer considers a figure based solely on how it looks; instead, he considers it in terms of the properties it possesses. For example, a Level 2 individual will identify a rectangle, not because it looks like a door as in the visualization level, but because it has four sides and has equal (90 degree) angles or corners. Figures are not seen, then, as a collection of visual gestalts but as ideas possessing specified properties or characteristics. Moreover, a rectangle is a symmetric figure, both in the standpoint of bilateral line symmetry and rotational symmetry. Although properties of figures are acknowledged, Level 2 individuals do not, in Van Hiele's words, "logically order" their thinking about geometric properties. That is to say, a quadrilateral with equal sides is not necessarily one with equal angles in the mind of the Level 2 individual. Level 2 thinking moves beyond merely identifying a shape or figure based solely on its appearance from a visual perspective, but it falls short of considering figures whose properties are logically ordered.

Level 3—Informal Deduction

Again, as in the second level, the third is often referred to as the informal deductive level by some researchers (Hoffer 1983; Fuys, Geddes, and Tischler 1984; Van de Walle 1998; Van Hiele 1999) and the abstract/relational level by others (Clements and Battista 1992). In Level 3, individuals are actually able to make so-called logical distinctions between properties of various figures. So, in this case, the individual is able to understand the notion that a square is one form of a rectangle for the very reason that the former possesses the same properties as the latter. At the same time, they realize that not all rectangles possess the same properties as squares, the sum of all angle measures of a triangle is equal to 180 degrees, and the sum of all angle measures of a quadrilateral is 360 degrees.

One major premise behind Van Hiele's model is the idea that geometric knowledge is built on geometric truths and the understanding of axiomatic logic. Based on this premise, the levels beyond the informal deductive or abstract/relational level are founded on the presupposition that geometric ideas are based on formal deductive reasoning or that thinking deductively is an a priori characteristic of performing successfully in geometry.

For the Van Hieles, the manifestation of geometric truths is based on logical deduction. In Level 3, although individuals can order properties and base their reasoning on the structure of a particular figure or whether it satisfies the definition of that figure, they are unable to establish theorems based on axiomatic logic and deductive reasoning. According to Van Hiele himself (1999), most students are unable to surpass this level of geometric thinking.

Level 4—Deduction

Individuals in Level 4—the deductive (Hoffer 1983; Fuys, Geddes, and Tischler 1984; Van de Walle 1998; Van Hiele 1999) or formal deductive level (Clements and Battista 1992)—demonstrate the ability to construct proofs of a theorem. They are able to justify the conclusion of a proof based on a systematic list of givens and statements, and while doing so, they are able to identify undefined terms and make sense of them by reasoning deductively through the use of axioms and definitions. Level 4 individuals are able to reason in terms of the relationships between properties of different classes of figures, not the properties within one class (as in the third level).

Level 5—Rigor

Level 5, the rigor level (Hoffer 1983; Fuys, Geddes, and Tischler 1984; Van de Walle 1998; Van Hiele 1999), is referred to by Clements and Battista (1992) as the metamathematical level. At Level 5, individuals are able to identify the relationships between different mathematical systems. Unlike Level 4, where students are able to use the relationships between properties of different figure classes within one mathematical system, Level 5 individuals are able to appreciate the relationships between two or more mathematical systems and produce or run comparisons between more than one axiomatic system.

Educational Concerns

Despite the extensive research on the Van Hiele levels of geometric thinking, a number of criticisms of their theoretical position have also appeared. First, a number of researchers have argued that although each Van Hiele level is qualitatively different from another, it would be very difficult from an educational point of view to determine when a student has achieved a higher level of geometric thinking. For example, at what point can a teacher accurately conclude that one of her students has reached the third level of geometric thinking? Moreover, is it possible for a teacher to conclude level transition? And if so, what measurement is used to determine this?

Another issue is that Van Hiele level transitions do not occur at approximately the same time during development for all people. How, then, is it possible to cover topics in geometry when level transition is an individual phenomenon?

Clements and Battista (1992) propose an additional Van Hiele level, one that precedes Van Hiele's first level. They refer to it as Level 0, or the pre-recognition level. They describe children (or adults) who belong to this level as having limited ability in recognizing all shapes. For example, a child may be able to distinguish between a square and a circle but unable to recognize the distinction between a hexagon and an octagon. Some individuals, then, may refer to a stop sign as a hexagon rather than an octagon.

Summary

Unquestionably, Piaget's influence on the study of spatial thinking and geometric thinking is profound. Moreover, there are numerous studies that challenge the Piagetian argument on children's conception of space and geometry. A large cross-section of these studies also maintains the Piagetian program as a staple of their methodological approach. We see this evidence, for example, in Van Hiele's framework of geometric levels of development and even in Baillargeon's important work conducted with the intellectual development of infants.[1]

But not all cognitive development specialists take the Piagetian perspective at all. We now discuss the Vygotskyan perspective, followed by the nativist perspective, and finally the interactionist perspective proposed by Newcombe and Huttenlocher (2003). We then define our agenda with regard to spatial and geometric development as it occurs in the everyday setting without the impingement of a child's completion of specified tasks.

VYGOTSKYAN PERSPECTIVE

The Vygotskyan perspective, according to Newcombe and Huttenlocher (2003), is one that is intrinsically associated with cultural implications of cognitive development and the ways in which spatial sense contributes to that development. For the proponents of this perspective of spatial thinking, culture is the sine qua non on which any subtopic of cognitive study depends, including that of spatial and geometric thinking. Vygotskyan researchers posit that mapping becomes more cognitively accessible when it is contextualized for the individual reading the map. Lack of contextualization limits the individual's cognitive ability to identify and decipher the meanings and symbolic representations associated with maps. Given Vygotsky's commitment to a Marxist program in psychological study, social environments are seen as essential in cognitive development.

Vygotskyans generally implement the scaffolding metaphor to illustrate this point even further. The scaffold serves to mediate between the child's misunderstandings of a given subject and the actual attainment of that knowledge. The Piagetian perspective views mapping in relation to spatial thinking as an individualistic phenomenon, only reached once the child surpasses projective space and understands the precepts of Euclidean space. However, the Vygotskyan method focuses on the expert-apprentice model, whereby researchers concern themselves with individual situational factors in spatial thinking that involve experiential learning within a sociological context.

A number of Soviet mathematics educators and researchers have continued along the path which Vygotsky had already started. One such researcher, the former Soviet psychologist I. S. Yakimanskaya (1971, 1991), expounds on the cultural relevance to mathematical thinking, particularly with regard to geometry, dimensionality, and perspective taking.

Yakimanskaya's contributions to the area of spatial and geometric thinking are not fully acknowledged, perhaps because her research program was overshadowed by other Soviet psychologists of the time. Nevertheless, many of her views on spatial thinking were brought to light by a number of American psychologists and mathematics educators, particularly those affiliated with the University of Chicago (under Izaak Wirszup) and the University of Georgia (under Jeremy Kilpatrick), who were interested in confirming or expanding on theoretical positions that warrant exploration.

Yakimanskaya's Theoretical Position

Yakimanskaya's position on spatial and geometric thinking seems to be directly linked to the tenets of Soviet psychology and philosophy. Like earlier Soviet psychologists (in the spirit of Vygotsky, Luria, and Leontiev),

Yakimanskaya's research agenda is founded on the Marxist-Leninist philosophical underpinnings of Soviet academic scholarship. Within this realm, the notion of practicality is of great importance. In directly referring to Lenin, Marx, and Engels, Yakimanskaya emphasizes the importance of practicality in her research on spatial thinking by arguing that thinking in general is based on one's needs, urges, and motivations. For her, these human characteristics are directly associated with societal and environmental conditions in which an individual survives. Within this framework, she posits that the development of spatial thinking is brought on by the practical need to orient one's self in the real world. According to Yakimanskaya, then,

> The epistemological function of "spatial thinking" is to help identify spatial properties and relations and use them in the course of solving problems related to orientation in real (physical) and theoretical (geometrical) space. . . . In its most highly developed form, spatial thinking utilizes images whose content is the reproduction and modification of the spatial properties and relations of objects, including their shape and size and the relative position of their parts. We understand spatial relations to mean the relations between objects in space or between the spatial attitudes of these objects. (1991, 17)

In light of her argument, Yakimanskaya considers advanced levels of spatial thinking as engendering frames of reference. Accordingly, like Piaget, she believes that spatial thinking is not a static phenomenon, the result of a passive glance at objects, or viewing objects as isolated geometric shapes. Rather, spatial thinking requires an individual to actively and dynamically manipulate objects. In other words, spatial thinking is only accomplished and spatial properties observed through the course of activity.

Yakimanskaya's Levels of Geometric Thinking

The Van Hieles were not the only theorists who attempted to develop a theory of geometric thinking based on hierarchical levels. A number of Soviet psychologists, including Yakimanskaya, also attempted to develop levels of spatial and geometric thinking. Yakimanskaya did not explicitly discuss levels of geometric or spatial understanding in her book. Nevertheless, she does outline a hierarchy of spatial thinking. However, Yakimanskaya's subjects are primarily former Soviet school-aged children between the ages of seven and sixteen years.

Level 1

Children age eight and younger are discussed only briefly. In Level 1, Yakimanskaya argues that children of these ages are unable to view objects in their various perspectives—i.e., viewing objects from the top and each of the sides—and they find it extremely difficult to manipulate objects to solve geometric problems.

Level 2

Yakimanskaya writes extensively on children ages nine and above. Although Level 2 individuals develop an abstract knowledge of objects, children ages nine to about twelve years resort to the prototypical geometric forms used by the teacher, usually with little or no attempt in selecting several different versions of representation. Another feature concerning Level 2 children is their need to use various types of learning aids, such as colored pencils or chalk, in solving geometric problems and differentiating between various spatial relations. Although students in this age range seem able to apply models when solving geometric problems, they are unable to use more complex schematic outlines and sketches as a means of reasoning geometrically. Finally, students in this age range use two-dimensional representations in geometry. When transformations of figures happen to take place, students generally displace these figures within the same two-dimensional plane.

Level 3

The next level in Yakimanskaya's hierarchy describes students between the ages of twelve or thirteen and seventeen years. Unlike their younger peers, these students manipulate both two- and three-dimensional images and identify representations of both plane and solid geometric figures. These students use learning aids far less often than younger students and resort to them only when attempting to solve difficult problems. Yakimanskaya is essentially arguing that younger children have a more difficult time perceiving and representing three-dimensional shapes or solids.

Unlike the Van Hieles, Yakimanskaya's focus on levels of spatial and geometric development is not on the progression from intuitive forms of spatial thinking to proving highly complex forms and systems of geometry through deductive reasoning. Nor does her model focus attention on space as an a priori form on which geometric principles depend. Instead, her levels and transitions—or cut-off points—have been developed with a concern for the ways in which individuals differ in terms of their perspective regarding various two- and three-dimensional objects and how they progress from centering on one aspect to selecting from a variety of ways of representing geometric phenomena.

Further, with her attention on school-aged subjects, Yakimanskaya's levels, unlike Van Hiele's levels, are dependent on age; in her sample, older children are much more adept than their younger peers at manipulating geometric ideas to solve both practical and abstract geometric problems, whereas in Van Hiele's levels, the chronology of the levels is what is important, not necessarily the age of the child. To extend on this difference between the two models, Yakimanskaya seems to ignore *décalage*, or the irregularities that occur when a child's ability in a knowledge area differs from the characteristics of a particular stage of development. In addition, she is perhaps one of the first researchers to study the development of children's spatial and geometric thinking in terms of its practicality, the fields and occupations in which geometric thinking plays a major part. Geometric thinking in Yakimanskaya's terms integrates the practical uses of geometry (the role of perspective as it is applied to architecture, drafting, or engineering—topics which Yakimanskaya herself studied in depth) with the importance of abstract knowledge instead of solely underscoring the latter.

In summary, Yakimanskaya believed that the development of spatial thinking is a social process that is directly influenced by learning and teaching practices. Moreover, she embraced the Marxist-Leninist view of intellectual development in general—that one's spatial thinking develops as a result of the needs and motivations of society at any given time. Her emphasis on the social influences of the development of spatial and geometric thinking is informative in that the type of intellectual activity in which an individual is involved may be directly related to environmental and contextual conditions.

However, unlike the present study, Yakimanskaya seems to gloss over a crucial period in the life of the child—the years preceding formal schooling. There is a lack of discussion on four- and five-year-old children's spatial and geometric thinking in the everyday context.

Pinxten's A Posteriori Universalism

Strangely, researchers on spatial thinking and representation often discuss the cultural implications of Vygotsky's framework of intellectual development, yet ignore another, more recent body of research—that by the Dutch anthropologist Rik Pinxten—that investigates ideas about space from the perspective of the non-Westernized culture. In *Anthropology of Space*, Pinxten, van Dooren, and Harvey (1983) outline a framework of spatial ability that views spatial sense from a universalist standpoint rather than solely a Western one. Newcombe and Huttenlocher (2003) do not refer to Pinxten, but they allude to the cultural implications of spatial development through the work of Vygotsky.

Unlike Piaget's adherents and other present-day developmental psychologists focusing on spatial thinking from both the Kantian and Piagetian perspectives, Pinxten challenges the idea that space and spatial thinking are entirely a priori constructions. Instead, he argues in favor of cultural boundedness of epistemological systems. That is, the nature of knowledge with regard to universal concepts—like space—is dependent upon the norms or patterns of a particular culture. At the same time, his research concerning the development of a posteriori universals enables researchers to analyze the similarities between two or more cultural groups.

Pinxten discusses cultural universals of spatial thinking and presents an argument for a culturally-bound geometry curriculum in the early grades. He addresses this curriculum specifically toward Navajo children but contends its usefulness in the learning of space and geometry for most populations. Pinxten challenges the notion of the strict universality of so-called Western geometry and instead demonstrates how the Western conception of geometric and spatial thinking is incommensurable with that of the Navajo perspective.

Prior to the publication of the *Anthropology of Space* (Pinxten, van Dooren, and Harvey 1983), Pinxten developed a system for understanding universal aspects of space so that researchers can identify spatial behaviors characteristic of all cultures studied. He calls this system the Universal Frame of Reference, or UFOR (Pinxten 1976). Inspired by Berlin and Kay's (1969) use of the Munsell card to analyze the universal semantic descriptions of color, Pinxten's UFOR was created as a means of identifying universal spatial relations through semantic categorizations of specific spatial concepts.

It was previously mentioned[2] that Pinxten distinguishes between three types of space: physical, sociogeographical, and cosmological spaces. In doing so, Pinxten was able to categorize the list of 118 entries of the UFOR among these three groups. Some entries exist in all three divisions while others do not. One example of the former case in Pinxten's entry list is "Near, Separate, Contiguous" (entry nos. 102, 202, and 302). Given that it exists in the UFOR, the notion of "Near, Separate, Contiguous" as Pinxten has discovered, is a universal spatial characteristic existing in all three spatial divisions. The characteristic of "Relations between earth-sun, earth-moon, planets-earth, planets-sun" (entry 335) however, only exists in one space division—that of cosmological space.

Perhaps the most important reason to discuss Pinxten's framework is that his categorization of universal spatial concepts of the UFOR was developed a posteriori. That is, the UFOR is a product of a great deal of detailed analyses from fieldwork. Each code or category is based not on a priori assumptions or "truths," but on an empirical approach used while studying the spatial characteristics of several distinct cultures. In explaining his rationale for the UFOR, Pinxten states,

> Piaget described the spatial system of the Western child as a logical and hierarchical structure. . . . It is by no means obvious that this structure . . . is univer-

sal. A first glance at the Navajo spatial model in the present model . . . or at the spatial knowledge of other cultures . . . immediately makes clear that neither the strict logical structures nor the hierarchical ordering of notions, need to be present in non-Western systems. Therefore, the relationships between each and every notion of space cannot be presupposed by the researcher. (Pinxten, van Dooren, and Harvey 1983, 185)

For Pinxten, the universality of spatial thinking is situated not solely in the tenets of the Western philosophical tradition regarding the meaning of space and geometry. Instead, it is based on empirical data collected from both Western and non-Western cultural systems of knowledge. The UFOR consists of all the common elements between the cultures that Pinxten had studied. Pinxten's view diverges from Kantian tradition, which considers the form of space an a priori structure. Moreover, he argues that philosophers and researchers in the spirit of Kant and his predecessors value the notion of spatial structures solely from the perspective of the so-called Western scholastic tradition.

Researchers and educators interested in studying preschoolers' mathematical behavior from the perspective of the subjects being examined—the children themselves—can learn a great deal from Pinxten's framework. The method for developing codes in the present study has been devised from some of the procedures Pinxten used. For one, children were analyzed in great depth in terms of their spatial and geometric thinking activities before actual codes were fully developed. Also, the development of the codes was based not on terminologies associated with academic mathematics but on the spontaneous mathematical (spatial and geometric) behavior of the four- or five-year-old child in her context rather than the adult's. It should be mentioned, however, that Pinxten is not the only anthropologist who used the bottom-up approach; other anthropologists, too, such as Geertz (1973), favor this method of studying various populations.

NATIVIST PERSPECTIVE

The nativist perspective in spatial thinking embraces the notion of a genetic component to spatial development. Nativists argue that spatial thinking is a universal attribute, in the same manner that Chomsky argues in favor of the theory of universal grammar.

Nativist theorists and researchers generally will argue the existence of innate factors which contribute to a particular intellectual ability. A number of psychologists who study mathematical cognition purport a nativist perspective. Starkey, Spelke, and Gelman (1980) observed that six-month-old infants can discriminate between two everyday objects and three everyday objects when looking at pictures of these objects on slides. In her well-known empirical research, Wynn (1995) concluded that infants as young as two or three days old can discern between different numerosities (e.g., one object versus a set of objects—more than one).

So, how would one convincingly show that spatial abilities are innate? One way is to show that infants are capable of discriminating between spatial or continuous quantities, in the same way it was shown that they can discriminate with number. Mix, Huttenlocher, and Levine (2002) allude to this when they argue that very young infants' alleged discrimination in numerosity is really a reflection of their abilities to discriminate between size or amount. Gao, Levine, and Huttenlocher (2000) find that infants seem to be able to discriminate between different amounts of liquid that is placed in a clear container.

A second way to buttress a nativist argument is to show that blind children possess spatial abilities. That is, if people do not have access to their visual senses, can we show that spatial abilities are present, even from early ages? Landau, Gleitman, and Spelke proposed this position by exposing a single blind child to a set of spatial encoding tasks (Landau, Gleitman, and Spelke 1981; Landau, Spelke, and Gleitman 1984). Newcombe and Huttenlocher (2003) dismiss this argument, first on the grounds that their study was based solely on one case and second, that a growing body of research seems to indicate that blind children's spatial abilities seem to improve over time, thereby demonstrating developmental and environmental inputs.

A third way to support the nativist claim is to demonstrate that the brain is pre-wired to think spatially and geometrically. We see this most clearly in modularity theory, originally proposed by the theorist, philosopher, and cognitive scientist Jerry Fodor (1983). Modularity theorists, when specifically referring to mind and cognition, contend that specific abilities can be associated with specific areas of the brain. This has been shown to be the case with the sensory organs. For example, the part of the brain that supports vision is the primary visual cortex, located in the occipital lobe in the brain's posterior. Another important example is the auditory sense, in which sound intensity—loudness and softness—can be found in the temporal lobe of the brain. Unlike vision, sound intensity, and virtually every other sensory field, the auditory phenomenon of pitch—the human's ability to seek out a tone of a certain number of vibrations per second (i.e., between 50 and 18,000 hertz)—is unique; the location of the brain that determines 440 cycles per second is close in proximity to the location that enables one to hear 450 cycles per second. Likewise, the location that enables one to hear 450 cycles per second is next to the location of the brain that enables one to hear 460 cycles per second, and so on.

So, modularity with regard to sensory mechanisms and their prospective locations in the brain have been shown to be accurate in the areas of medicine, biology, and psychology, ever since the physiologists of the late nineteenth century have studied the brain's interior. More recently, however, modularity with respect to cognitive processes has become an important research area for philosophers, psychologists, and cognitive scientists.

How does modularity theory play a role in human cognition with respect to spatial and geometric knowledge? Subsequent to Fodor's theoretical position, Ken Chang (1986) investigated spatial abilities in rats. Chang found that when the rats were disoriented while looking for food, they were impervious to odor or color, yet they seemed to discern where to search for the food based on the geometric characteristics of the enclosure. These studies were the foundational works for later studies associating modularity to spatial cognition in humans (Hermer and Spelke 1994).

The general environment that nativists provide to support their thesis of modularity of mind goes something like this: An experimental study is often undertaken in which young children between the ages of three and twelve years are asked to search and attempt to find a hidden object— usually a toy or prize of some kind. The experiment takes place in an environment that is usually constricted to one or two rooms, and each room varies in terms of several factors which include wall color, room size, room organization and interior decoration based on children's curiosities and interests, and spatial features of the room's layout having to do with specific geometric characteristics of the room in question (most often the geometric features of the walls). The modularity theorist's general conclusion is that children will search for the toy by reference to the geometric layout of the room and ignore the other variables having to do with color, size, and organization.

In general, the nativist perspective emphasizes heritable, possible genetic, or brain-based origins of concepts and intellect at the expense of environmental or developmental (stage related) factors.

INTERACTIONIST APPROACH

The interactionist approach in the development of spatial thinking was introduced by Newcombe and Huttenlocher (2003). This approach suggests that spatial thinking, among other cognitive domains, is a construct that is influenced by a nativist, developmentalist, and an environmental influence. For Newcombe and Huttenlocher, human biological factors interact with environmental and contextual factors. Eventually, this interaction will influence the development of spatial thinking during early and middle childhood.

The supporters of an interactionist approach initially examine the ways in which adults think about space and spatial structures. Doing so provides a general overview of how one might approach the origins of spatial cognition. Newcombe and Huttenlocher (2003) refer to the process of spatial coding as a way to determine the spatial abilities of individuals at various age levels. Their application of spatial coding emanates from the works of Piaget and Inhelder (1954, 1956/1967), who held that adult competence at any mental task was an end whereby one would be able to identify the means—that is, developmental factors contributing to a particular cognitive ability.

Newcombe and Huttenlocher, at the same time, caution the reader not to overextend the eclectic nature of the interactionist approach. To do so would be possibly to lose oneself in the multifaceted characteristics of various outlooks. For example, an overemphasis on contextual factors that impinge on spatial thinking muddles the equally important factors having to do with biological mechanisms that influence human spatial thinking processes.

EVERYDAY MODEL OF SPATIAL DEVELOPMENT

To this point, we have discussed four different perspectives on spatial cognition, all of which have some overlap in content. Nevertheless, as illustrated above, there are numerous differences between them. For example, the Piagetian perspective clearly articulates spatial development from an individualistic standpoint, somewhat removed, though not entirely, from context or environment. The Vygotskyan perspective elaborates and emphasizes the role of environment and environmental impact on spatial cognition. For this approach to be legitimate, one must consider the role of context as the key factor in spatial development. There is a good deal of overlap between the Vygotskyan approach and Rik Pinxten's a posteriori universalist framework. Both urge the necessity of cultural and contextual factors in spatial development. The latter approach, however, emphasizes the importance of universal frames of reference with regard to spatial thinking. That is, space and spatial thinking is not the result of a priori assumptions. Rather, mental constructions of space are developed after the fact—a posteriori—and are culturally bounded.

We argue that none of the previous four perspectives—Piagetian, Vygotskyan, nativist, and interactionist—purport to children's own constructions of spatial activities. To be sure, the cultural and contextual approaches are limited when considering infant and early childhood development and young children's constructs of space. Accordingly, they do not tell us very much about the culture of the child, in particular, the child's perspective of space and geometry.

The Topological Primacy Thesis v. The Everyday Model

Indeed, Piaget and Inhelder's contributions to the subject of the develop-ment of spatial and geometric concepts were prodigious. To elaborate on the child's development of spatial thinking from both a Wernerian and Piagetian perspective, concepts of space are constructed by the child through hierarchically integrated equilibrations, whereby the child interacts with and adapts to her own environment using the continual processes of assimilation and accommodation. Despite the criticisms of the topological primacy thesis, Piaget and others before him maintain that the child's con-struction of space is not merely the accumulation of spatial facts strung together but is a highly complex network and process of development that is not necessarily based on experience alone.

But what Piaget did not do, nor anyone after him, was to examine young children's spontaneous spatial and geometric thinking in the everyday con-text through naturalistic or contextual methods. In fact, few researchers today examine mathematical cognition in the everyday context. Only two research programs come to mind. First, Ginsburg and his colleagues (Gins-burg, Inoue, and Seo 1999; Ginsburg, Pappas, and Seo 2001; Ginsburg et al. 2003) have established codes for identifying young children's overall mathematical behaviors during free play. And second, Gerdes (1988, 1999) and his colleagues (see Mapapá 1994) have identified methods for studying the rather elaborate mathematical knowledge of merchants and artisans in Mozambican society as well as the mathematical abilities of those in numerous cultures in various parts of the African continent. Indeed, Pia-get's clinical method allows researchers to tap in to "uncharted" territory— the process in which young children develop ideas about space and geometry. The clinical method is more informative than most (if not all) standardized methods, which only identify children's "correct" answers to questions involving space and geometry. However, as powerful as the clini-cal method (i.e., the clinical interview) can be, it is not suited for identify-ing spontaneous mathematical activities. To do so, one would need to employ an alternative method to standardized assessment that would sum-mon these very characteristics of children's everyday behavior. Contextual observation, a type of naturalistic observation (see chapter 4), is one such method that allows the researcher to identify spontaneous mathematical activity.

Piaget's theory on spatial thinking influenced a number of researchers who have followed him. Subsequent researchers have studied and imple-mented his contributions to the field, and several of them have developed their own theoretical frameworks on spatial and geometric thinking, usu-ally involving models based on levels of spatial and geometric knowledge and reasoning.

CHAPTER TOPICS FOR DISCUSSION

1. Similarities between the Vygotskyan perspective of spatial development and Rik Pinxten's a posteriori universalism abound. But there are key differences between the two perspectives as well. Identify at least three differences between the two theoretical frameworks of spatial thinking and explain their significance with regard to child development and learning.

2. Discuss Newcombe and Huttenlocher's interactionist approach to spatial cognition. Although Newcombe and Huttenlocher seem to propose an eclectic approach that provides equal weight to heritability (nativism), development (Piagetianism), and environmental conditions (Vygotskyanism), identify possible characteristics that they may have possibly omitted or overlooked.

3. What is meant by Pinxten's use of the term *a posteriori universalism* with regard to space concepts? And how does his definition compare and contrast with the notion of a priori spatial and geometric concepts proposed by the German philosopher Immanuel Kant and espoused today?

4. Compare and contrast Werner's organismic theory of spatial development with Piaget and Inhelder's topological primacy thesis.

5. Compare and contrast Yakimanskaya's practicality theory with Van Hiele's levels of geometric development. One way to approach an explanation for this comparison is to consider their different perspectives of spatial thinking.

6. Identify the strengths and weaknesses of the nativist approach. Are there any philosophical arguments that can support the notion that spatial cognition is a heritable phenomenon?

7. A large section of this chapter considers research that challenges Piaget's topological primacy thesis. But criticisms of other perspectives are not as sweeping and comprehensive as those that critique Piaget's position. Consider one of the other perspectives, particularly the Vygotskyan, nativist, interactionist, or everyday perspectives, and identify its strengths and weaknesses as a theoretical approach to spatial thinking.

NOTES

1. See Smock (1976) for a more detailed discussion of Piaget's theory on the development of space concepts and geometry.

2. See the section defining spatial cognition.

3

Children as Architects: The Identification of Architectural Principles Underlying Young Children's Geometric Constructions

> Children's perception of stability can be seen when they test their structure by placing a block gingerly or by placing it tentatively.
>
> Kristina Leeb-Lundberg (1996, 43)

Researchers of numerous papers and texts on cognitive development have argued that young children's cognitive behaviors appear to approximate those of scientists and mathematicians. In fact, there is a large body of literature on inquiry learning in science and mathematics curricula. What is provided in this chapter is a formal analysis of these natural behaviors displayed by young children with respect to the formal study of architecture: we identify the principles that underlie young children's geometric constructions.

In chapters 1 and 2, we outlined a general overview of the meaning of space and spatial thinking, as well as the major theorists and researchers who have contributed to this rather broad area of study. The theme of the present chapter concerns the study of architecture and how spatial and geometric thinking influence the emerging architectural principles behind young children's block constructions. Despite the paucity of research on the subject, a number of explanations seem to account for the many connections between the mathematics in preschool children's block constructions and the work of professional architects. We elucidate on these explanations in the following sections.

The first part of this chapter focuses on the historical implications of the link between spatial and geometric thinking and architectural principles. We next introduce the topic of spatial and geometric thinking through block play in a historical context, followed by a discussion of the interconnectedness between spatial and geometric thinking with architectural principles and how this is clearly identified through young children's Lego and block play. In the second part of the chapter, we discuss a professional architect's observations of nine videotaped excerpts of young children engaged in everyday, spontaneous free play with Legos and blocks. Her analyses of the children's constructions further support the intrinsic connections between young children's Lego and block constructions with emergent architectural principles.

ARCHITECTURAL PRINCIPLES

Historical Foundations

To begin with, historical evidence substantiates the connections between young children's spatial and geometric thinking and emergent architectural principles. Balfanz (1999), for example, discusses how Friedrich Froebel's Gifts, both three- and two-dimensional materials that were designed and intended to promote young children's understanding of geometric concepts, influenced numerous individuals in different mathematically related fields. In architecture, as shown in Brosterman (1997), Frank Lloyd Wright expressed his indebtedness to Froebel's ideas and techniques on numerous occasions. In one of his autobiographies, Wright recalled working with Froebel's Gifts to create geometric designs and models of buildings, which he further contended had a profound impact on his career. Wright was not the only architect who explicitly recognized Froebel's influence on later thinking. The Swiss architect Charles-Édouard Jeanneret, too, acknowledged the importance of Froebelian Gifts as an important catalyst for his later endeavors in architecture. Jeanneret, better known by the pseudonym Le Corbusier, whose kindergarten experience was greatly influenced by Froebel, designed buildings that explicitly demonstrated Froebel's creative approach to learning geometry. The notion of early experiences on later career choices has also been investigated by Anne Roe (1951a, 1951b, 1952) in her interviews of eminent scientists (see below).

The Process of "Doing" Architecture

Another reason for the connection between architecture and the mathematics inherent in block building has to do with the idea that mathematics does not only exist in writing alone, as most of us see it printed in mathematics journals or textbooks. These are merely the written records, the fruit of the mathematician's labor and efforts (Dewey 1924). Mathematical thinking, then, involves the *process* of arriving at results, answers, conclusions, or proofs, and not solely the results, answers, or proofs themselves. To be sure, this process requires a great deal of thinking and intuition on the part of the mathematician. In a similar fashion, research in mathematical thinking clearly suggests that young children also possess a rich knowledge of mathematics based on intuitive processes (Gerdes 1999; Ginsburg, Inoue, and Seo 1999). And this knowledge occurs during the construction of concrete objects or ideas—that is, prior to the finished model of a skyscraper, airport, garage, and so forth.

In addition, one can identify parallels that exist between the construction of the architect's blueprint and the intuitive nature of a preschooler's or mathematician's mathematical thinking. Indeed, before the blueprint is completed (let alone the building itself), the architect's mind is filled with ideas, ranging from deciding which geometric design will be suitable (perhaps based on the client's wishes) to creating a building that will not interfere with any real-life obstacles (e.g., power lines and zoning restrictions).

The Geometry of Architecture

Finally, and perhaps most important from the perspective of content knowledge, one cannot deny that the field of architecture, architectural principles specifically, is rich in spatial and geometric concepts. The intimate connection between geometry and architecture had been noted for centuries; it is clearly and explicitly illustrated in the writings of Marcus Vitruvius Pollio (1914/1960), a Roman architect and engineer who lived in the first century BC, as well as in the first of eight books on architecture of Sebastiano Serlio, written in 1545 (1611/1982).

For architects, then, from antiquity to the present, the relationship between geometry and architecture is clear (Blackwell 1984); geometric reasoning is an essential component for determining form and function of a structure before its construction, and the finished product possesses characteristics that stimulate geometric thinking on the other. An architect, for example, cannot dismiss the role that symmetry plays in the construction of a suspension bridge or the building of a skyscraper. Moreover, she cannot ignore shape and contour when dealing with a building's aesthetic quality or a client's interests. Precise measurement is also essential, given that a building must remain erect under various physical conditions.

At the same time, we see these ideas clearly emerge in the thinking and cognitive processes of young children as they construct models of bridges, buildings, tracks, and roads. Though not explicitly associating architectural principles with children's block play, a number of sources shed light on how these principles, along with their spatial and geometric underpinnings, are essential to ensuring a structure's durability and strength, its aesthetic design, and its usefulness (Allen 1995; Ching 1996; O'Gorman 1998; Salvadori 1980, 1990). In addition, a number of resources are geared toward children's actual involvement in architectural design (Abhau, Copeland, and Greenberger 1986; Cogan et al. 1988; Lupton and Miller 1991; New York State Education Department 1982; Slafer and Cahill 1995). The next section is a review of some pertinent research in block play and how block play may influence spatial or geometric cognition and the development of architectural principles.

GEOMETRIC THINKING
THROUGH BLOCK PLAY

Widespread interest in research on pedagogical techniques of space and geometry did not occur until the twentieth century; nevertheless, a number of prominent thinkers and educators of the late eighteenth and nineteenth centuries developed ways that foster children's thinking about the world through the use of specific objects. These objects were also essential in developing young children's ideas about space and geometry.

Geometric Thinking through Blocks in the Late Nineteenth Century

Perhaps the most important aspect of Froebel's connection with young children's involvement in geometric activity is his invention of twenty Gifts. These Gifts consisted of both two- and three-dimensional objects created specifically for the purpose of allowing the young child to explore and develop her mind through both mental and physical manipulation of objects. Following Froebel, blocks have become one of the most popular of toys and play materials for children in both Europe and the United States (Provenzo and Brett 1983; Hirsch 1996). In the late nineteenth century, the Crandall family had become one of the most successful manufacturers of children's blocks, credited for the creation and development of the interlocking block.

The Crandalls were by no means without competition, however. Friedrich Richter's Anker-Steinbaukasten, or anchor block (made of highly compressed sand), had become quite popular in the United States in the late nineteenth century after its success in Germany and the rest of Europe. The importance of the Richter blocks, which were founded on the principles of Froebel's Gifts and Occupations, lay in their construction, which seems to foster young children's intellectual development and flexibility in geometric thinking (Brosterman 1997). Richter's "Stereometry made easy" (stereometry refers to the measurement of solid geometric figures) allowed children to not only explore with solid geometric blocks but extend the notion of shape identification to the actual measurement of solid bodies.

Montessori's Kindergarten

Maria Montessori, too, implemented blocks in her program as a means of developing geometric thinking and reasoning in the early years. Unlike earlier educators, Montessori, an Italian educator (trained as a physician), instilled an element of free choice in her method of facilitating young children's learning (Balfanz 1999). Through her method, children developed ideas of various geometric shapes (circles, squares, triangles, ellipses, trapezoids, rhombuses, hexagons, and so forth) through exploratory activity. This is not to say, however, that her exercises and activities for children were deprived of structure; in fact, "The Montessori Method" contains nearly 400 pages of sequenced lessons that are to be balanced with the child's free choice activities. Montessori's method grew in popularity in Europe at the turn of the century and by 1912 had become a success in the United States.

By the end of the 1920s, Montessori's pedagogical methods fell into disrepute, particularly with the critiques of several educational psychologists of the time, William Kilpatrick and Edward L. Thorndike from Teachers College, Columbia University, in particular (Balfanz 1999). While interest in educational theories in associationist psychology had waxed in popularity, the acceptance of the Montessori method, despite its earlier success, had begun to wane. Kilpatrick wrote a scathing critique of Montessori's methods, describing them as insensitive to the social needs and development of the child. Moreover, he believed that her materials lacked a sense of differentiation and did not allow for creative expression on the part of the child. Thorndike, too, was a leading critic of the Montessori method and any other method or theoretical position emphasizing intellectual development at the expense of social development and personal hygiene in the early years. Nevertheless, despite overwhelming criticism, Montessori's method was not without merit in terms of the way her program and materials helped shape young children's spatial and geometric thinking and competencies.

Caroline Pratt and the Unit Block

Froebel was perhaps one of the first individuals to connect young children's cognitive skills with their use of hands-on block materials—the Gifts or Occupations. After Froebel, the most noted individual who encouraged the inclusion of blocks (particularly unit blocks) in the educational curriculum was Caroline Pratt. Unlike Montessori, whose emphasis was on an educational theory where blocks played merely an incidental function, Pratt made the unit block set a staple of her educational curriculum and agenda. Much of Pratt's curriculum and educational ideology was based on intensive observation of children's cognitive behaviors during free play (see Provenzo and Brett 1983). Her educational program, then, was founded on the notion that children's learning stems from spontaneous activity. Pratt's interest in children's spontaneous learning intensified after observing a kindergarten class facilitated by Patty Smith Hill. Pratt was inspired by the children's use of floor blocks in Hill's classroom, and their ability to construct houses, buildings, cars, and wagons. Hill's maple floor blocks were manufactured in such a way as to represent real-life objects or phenomena. Some blocks were in the shape of circles (for the wheels of a car), while others were small $3'' \times 3'' \times 3''$ cubes and $36'' \times 3'' \times 3''$ rods. In her book, Pratt alludes to blocks as a central role in children's geometric thinking.

> Of all the materials which I had seen offered to children . . . these blocks of Patty Hill's seems [sic] to me best suited for children's purposes. A simple geometric shape could become any number of things to a child. It could be a truck or a boat or the car of a train. He could build buildings with it from barns to skyscrapers. I could see children of my as yet unborn school constructing a complete community with blocks. (1970)

Despite her penchant toward Hill's floor blocks, Pratt nevertheless strove to produce a type of block that did not necessarily resemble real-life models or phenomena. Instead, she searched for a block in which children were able to express their creativity—that is, children needed generic blocks to have the opportunity of imposing their own rules on constructing larger life-like objects. Shortly after the founding of the City and Country School in New York City, Pratt invented blocks based on a unit system with proportions of 1:2:4. Pratt's creation led to the prototypical block set that most American preschools have been using for the past several decades.

Although Pratt alluded to the power of blocks in building young children's cognitive skills and understanding of geometry, little research had been devoted to blocks and their possible connection with spatial and geometric cognition by the end of the 1920s. Despite the convincing arguments made by those who embraced and championed young children's use of blocks and the Froebelian Gifts, there was little evidence supporting types of play or activity engendering spatial or geometric thinking through a cognitive or developmental perspective. It was not until the 1940s, with the work of Werner and Piaget, that an understanding of the development of spatial and geometric concepts was fully considered.

Research on Block Play

The role of objects, blocks or Lego pieces in particular, in early childhood education has only recently become a central theme in developmental psychology and early childhood education literature. Two pioneering books in this area include the work of Provenzo and Brett (1983) and Hirsch (1996). Brosterman (1997) is helpful in establishing the historical background regarding the connection between these two areas. Thus far, studies and monographs related to the ways in which blocks can serve as a learning device have been discussed. However, few studies, if any, examine how blocks may serve as a cognitive device in enhancing children's spatial and geometric thinking. Two of the few studies that seem to explore this area are Reifel's discussion (1984) of children's block play development and Forman's analysis (1975) of the procedures that children use when juxtaposing blocks. Reifel presents a provocative framework for educational practitioners and researchers in understanding children's own ideas about spatial relationships. Basing his thesis on Piaget's theory of intellectual development as it relates to children's conception of space, Reifel organizes children's development of block constructions into several stages. Before discussing more advanced types of block constructions, Reifel treats particular spatial representations with blocks as discrete components within a developmental progression.

Following Piaget's argument that children acquire knowledge of proximity of objects before they develop an understanding of enclosure, Reifel argues that children's initial block constructions, mostly prior to four years, are a result of the process of either piling blocks on top of one another to create vertical structures or placing individual blocks by or next to other blocks in a horizontal fashion. During and after the fourth year, children progress to another level in which defining characteristics of block construction include the necessity for inner space. Constructions of this kind include various types of enclosed or arch-like structures. His framework, then, involves four elemental block structure types: the stack, in which individual blocks are placed on one another (vertical); the row, in which individual blocks are placed by one another (horizontal); the flat enclosure, in which blocks are placed by one another in such a way that produces inner space, surrounded by blocks touching one another; and arch-like enclosure, in which one or more blocks are suspended by at least two other blocks.

Despite Reifel's attempt to develop stages in the progression of spatial representations with blocks, he omits the child's development of order and continuity—two crucial spatial relations in the child's understanding of space and subsequent conceptual formations of geometry. Also, Reifel seems to overlook the connections between block building, geometry, and formal and informal mathematical learning—connection with formal concepts and procedures. Finally, as described below in the section on architectural principles, the enclosed structure, which Reifel refers to as "arch[ed]," is not based on the same principles that architects or engineers—and, as seen below, preschool children in their everyday context—use for the building or construction of arches or vaulted buildings. Instead, Reifel's enclosures that he calls "arches" are closer in resemblance to the trabeated system of building—that is, the use of posts and beams (or the appearance of a rectangular arrangement of objects or material) whose physical condition is based on both tension (beams) and compression (post and beams), as opposed to a circular or semi-circular one whose physical constraints are those based on compression alone.

Forman's work (1975) on children's use of blocks presents a unique and alternative picture to what we have described above. His study is, for the most part, a highly detailed examination of the array of transformations children make with geometrically related objects, mostly blocks. His main thesis is to show that the emergence of equivalence relations ($A = A$) can be demonstrated through infants' and young children's (seven to thirty-two months) manual manipulations of objects, play blocks in this case. Forman contends that the human characteristic of bilaterally symmetric hands serves as a foundation for young children understanding equivalence between objects. With one of Forman's subjects, the child identifies a semi-circular block and "determines" that a "circle is broken." The child subsequently searches for another semicircular block to "complete the circle." Initially, however, the child superimposes both pieces, rather than forming a bilateral symmetry with the semicircular ends touching—that is, the circle itself. The developmental progression, Forman suggests, starts with the child producing her structure based on the physical constraints of the objects themselves; it then develops into the situation where physical constraints become secondary to governance—that is, rules of order and continuity that restrict and determine the structures that are produced. Forman also concludes that the findings of his sixty-six children show what he calls "the gradual atemporalization of successive states and the dissociation of the logical from the contingent" (1975, 55). In other words, the children seem to build structures for inspection—identification of junctures or separations of blocks—well after the construction of the structure has ended. At the same time, rules do not govern the actual construction as a whole. Forman's thesis here seems to corroborate much of Piaget's work discussing children's use of syncretism—linking together unrelated events or ideas—a common attribute of the preconceptual substage at the end of the sensorimotor and beginning of the preoperational period of development.

Again, little has been examined regarding spatial and geometric thinking and its connections to block construction, and even less in terms of connections with inherent architectural principles. Additional discussion on children's block constructions may be found in Hirsch's well-known *The Block Book* (1996) or Provenzo and Brett's *The Complete Block Book* (1983) and even more recent books by MacDonald (2001) and Wellhousen and Kieff (2001). Yet even these important publications only marginally and indirectly mention the mathematical connections with block constructions. Perhaps these principles are self-evident to the researcher or educator. However, based on our experiences and work in the field, mathematical and scientific principles are not evident to many parents. Our attention now turns to a professional architect's perspective of young children's knowledge of emergent architectural principles when using blocks in the everyday context.

A PROFESSIONAL ARCHITECT'S PERSPECTIVE OF YOUNG CHILDREN'S LEGO AND BLOCK PLAY

In this chapter, we have thus far examined the somewhat scanty research corpus connecting the ideas between architectural phenomena and the spatial and geometric constructions of young children. We have attempted to establish the inextricable link between block play and cognitive development with regard to spatial and geometric thinking and architectural principles. The early childhood and mathematics education communities have taken the putative stance and essentially intuitive position that children's engagement with blocks contributes to intellectual growth, particularly in mathematics and science. Again, the books mentioned above on block play generally subscribe to this constructivist model of mathematical thinking— namely, that one's use of Legos and blocks serves as part of the foundation on which prior knowledge is summoned to solve more complex problems in later years.

It is difficult to determine, however, whether young children's exposure to blocks and block-like toys in the preschool years is a predictor of future success in mathematics and other academic subjects during elementary school, secondary school, or college. Only one study to date has examined this issue in some detail. In their approximately fifteen-year longitudinal study, Wolfgang, Stannard, and Jones (2001) made a bold attempt to determine the likelihood that block play influences future achievement in mathematics and other subjects. Their experimental study included thirty-seven four-year-old children who were engaged in play at a preschool in 1982. At the time, the researchers used the Lunzer Five-point Play Scale (1955) to determine a measure for block play and used the McCarty Scales of Children's Abilities (1972) to control for social class, IQ, and gender. Their findings show no influence of block play on children in the third and fifth grade levels. Yet, at the seventh grade, they found a statistically significant relationship between block play and high mathematics achievement. Further, they found a statistically significant relationship between block play and high overall academic achievement at the high-school grade levels.

Wolfgang, Stannard, and Jones's (2001) study is indeed an ambitious undertaking. Yet, experimental studies such as this one are not necessarily the most reliable indicators of the influence of block play on cognitive development for several reasons. First, there is little indication as to the amount of time the children who frequented the block area were engaged in block play. It is possible, then, for a child with a high Lunzer score to engage in block play for less time than another child with a low Lunzer score. Second, the Lunzer scale (1955) uses mentalistic terms such as "highly insightful," terms that submit to subjectivity when describing a child at the highest Lunzer score during block play. Third, given that individual contexts and environments change over time, the tracking of thirty-seven children (a modest sample size) over the course of fifteen years may lead to misleading results simply due to the rather long time period. Fourth, the lack of significance in the elementary school years may be directly related to students' generally high academic scores during this period of schooling when compared to the high-school period. Fifth, number use and calculation tend to be the central foci of elementary-school mathematics curricula. Topics associated with block play—namely, spatial and geometric skills—are not emphasized during this period. Sixth, it is difficult to ascertain what accounts for "successful" achievement at the high-school level.

Another question with studies of this type has to do with a basic problem in cognition—exposure to environmental stimuli. In his classic article "Cognitive Maps in Rats and Man," Tolman (1948) demonstrates that learning occurs as a result of experience with particular objects or exposure to various stimuli in different settings. One of Tolman's foundational arguments was that one's exposure to a given environment is directly correlated with conceptual knowledge and gains. That is, the more one is exposed to various stimuli within an environment, the more likely one is able to know and remember the characteristics of that environment. The seemingly long durational gap between the time that participants in the Wolfgang, Stannard, and Jones (2001) study engaged in block play and the time that these same individuals entered elementary school and secondary school does not answer to one of the essential questions having to do with cognitive development: If these participants became less exposed to blocks over time, then how can gains in cognitive abilities or levels of development as a result of block play be determined two years later? Five years later? Or ten years later during high school?

Existing evidence from the literature is a valuable way to support the argument that young children's Lego and block constructions do, in fact, have underlying architectural principles. But it by no means represents the essence of how children actively engage in spatial, geometric, and even architectural thinking while constructing with Legos and blocks. As popular as blocks are with young children, it is surprising to find little evidence connecting the ideas between architecture and spatial and geometric constructions.

To better appreciate young children's cognitive propensities during block construction, we have identified three primary methods for tapping these areas. First, we invited a professor of architecture to observe the videotaped excerpts of young children between the ages of four years zero months and six years zero months who are engaged in free play activities—specifically children engaged in Lego and block constructions. This method is fully discussed in the present chapter. The second method is an empirical investigation that provides a broad overview of the time children spend engaged in spatial-geometric, architectural, and scientifically related activities during free play. This empirically based method is examined completely in chapter 5. The third method we have implemented, in contrast to the second, is case study analysis. In using this method, we selected four children between the ages of four and six years, who demonstrate overt use of Legos, blocks, or some other tool for construction. As we have asserted in a number of places throughout this text, we contend that the Lego and block area at home or at school represents a fertile environment whereby researchers in psychology and education can tap young children's emergent ideas about space, geometry, and other mathematical and scientific principles related to architecture. After selection, we examined each of the four children in great detail in a way that captures the cognitive, social, environmental, historical, and political implications of what the child is doing and identifies spatial, architectural, and scientific concepts embedded within each construction. We examine four cases in chapters 6 and 7.

One of the important considerations in this investigation is our interest in the spatial-geometric and scientific principles in the construction of young children's Lego and block structures. We also ask if there are any underlying emergent architectural principles that are embedded within these constructions. To do this, we invited a professor of architecture at Columbia University who is also an architect from a major architectural firm and a senior lecturer of architecture at Barnard College in New York City to view a sample of videotaped excerpts of young children engaged in spontaneous Lego- and block-related free play activities. Table 3.1 presents some overarching emergent architecturally related concepts. Each videotaped excerpt includes a target child on whom we focused our attention and the target child's peers or teachers. All the target children mentioned below are engaged in Lego or block constructions. Each analysis below provides a fairly brief description of what had ensued in each videotaped excerpt, fol-

Table 3.1. Architectural concepts and principles from young children's constructions

Balance	Cantilever principle
Vertical space	Symmetry (ornamental v. balance)
Connections/distinct places of connection	Interlock
Parallelism	Functionalism
Tangent lines or perpendicularity	Enclosure (interior v. exterior space)
Scale/proportion	Proximity
Spatial layering	Order
Geometry/patterns	Continuity

lowed by the professor's comments on what the child (or group of children) was doing with the Legos or blocks and how the child's actions are interpreted in terms of emergent architectural principles.

Thelonius

Description

Thelonius is involved in the construction and reconstruction of a train track structure and the areas in which the structure traverses. Unlike Nat, who we discuss below and in chapter 6, Thelonius engages in somewhat cooperative play, building the train track system with other boys in the Lego and block area of the preschool (see figure 3.1).

Analysis

Upon observing the episode with Thelonius and other male children constructing and reconstructing a train track structure, the professor stressed the importance of materials, directing our attention to the Brio set that the children were using. Given that the Brio toy manufacturers developed pieces with specific construction functions, the professor indicated that for the bridge within the structure to function, some parts serve as mediating pieces between the lower or ground level and the upper or bridge level. She also noted that the concept of balance was evident in the excerpt because the boys were forced to engage in trial-and-error situations where parts of the structure would collapse. Architects can identify the strengths and weaknesses of certain constructions when they use "sections" or draw a blueprint that demonstrates the structure when it is "sliced" in half.

Another principle the professor felt was essential in architectural design is the notion of connecting or attaching objects together. All toys have different kinds of connecting devices or mechanisms. Further, different principles become more apparent depending upon the kinds of materials that are

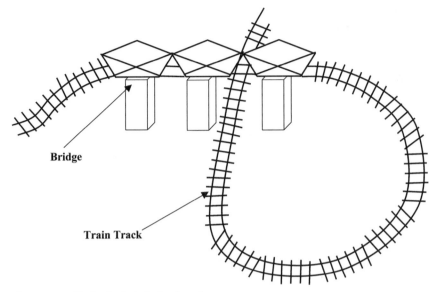

Figure 3.1. Thelonius's train track system

being used. She added that when there is enough flex, one can test the material's strength. This notion again summons the trial-and-error actions of children engaged in constructions. A final issue raised about Thelonius's train track system was the idea of scale: the relation of one's body to the structure being built, or the proportion between the builder and the building.

Fernando

Description

We examine Fernando's videotaped excerpt in much greater detail in chapter 7. Nevertheless, we introduce Fernando here, given his uncanny sense of skyscraper construction, mostly in terms of the longevity of his structures. In brief, within one episode of Fernando's videotaped excerpt, Fernando and Gabe are engaged in competitive play. The object of their game is to build the tallest vertical Lego structure, seemingly as quickly as possible. Each of the two children, at one time or another, manages to exceed the height of the other child. The main difference, however, is that Fernando's structure is a linearly vertical structure, made mostly of stacked Legos with sides generally perpendicular to the floor. Gabe, too, builds his structure rather quickly, but unlike Fernando's "engineering" method, Gabe employs the cantilever principle, which exhibits extensions of Legos as the structure increases in height. Accordingly, the sides of his structure do not always form perpendicularly to the floor. We also observe from videotaped analysis that Gabe's structure collapses much more frequently than Fernando's structure. At the same time, although Fernando's structure seems more secure, the structure falls as it exceeds the height of its architect—Fernando himself (see figure 3.2).

Analysis

Both Fernando and Gabe built very high structures that exceeded their own body height. According to the professor, because both structures are built with Legos, the structures will fall the higher they get. Different materials will have different structural limits. Also, the children are sensitive to the base of their structures, which is perhaps the reason why they build from underneath—that is, they will add Lego pieces to the bases of their constructions until they complete their structures.

Fernando's Structure   **Gabe's Structure**

Figure 3.2. A comparison of Fernando and Gabe's Lego constructions

Kathryn

Description

While engaged in solitary play, Kathryn constructs a block structure that is emblematic of an open-air "high-rise" building with ornate attachments (see chapter 6, figure 13). Adjacent to Kathryn's structure is a structure that resembles an airport, which was constructed by one or two other girls (see figure 3.3). The preschool to which Karen belongs instituted guidelines governing the days on which boys and girls were allowed to play in the block area. Perhaps this has something to do with the overwhelming number of days that boys engage in block play when compared to girls. To ameliorate this problem, the teachers introduced a system whereby the block area is used on alternating days based on gender (i.e., girls play in the block area on one day, and the boys the next, etc.).

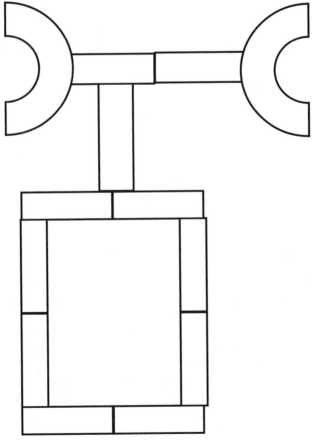

Figure 3.3. Bird's eye view of girls' airport structure

Analysis

Perhaps equally as interesting as Kathryn's structure is the construction produced by another girl (or group of girls). This particular structure resembles an airport. For the professor, the children clearly want continuity of the outer ring of the airport structure. This outer ring consists of Y-shaped (decorative) blocks that resemble an aircraft hangar. The important feature of the structure is the arch-like appearance. Yet the children's construction of this arch-like structure is based on the connecting of two Y-shaped blocks.

Two important ways to analyze children's structures are to see the final product and to observe the children as they build the structure. The observation of Kathryn and the girls beside her led us to the interesting idea of setting up a room with several stations, each having different materials and controlling it as children are involved in play.

Children seem to understand the notion of cantilever, or two pieces with no support at the ends. With blocks, there is nothing to help the structure "lock" into place. Some children, regardless of gender, seem to build vertical structures, while others, such as the girl who built the airport structure, tend toward the horizontal. The professor mentioned that units have certain width, and width has a certain constant. An interesting dichotomy concerning Kathryn's structure is the difference between solid upward structures and open upward structures. Although her structure demonstrates symmetry at the top, Kathryn's perspective of her structure may be entirely different from that of an adult's.

David

Description

David is a four-and-one-half-year-old boy from Taipei, Taiwan. In this videotaped excerpt, David is engaged in solitary play while constructing a vertical structure—assumed to be a skyscraper. Unlike some of the other skyscraper constructions described in this text, David's is unique in that he does not construct it straight up; that is, he does not create a vertical structure merely by stacking Legos one on top of the other (as does Fernando), nor does he develop his structure using the cantilever principle (like Gabe). Rather, David builds his structure with a small and seemingly unstable base. Yet, his structure remains erect because it is almost entirely symmetric. Moreover, the symmetry of the building structure is maintained through David's method of Lego block attachment: David uses both hands simultaneously, with one Lego piece in each hand, to attach Lego pieces on both the left and right sides of his structure. Eventually, David's structure almost resembles a building having the appearance of the human body (see figure 3.4).

Analysis

According to the professor, there seems to be a profound difference of symmetry between Kathryn's structure and David's structure. For Kathryn, symmetry is ornamental. Not so for David. His structure's symmetry is essential in terms of balance. What is unique for David is the way in which he adds Legos to his skyscraper structure—using both hands simultaneously. David's structure is symmetrical in principle, yet it does have some deviations. Pieces interlock in more than one way, and the structure seemed to bend a little bit. Interestingly, the professor mentioned that pieces pro-

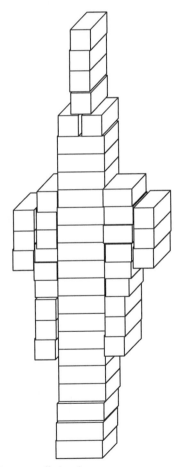

Figure 3.4. David's "skyscraper" structure

truding from a structure make that very structure stronger than one that is constructed "straight up." David could have created the tallest structure if he had started wider at the bottom.

Andy

Description

Three boys, Andy, David, and Jimmy, are engaged in free play involving the use of Legos. As the videotaped segment progresses, one can observe David and Jimmy doing most of the work in terms of the construction of a parking garage. Andy seems to be the child, however, who is doing most of the "engineering," describing what he wants the building to look like. Based on the construction of the boys' garage, given that it has an irregular roof, it seems they begin from the sides and work their way to the roof, which is eventually connected (see figure 3.5). Once the initial structure is built, David and Jimmy continue to work on the garage and attempt to fit their toy cars within it. Andy attempts to fit his toy car in the garage, and subsequently, there is a good deal of bickering among the three children with regard to the sizes of each of the three cars and whether certain cars have large enough spaces within the enclosed garage.

Analysis

The uniqueness of Andy's (and the others') structure is the idea of enclosure. What contributes to this phenomenon is the importance of language.

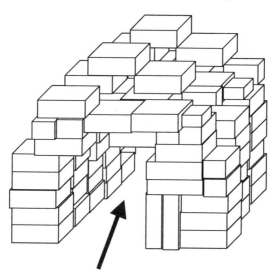

Entrance for Cars

Figure 3.5.   Andy's garage

The conversation, in fact, dealt with a real-life situation common in a large metropolitan area like Taipei—the problem of parking and keeping one's possessions "dry from the rain." One of the most important aspects of their construction was the very notion of covering or enclosing the structure almost entirely, with the exception of the entrance for the cars.[1]

Therefore, function plays a unique role in Andy's segment. The example also supplies evidence of the impact of culture and experience on behavior. The professor was most impressed with the number of words associated with spatial thinking in this segment. Statements such as "If you don't move your car further inside, my car won't fit" are clear evidence of spatial language, though not necessarily typical "spatial language" discourse (words to indicate location and direction to find particular objects).

Gabe

Description

Gabe is four-and-a-half years old. In this videotaped excerpt, he is involved with two other children in the construction of a "monster's house." Gabe, with some help from his peers, constructs the house out of blocks. A particular type of block is used for the actual structure and a second type is used to support the structure. Another interesting aspect of Gabe's monster house is the connection between parts of the house and its subparts—that is, the parts of the part. So, for example, the house has a door (a part of the house) as an entrance, and the door is opened as if it had hinges (the part of the part of the house) that connect the door with the remaining structure (see figure 3.6).

Analysis

Gabe's structure is unique in that he had stacked narrower blocks for the back wall of the monster's house. When a child runs out of a particular kind

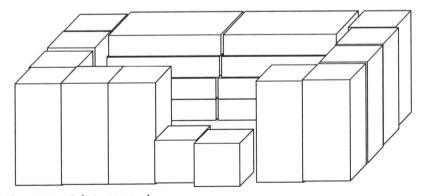

Figure 3.6. Gabe's monster house

of block, he will often find other block types that are somewhat similar to serve as a surrogate to the original block type. So, in this case, Gabe uses two stacks of flat unit blocks to take the place of the more common wider unit block that is used for the side walls. Furthermore, the door to the house was used as if it had real hinges attached. Of course, in our environment, hinged doors are the norm. Gabe also pays close attention to the base of the structure, as it is perhaps the most important part of any building or architectural design.

Nat

Description

In chapter 6, we elaborate on Nat's videotaped excerpt and examine his spatial and geometric tendencies in a case study analysis. Nat is five years and one month old. He is constructing a very elaborate "roller coaster" structure in mostly solitary play. Nat uses materials that resemble pieces of train track. In addition to these track pieces, Nat uses typical play blocks: Unit blocks in the shape of bricks, half unit blocks, and quadruple blocks (approximately four times the length of unit blocks). The unit and half unit blocks are used to support the track structure, while the quadruple blocks are placed in a position resembling a flat landscape on which the track can be situated (see figure 3.7).

Analysis

Nat employs the cantilever principle, which is based on one's knowledge of how to position posts (vertical girders) and beams (horizontal girders). In Nat's case, the cantilever principle involves the overlap of track pieces onto and beyond the edges of the unit blocks, showing the cantilever model using blocks. Nat seems to have an intuitive understanding of heights—he needed to remove one of the "landscape" (long) blocks in order to continue his roller coaster structure. The notion of landscape and that the long connected blocks represented a sort of landscape for Nat seemed essential in the continuation of his structure.

Tina

Description

Tina is four years and seven months old and from Taipei, Taiwan. While engaged for the entire segment in solitary play, Tina manipulates pieces from a Lego-like play set. The main difference between this set and the typical Lego play set is that it contains flat two-dimensional-like pieces that can

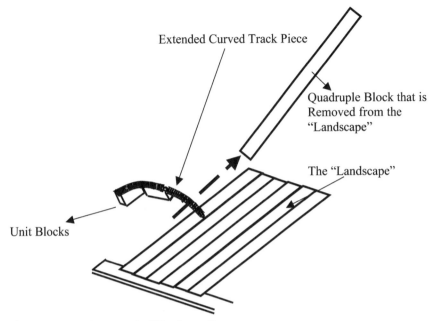

Extended Curved Track Piece

Quadruple Block that is Removed from the "Landscape"

The "Landscape"

Unit Blocks

Figure 3.7. Nat's removal of "landscape"

be attached together by snaps on the sides of each piece. This type of play object, then, allows children to construct three-dimensional figures out of two-dimensional squares, rectangles, and triangles. Tina is engaged in constructing cubes and pyramids out of her two-dimensional snap pieces. She then attaches them to long plastic rods, so the finished product has the appearance of a "magic wand" structure (see figure 3.8).

Analysis

Tina's case is unusual for two reasons. For one, it does not seem as if her intentions are to construct buildings, skyscrapers, or garages. Second, the play objects that she uses are not typical in most preschools in the United States. Yet, at the same time, Tina's cognitive behaviors seem to indicate a prime example of the creation of three-dimensional objects with hollow space. Indeed, the toy objects that Tina uses seem quite conducive to the construction of three-dimensional geometric figures.

Alejandro

Description

Alejandro and Harry, both between four years six months and five years of age, attend a daycare center in New York City. Both are engaged in the

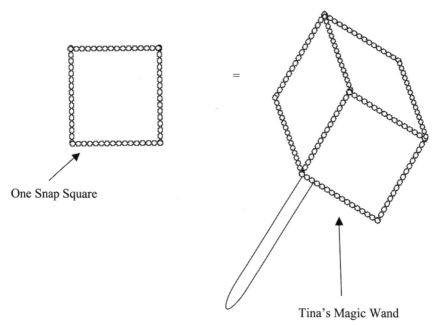

One Snap Square

=

Tina's Magic Wand

Figure 3.8.   Tina's magic wand constructed of snap squares

construction of a very large garage. In the process of constructing their
garage, both Alejandro and Harry use as many types of blocks as are available to them. The initial foundation for the garage, which was very close
to a wall, is razed and subsequently moved to a more open location. The
foundation for the garage consists of four equidistant cylindrical blocks
with four quadruple blocks serving as beams. This foundation is able to
withstand a great deal of weight—over one hundred block pieces of all sizes
and shapes. The end result is a garage built in the shape of a large rectangular solid. The structure, however, is hollow on the inside (see figure 3.9).

Analysis

The professor was quite impressed with Alejandro and Harry's garage
structure. Unlike Andy's garage structure, Alejandro and Harry are not really
concerned with access. The professor described their structure as having a
sort of logic—localized logic. They perceive it according to the surfaces they
are working on, centering their attention to the structure on one side at a
time. The details and joints are "clean," and the structure has a very strong
base. They aligned it perfectly. According to the professor, they created a
foundation for their garage that represents, in essence, an archetype that
most architects would prepare for a blueprint.

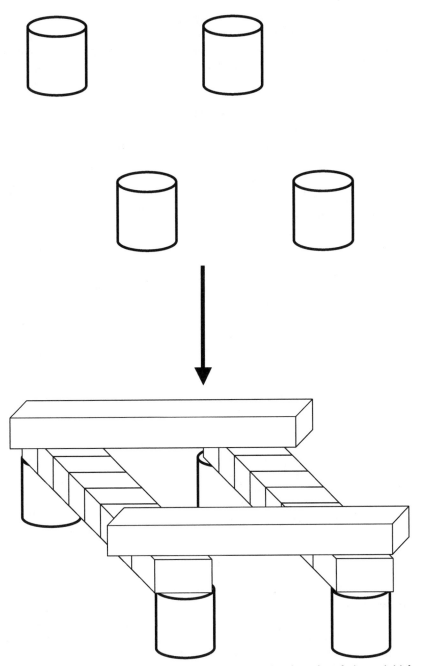

Figure 3.9. Alejandro and Harry's process of construction from foundation to initial spatial layering

The professor continued her discussion on physical foundations of structures. And while Alejandro and Harry's foundation seemed representative of the archetypal foundation for most buildings, she expanded on this concept by elucidating on other strong models for structural foundations. The pyramidal foundation, according to the professor, is perhaps the most secure. This conclusion is also supported by other eminent architects (Allen 1995; Salvadori 1980, 1990). The great pyramids at Giza in Egypt show that this stable foundation was evident to the architects of these tombs, built some three thousand five hundred years ago. In our time, some well-known skyscrapers that possess or emulate this foundation include the Bank of America Building in San Francisco and the Petronas Towers in Kuala Lumpur, Malaysia.

In general, the professor found existence of both engineering and architectural principles in these constructions of young children. She seemed impressed by the navigational language used by these children (e.g., *inside, outside, next to, how far*). According to the professor, the differentiation between interior space and exterior space is an elementary concept in architectural terms. She also suggested that mathematical ideas in the structures of children or architects are possibly dependent on the materials that are used during construction. A preschool environment that includes a plethora of toys and blocks reinforces the notions of right angles, circles, quadrilaterals, and a host of other mathematically related concepts associated with architecture.

CONCLUSION

In this chapter, we have investigated the architectural implications in young children's Lego and block constructions in two ways. We first examined the literature for connections between these two areas and concluded that the research and discussion of the symbiotic relationship between architectural principles and children's construction play is minimal at best. We then have attempted to link these two areas by examining the perspective of a professional architect, who happens to also be a professor of architecture at a major research university. This investigation proved to be important for a number of reasons.

First, Anne Roe's classic study of eminent scientists (1951a, 1951b, 1952) suggests links between early childhood science-related experiences and physical science–related careers. Roe's study of the lives of eminent scientists indicates that there were noticeable group differences between biologists and physicists and between natural scientists (e.g., biologists and physicists) and social scientists (e.g., psychologists). A pattern of psychosocial characteristics and basic common experiences that may be compared with personality formation emerged from her study. In general, Roe (1952) reports that the three characteristics of her eminent scientists were first-born children, sons of middle-class families, and were the sons of professionals. Further, Roe's scientists were persistent in their work and put in long hours. Roe (1952) suggests that the situations experienced by the scientists may have fostered personality attributes consonant with greater independence. Subtle differences in adjustment patterns have been recognized for physical scientists, biological scientists, and social scientists. Among the three groups of scientists in the study, the greatest similarities were found between the physicists and biologists. The physicists reported early extra-curricular interests that related directly to later career interests. As young boys they played with physical gadgets and Meccano sets, worked with electricity, and enjoyed experimenting that included tinkering with objects. However, early career interests were not as evident for the biologists. Roe (1981) suggests that the most significant trait mentioned in each study of either eminent or creative people working in science is independence. According to Roe:

> The most important single factor in the making of a scientist—the need and ability to develop personal independence to a high degree. The independence factor is emphasized by many findings: the subjects' preference for teachers that let them alone, their attitude toward religion, their attitude toward personal relations, their satisfaction in a career in which, for the most part, they follow their own interest without direction or interference. (1981, 109)

Integrating the work of Roe with theories of psychosocial development provides a plausible explanation for human development with a propensity toward physical science–related activities. The importance of personality development being affected by common experiences early in life is directly expressed by object relations theory. On the social level, Roe's study exposes how conflicts and sense of self developed during childhood and their effect on the external experiences of adulthood.

Chodorow (1978) argues the importance of a child's early social relations in determining psychological growth and personality formation. Chodorow explains that:

> Culture and personality theory has shown that early experiences common to members of a particular society contribute to the formation of typical personalities organized around and preoccupied with certain relational issues. To the extent that females and males experience different interpersonal environments as they grow up, feminine and masculine personalities will develop differently and be occupied with different issues. (1978, 51)

Roe's research integrated with object relations theory informs us of the importance of the early experiences for preschool children. The quality of the experience, the materials available, and encouragement by adults and peers establish an environment that allows us to observe the behaviors of children who demonstrate their intrinsic motivation. The key point here is to equate intrinsic motivation with Roe's scientists' personality trait of persistence. A concrete behavior that represents persistence, in our investigation, is time on task with Legos and blocks. An example of this concept is seen in our children who spend more than one-third of their free play time actively engaged in their spatial, geometric, and architectural activities (see chapters 4 and 5). Therefore, an environment rich in Lego-like materials and block resources that allows for the participation of all preschool children is one that is conducive to the development of spatial abilities, geometric skills, and physical science knowledge.

In addition, Farenga (1995) and Farenga and Joyce (1999a, 1999b) demonstrate the connection among informal science-related experiences, future interest in science, and the gender of young students. They constructed a regression model that tested whether science-related experiences, science attitudes, and gender predict future physical science participation as measured by the number of future physical science courses selected. This was of particular interest due to the young age of the students in the study. It was determined that gender, future career interest in science, and informal physical science-related experiences could explain approximately forty-two percent of the variance in physical science course selection. The inclusion of career interest was consistent with Roe's (1952) observation that early career interest was a trait of many physical scientists. A similar pattern also connects informal physical science-related experiences as a predictor of the number of physical science-related courses selected. This suggests a direct connection between previous experience in a field and interest in future participation. Simply put, the percentage of young children who selected future physical science-related careers is identical to the actual percentage of individuals who graduate with advanced degrees in these same careers.

What is also pertinent is that each of the studies found significant gender differences that parallel current employment statistics in the mathematical and physical science-related fields. This is significant when combined with the present study which demonstrates no gender differences in the physical science-related activities of spatial abilities and architecture in young children ages four and five (see chapter 5). However, significant gender-related differences were substantiated by Farenga (1995) and Farenga and Joyce (1999a, 1999b) for students as young as nine years. Thus, a pattern of socialization that identifies certain courses in physical science-related activities as male and female appears to take a firm hold between kindergarten and third grade (ages six through nine). These related findings are important since, as we suggest, blocks and block-like materials are the precursors for future interest with more advanced playtime materials, such as Erector

Sets, Kinex Blocks, and Lego Techniques. These free play activities prime the development of functionally related skills required in using architecturally related or engineering-related equipment. These physical science–related activities have also been linked to the development of spatial ability required by activities involving mathematical or scientific thinking.

In sum, the professor's perspective provides yet another example of how young children's mathematical and scientific thinking is inextricably associated with those of professional mathematicians and scientists. The story, however, is still by no means over, and there is much more to tell. In the next chapter, we provide our results from empirical investigation of young children's emergent spatial, geometric, and architectural behaviors in the context of everyday play. In chapter 5, we discuss our results as they relate to development (i.e., changes of age), gender, and socioeconomic class. Our investigations show that young children's constructions are closely tied with spatial-geometric, architectural, and scientific principles.

CHAPTER TOPICS FOR DISCUSSION

1. Based on the discussion of architectural concepts and principles in this chapter, compare and contrast these basic concepts with those of space and geometry and the scientific principles having to do with the inversely related forces known as tension and compression.
2. Of the nine children examined by the professional architect and professor of architecture, select three of these children and compare and contrast them in terms of their conceptions of space and ideas about science with their architectural products.
3. What is the relationship between Ann Roe's findings of the lives of eminent scientists and the importance of Lego and block play?
4. Explain how Friedrich Froebel can be credited with fostering geometric thinking activities for the purposes of curriculum and instruction.
5. In architecture, three primary conditions play a crucial role in the development and construction of any structure: strength or firmness; utility or functionality; and aesthetics. Select three of the nine children examined in the chapter and describe how the three architectural conditions—strength, utility, and aesthetics—may or may not be connected to the scenario provided.

NOTES

1. Incidentally, for Piaget, the concept of enclosure is considered one of five elementary spatial relations—the other four being proximity, separation, order, and continuity. See previous chapter for further elaboration.

4

Contextual Observation: The Assessment for Measuring Spatial, Geometric, and Architectural Thinking of Young Children (SPAGAR)

> We looked to the geometrical forms and patterns of traditional objects like baskets, mats, pots, houses, fishtraps, and so forth and posed the question: Why do these material products possess the form they have? ... It came out that the form of these objects is almost never arbitrary, but generally represents many practical advantages and is, quite a lot of times, the only possible or optimal solution of a production problem. ... The traditional form reflects accumulated experience and wisdom. It constitutes not only biological and physical knowledge about the materials that are used, but also mathematical knowledge, knowledge about the properties and relations of circles, angles, rectangles, squares, regular pentagons and hexagons, cones, pyramids, cylinders, and so forth.
>
> Paulus Gerdes (1988, 34)

In the above quotation, Paulus Gerdes refers to the reconstruction of nearly wiped out mathematical traditions used in Mozambican culture. But if we also consider the culture of the child and identify young children's spatial and geometric propensities, our methodology of contextual observation is complementary to the methodology that Gerdes and his colleagues have used over the years.[1] We have essentially looked for the "geometric forms" that have never been constructed and implemented in written or descriptive form by researchers. In the same manner as Gerdes in his methodological approach, we have found that young children's geometric constructions are almost never arbitrary and do possess many practical advantages. We can only recall Andy, David, and Jimmy's "garage" described in chapter 3 and the importance of resourcefulness and usefulness as they consider "parking" each of their toy cars.

Further, we have found that, like the Mozambican artisan or the mathematical researcher in the laboratory, the child's developmental knowledge of spatial and geometric concepts are based on accumulated experience. That we compare Gerdes's work with mathematical knowledge of Mozambican artisans and merchants with the culture of the child is no trivial matter. In fact, there are many more similarities among Mozambican artisans, professional mathematicians or physical scientists, and preschool children than differences in terms of the ways in which members of each group think through mathematical or scientific tasks and problems and the construction of physical structures.

With this methodological comparison, we now discuss the essential investigations we have conducted, and based on the outcomes of these investigations, we discuss what the teacher, parent, or researcher needs to look for in order to implement best practice in fostering and promoting young children's cognitive strengths in the area of spatial and geometric knowledge.

In this chapter, we provide a description of each of the thirteen codes within the spatial-geometry-architecture coding system (SPAGAR). The first part of this chapter provides the reader with evidence to support our assertions and beliefs that young children routinely engage in spatial and geometric prototypical behaviors during free play. The basis of our assertions is the SPAGAR coding system. The second part of this chapter describes two specific, yet interwoven, types of analyses used in naturalistic studies of spontaneous mathematical activity of preschool children in the everyday context—namely, empirical analysis and case study. We then present the outcome of our empirical investigation, which provides a general picture of the amount of time children spend engaged in spatial-geometric, architectural, and scientifically related activities during free play. We highlight these activities so that teachers and parents will have the opportunity to recognize these behaviors and implement and advance activities at school and in the home or other environments.

YOUNG CHILDREN'S EVERYDAY
MATHEMATICAL ACTIVITIES THROUGH
CONTEXTUAL OBSERVATION

The ideas for this chapter emanate from our years of experience working with young children, discussions with experts in the field, and the review of research which examines children's cognitive development and the importance of non-structured play. We have examined the pattern and shape and spatial relations in greater depth than other seemingly common mathematical ideas, like enumeration and magnitude, because children's free play reveals a greater amount of time spent on these activities.

What types of patterns do children explore? What types of shapes do they construct? And what kinds of architectural principles underlie their frequent play with Legos and blocks? In this chapter, we use the method of contextual observation as a means of identifying geometric and spatial concepts of preschool children in the everyday context. Similar to naturalistic observation, contextual observation is a method for recording samples of behavior that a student demonstrates while being engaged in an activity during free play. It supplies the situational context in which the behavior occurs. It includes what the children are doing (behaviors), what the environment can support (resources), and social interaction (peer or adult support). We integrate qualitative and quantitative measures to obtain a more robust understanding of children's abilities. There is something lost when aggregating numerous pieces of information about a child in order to come to a generalization about all the behaviors of children.

The basis for contextual observation is summarized quite succinctly in Donaldson (1978), who refers to *formal thinking* as "disembedded thinking." As Donaldson informs us, the term *formal*, which is often applied to written, scientifically based entities of thought, often can be misconstrued with the developmental periods to which Piaget refers in his theory of intellectual development. For Donaldson, to refer to an academic subject as *formal* obfuscates the meaning of a concept on contextual grounds. In other words, to say that a student learns the mathematical topic of place value in a formal way does not demonstrate the context (or changes of context) in which the student is learning the concept.

Donaldson uses the example of formal logic (as defined in mathematical terms) as a prime example of disembedded thinking. In one example, she illustrates the notion of disembedded versus embedded thinking through written symbolism. In the first case, using an example from Wason and Johnson-Laird's research (1972), four cards are shown with the letters E and K (one vowel and one consonant) and the numbers four and seven (one even number and one odd number). The student is then given the rule: "If a card has a vowel on one side, then it has an even number on the other side." Students are then asked which cards must be turned over to demonstrate the rule. Donaldson points out the disembeddedness of the problem, given that it might be rather difficult to determine that the correct answer is to turn over the cards with the E (vowel) and the seven (odd number). The E card (i.e., p) is to be turned over because in order to determine if the given rule is true, one must check that an even number (i.e., q) appears on the reverse side. The seven card is to be turned over due to the contrapositive—namely, if the number is not even (i.e., not q), then the reverse side is not a vowel (i.e., not p). The K card need not be turned over because the rule does not state whether a card with a consonant has an even or odd number on the reverse side. Similarly, the rule does not state whether a card showing an even number must have either a vowel or consonant on the other side. The reason has to do with formal logic, which states that categorical syllogisms—if p then q—are only true if p is true and q is true, or in the case where the syllogism, if $\sim q$ then $\sim p$ (read as "if *not q* then *not p*"), in which the negation of q implies the negation of p (contrapositive). This is indeed a concept that is disembedded from context.

In contrast, if we examine another example by Johnson-Laird, Legrenzi, and Sonino Legrenzi (1974), we find that it takes on virtually the same logical structure as the categorical syllogism without using abstract symbolism. In this case, the student is given the rule: "If a letter is sealed, then it has a five penny stamp on it." Four pictures were presented: a sealed envelope, an unsealed envelope, an envelope with a five-penny stamp, and an envelope with a four-penny stamp. Students are then asked to turn over the correct envelopes to demonstrate the rule. Given the embedded context of the conceptual problem at hand, most students are able to answer correctly—namely, the sealed envelope is turned over to determine if a five-cent stamp is on one side, and the four-penny stamped envelope is turned over to determine if the envelope is not sealed. The main point here is that Donaldson emphasizes the importance of context in the summoning of conceptual understanding and cognitive structures.

In our analyses, we have examined ninety four- and five-year-old children while considering the contextual factors which may affect the ways in which children encounter emerging spatial concepts and architectural principles. It should be evident that anything the child does is within the bounds of that individual's environment. Thus, cognitive development presupposes the contextual factors in one's environment and summons embedded thinking.

Two types of analysis were used to gather data. The first, an empirical investigation, involved the coding and interpretation of spatial, geometric, and architectural activity. The second form of analysis involved case studies of individual children who exhibited both unique examples of cognitive behaviors and of behaviors that can be identified within the general population of preschool children. The data collected were from five urban preschools, in which individual four- and five-year-old children were videotaped during free play. Further, they represent various socioeconomic levels (low-income, middle-income, and upper-income). One play center involved only low-income children, two accommodated both low- and middle-income children, one accommodated only middle-income children, and one took in only upper-income children. The number of children in each preschool classroom ranged anywhere from nineteen in one pre-school to more than thirty in another. In general, all the preschool class-rooms included centers for particular free play activities, including a Legos and blocks area, a dramatic play area, a reading area, and water and sand play. Although the preschool accommodating only upper-income children seemed to have greater quantities of play objects, for the most part all the preschools had the same types of materials.

The preschoolers, all of whom resided in an urban environment, were between the ages of 4.17 to 6.00 years (Mean = 4.97 and SD = .48). Of the entire group of children, thirty were from low-income households. Social class was based on whether the child was qualified for subsidized day-care expenses as described by an agency specializing in child develop-ment services. The children from low-income families ranged in age from 4.00 to 5.42 (Mean = 4.72 and SD = .45). The ethnic backgrounds of the low-income children were seventeen African-American, twelve Latino, and one of both African-American and Latino background. The middle-income group also consisted of thirty children, whose ages ranged from 4.00 to 5.92 years (Mean = 4.65 and SD = .48). The ethnic backgrounds of the middle-income group were twelve African-American, nine Latino, four White, two both African-American and Latino, and three Asian. The upper-income group, too, consisted of thirty children, whose ages ranged from 4.08 to 5.92 years (Mean = 5.03 and SD = .50). The ethnic backgrounds of all these children were White. Moreover, the upper-income preschool administration set two criteria for accepting children into their program: parents' level of income and a child's high score on an intelligence (IQ) test. In sum, low-income children were mostly African-American and Lat-ino while the entire upper-income population was White.

In examining the videotapes, we were careful to listen for the child's lan-guage in order to tap into the child's mathematical thinking, especially if the child used explicit mathematical language. Verbal data were collected using a cordless microphone. The child was then videotaped for at least fifteen minutes, regardless of his or her activity or location within the set-ting. In examining SPAGAR, over one thousand five hundred minutes of children's free play were observed. SPAGAR activity was coded based on one-minute intervals out of a total of fifteen minutes per target child.

SPATIAL, GEOMETRIC, ARCHITECTURAL (SPAGAR) CODING SYSTEM

The codes describing spatial thinking, geometric concepts, and architectural principles were developed by the researchers using both a top-down and bottom-up approach. That is, the development of these codes evolved from examining the literature on spatial and geometric thinking and identifying specific characteristics of mathematical conceptualizations used by mathematicians themselves (top-down). Moreover, observation and analysis of the videotape segments, in addition to numerous discussions and debates with several individuals involved in naturalistic observation methodology, served as a type of bottom-up approach that led to the creation of the codes described in this chapter. We have identified and defined a total of thirteen space-geometry-architecture (SPAGAR) codes. Our procedure is similar to Ginsburg and his colleagues (Ginsburg, Inoue, and Seo 1999; Ginsburg, Pappas, and Seo 2001), who developed their six mathematical category codes in a similar manner. Ginsburg's codes are classification, magnitude comparison, enumeration, dynamics, pattern and shape, and spatial relations (see table 4.1).

We define each of the thirteen SPAGAR codes next. A quick reference to each of the thirteen SPAGAR codes is outlined in table 4.2. Further, if a particular spatial or architectural domain contains codes, each code is defined after the domain under which it is listed. So, for example, after the symmetric telations domain is defined, the definitions of the three codes related to symmetry will follow—namely, line symmetry, plane symmetry,

Table 4.1.   Mathematics codes developed by Ginsburg and colleagues (Ginsburg, Inoue, and Seo 1999; Ginsburg, Pappas, and Seo 2001)

Code Name	Description
Classification	Systematic arrangement in groups according to established criteria. It involves activities such as sorting, grouping, or categorizing.
Magnitude Comparison	Comparison of two or more items to evaluate relative magnitudes. It involves activities such as measuring, ordering, or comparing by length, size, area, weight, height, depth, or volume.
Enumeration	Numerical judgment or quantification. It involves activities such as counting, subitizing, or explicit use of number words.
Dynamics	Exploration of the process of change or transformation. It involves activities such as adding and subtracting or motion exploration like rotations, flips, or turns.
Patterns and Shapes	Exploration of patterns and spatial forms. It involves activities such as detecting patterns, identifying shapes, exploring parts and attributes of shapes, drawing shapes, or creating patterns and shapes.
Spatial Relations	Exploration of positions, courses, and distances in space. It involves activities such as drawing maps, representing the locations of objects in space, or telling directions like left, right, front, above, or behind.

Table 4.2. Spatial/geometric/architectural (SPAGAR) code descriptions

Code Type	SPAGAR Code	Description/Example
	Spatial Relations	
Symmetric Relations	Symmetric relations include arranging smaller objects or drawing a completed figure in which both halves of the completed (or semi-completed) arrangement or figure are each other's mirror images. An object is placed (or centered) equidistant from the sides or ends of a larger object or structure.	
	1) Line Symmetry	• Drawing a picture of a butterfly. • Placing a magnet onto another magnet that has originally been set on a magnetic surface.
	2) Plane Symmetry	• Constructing a Lego skyscraper in which one side is a mirror image of the other
	3) Rotational Symmetry	• Constructing a pinwheel or other object in which a rotation does not change the object's disposition.
	4) Patterning	• Arranging a group of objects in a way that demonstrates a subject-imposed rule-governed activity or consistent relationship. Repeating similar objects in line or row form.
Figural Relations	Figural relations includes figure identification and shape matching. These two codes are complementary and inversely related; the former has to do with objects that are present in the mental schema, while the latter deals with the child's adjustment to newly introduced geometric properties.	
	5) Figure Identification	• Demonstrating a child's use, description, or representation of geometric shapes that may be encountered in formal schooling.
	6) Shape Matching	• Using geometric properties—size, shape, or contour—to complete rule-governed activities, such as puzzles and other similar play objects.
Direction/ Location	7) Direction/ Location	• Deliberate evidence—words or actions—making navigation, place, or location explicit (e.g., over, under, behind, on top of, left, right; building track under a bridge).

	Architectural Principles	
Architectural Principles	This code type involves children's use of six general ideas that are found in construction of both children and architects and civil engineers.	
	8) Enclosure	• Creating or producing an arrangement of interlocking, touching, or continuous objects, thus forming an inner space.

Table 4.2.   Continued

Code Type	SPAGAR Code	Description/Example
		Architectural Principles
Architectural Principles *(continued)*	9) Foundation	• Systematically arranging objects to form a base for a potentially large structure; it is evident when a child uses more Legos or blocks at the base of a structure than anywhere else.
	10) Trabeated Construction	• Systematically arranging objects to form a base for a potentially large structure; it is evident when a child uses blocks or similar objects as post and beams to possibly support additional levels or "floors" of a structure.
	11) Posting	• Systematically arranging objects to form a base for a potentially large structure; it is evident when a child uses objects for supporting bridges, roadways, or track.
	12) Engineering	• Contriving or manipulating objects skillfully or artfully, which can involve informal or formal measurement or estimation.
	13) Proportional Reasoning	• Recognizing a model's size with respect to the real-life object or its representation.

and rotational symmetry. The first seven codes (line, plane, and rotational symmetry; patterning; figure identification; shape matching; and direction/location) fall under spatial and geometric relations, while the remaining six codes—enclosure, foundation, trabeated construction, posting, engineering, and proportional reasoning—fall under architectural principles. The following section discusses how we define and interpret each of the codes in the SPAGAR system.

SEVEN SPATIAL CODES

Symmetric Relations

Various descriptions of symmetry differ considerably, and in some cases, diverge in meaning altogether. In the most general sense, the domain of symmetric relations is defined here as the arrangement of objects such that whatever form these objects take on one side of an axis is mirrored on the other. This situation is an example of what is frequently referred to as bilateral symmetry. According to Hargittai and Hargittai (1994), the more generalized term for this kind of symmetry is called point-group symmetry: that is, one side of a construction is a reflection or replica of the other side.

In this sense, symmetric relations also involve balance; as described by O'Gorman (1998), balance provides both a sense of unity (in terms of aesthetics) and firmitas, or structure. That is, it is common to associate balanced structures with symmetric ones—the notion of one side of a structure as a mirror image of the other (symmetry) is balanced by its very nature. In addition, as an architectural principle, balance and symmetry are two important attributes of a strong and stable structure.

However, symmetric relations can take numerous other forms as well. We see them in many examples in the everyday world. Some of the forms of symmetry that are not associated with the typical mirror image, or bilateral, definition are rotational symmetries (e.g., windmill, yin-yang), symmetries that involve repetition (see patterning below), and even those that involve proportionate objects or figures, which are magnified by the same number.

So, given the expansiveness of symmetric relations, what kinds of symmetries do four- and five-year-old children exhibit during free play? The idea of symmetry is clearly illustrated in children's Lego or block building or in their drawings. Through extensive observation, we have identified four types of symmetry in preschool children's free-play activity: line symmetry, plane symmetry, central/rotational symmetry, and patterning. With line symmetry, involving structures in two dimensions, an object is placed (or centered) equidistant from the sides or ends of a larger object or structure. Centering, a form of line symmetry, refers to the placement of an object so that a structure demonstrates a symmetric appearance. It involves the aesthetics of symmetry and perhaps shows less complexity (see figure 4.1).

Examples of plane symmetry involve structures in three dimensions, whereby one side of the structure is a mirror image of the other (see figure 4.2). Rotational symmetry occurs in children's constructions when an object of the structure appears as if it can be rotated around its axis, and it appears in the same position two or more times. One example of rotational symmetry would be the occurrence of a child drawing a pinwheel or a

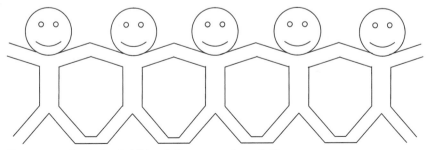

Figure 4.1. Example of children's line symmetry activities

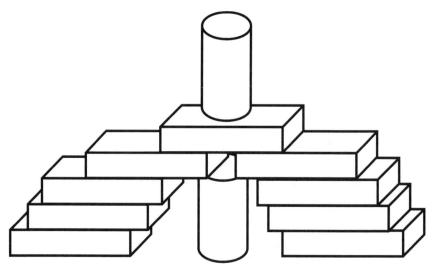

Figure 4.2.   Example of children's plane symmetry activities

windmill or creating a rotational object out of Legos or blocks (see figure 4.3).

Patterning

Patterning is defined as a type of symmetry in which a group of objects is arranged in a way that demonstrates a subject-imposed rule-governed activity or consistent relationship. The child arranges objects according to a rule, thus creating an intrinsically or extrinsically derived pattern. In addition, "space-group symmetry"—the repetition of similar objects in line or row form (Hargittai and Hargittai 1994)—is associated with this spatial characteristic. As Hargittai and Hargittai suggest:

> Space-group symmetries are created by simple repetition of a basic motif, and describe the most economical growth and expansion patterns. Border decorations are examples of one-dimensional space-group symmetry in which a pattern can be generated through translational symmetry by repeating a motif at equal intervals. Repetition can be achieved by a shift in direction, or it may be done by reflection, rotation or glide-reflection. Helices and spirals display one-dimensional space-group symmetries although, as a spiral staircase, they may extend to three dimensions. (1996, 81)

In accordance with Hargittai and Hargittai's findings, the forms of symmetry that we have observed among young children's spontaneous, everyday activities during free play are, for the most part, unforced and not strictly

Figure 4.3. Example of children's rotational symmetry activities

rigorous in mathematical terms. Figure 4.4 exemplifies what children can produce with regard to rule-governed pattern constructions.

Geometric Relations

There are two types of geometric relations in the SPAGAR coding system: figure identification and shape matching.

Figure Identification

Figure identification concerns the identification of figures, patterns, or shapes in either two or three dimensions or awareness of their properties (e.g. circle, square, cube, or pyramid). Unlike shape matching (see below), with figure identification, the child has most likely assimilated the structure or geometric form that has been identified. Two examples from the video-taped segments should help explain the general meaning behind figure identification because a good deal of figure identification is derived from verbal evidence that the child provides.

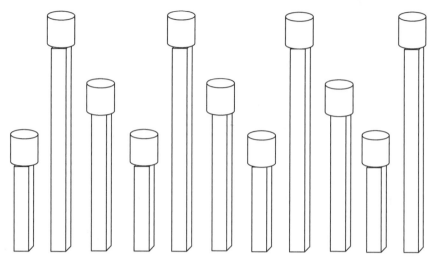

Figure 4.4. Example of children's patterning activities using both rectilinear and cylindrical blocks

In one segment, for example, Alejandro asks Harry for the "circle thing" in order to build a make-believe garage. Alejandro and Harry plan to use four "circle things"—cylindrical blocks—in order to establish a foundation to their garage. In another segment (not part of the segments analyzed in depth), Les and Samantha, two three-year-old children, construct a large rectangle on the classroom floor out of different length rectilinear blocks. They refer to the final construction as a "big square"; although opposite sides appear parallel and create ninety degree corners, not all sides are equal in length. Nevertheless, Les and Samantha's reference to the constructed figure as a "square" demonstrates the children's command of different shapes and how the square-like features of their construction seem to stand out.

Shape Matching

Shape matching concerns the use of geometric properties—size, shape, or contour—for completing rule-governed activities, such as puzzles and other similar play objects. Unlike figure identification, shape matching involves accommodation; the child must adjust to certain geometric properties that may be imposed by the object in order to solve the task at hand.

In one videotaped segment, Dean demonstrates his expertise in arranging puzzle pieces so that the entire puzzle is complete. When Bart, another young child, approaches Dean and observes how fast Dean can put his puzzle together, he challenges Dean to a race to see who can complete each individual puzzle faster. This scenario demonstrates two children's involvement in a shape matching activity: Clearly, the children need to adapt to the rule-governed characteristics of the two puzzles in terms of the different sizes, shapes, and contours of each of the pieces.

Direction/Location

Direction/location involves words or actions relating to navigation, place, or location (e.g. over, under, behind, on top of, left, right; building track under a bridge). It demonstrates deliberate evidence of making navigation explicit or using prepositions of navigation or other symbolic means in expressing geographical location. For example, Harry approaches Cecil, who is experimenting with a Lego wheel and the color spectrum when the Lego wheel spins. The Lego wheel is constructed from a circular hub and individual rectangular Lego pieces, each having a distinct color, attached to the side of the hub. Harry asks Cecil where to find the hubs. Cecil verbally directs Harry to the appropriate location using works like "Go right" then "straight ahead" followed by "into the kitchen, in the cabinet and below the counter." In this case, navigation was clearly made explicit.

SIX ARCHITECTURE CODES

The six architectural codes in the SPAGAR coding system are enclosure; foundation, trabeated construction, and posting (all are in the support category); engineering; and proportional reasoning.

Enclosure

Children demonstrate enclosure when they create an arrangement of interlocking, touching, or continuous objects, thus forming an inner space. Enclosure can involve two-dimensional inner space, three-dimensional inner space, or structures that may be partially built to enclose (like an amphitheater model) but serve the function of covering or enclosing one or more objects (see figure 4.5).

With the possible exception of studies of block play and block construction, little has been researched in the area of children's constructions involving enclosures. One exception is in connection to Erik Erikson's observations of young children's constructions when comparing boys with girls. In *Childhood and Society* (1963), Erikson suggests that young girls tend to construct blocks as enclosures or in an open air fashion, whereas boys are more inclined to construct in ways which demonstrate compactness and verticality. Although we noticed this tendency among boys and girls in our videotaped analyses (see the case of Kathryn in chapter 8 and the case of

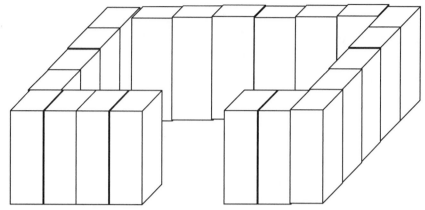

Figure 4.5.   Example of children's enclosure activities using rectilinear blocks

Fernando in chapter 9), we also have observed boys engaged in more or less horizontal, open-space construction and some girls engaged in more compact, vertical constructions.

Supports

The category of supports is defined as a systematic arrangement of objects forming the base of a potentially large structure. The child's intention is to use a base to support a structure above it. Three types of supports construction are evident in children's free play: foundation, trabeated construction, and posting. Foundation is a systematic construction of objects forming a base of a potentially large structure. The intention is to create a strong base so that a structure remains erect. Foundation is evident when a child constructs a base for a larger structure without attending to post and beam (perpendicular) construction (see figure 4.6).

Trabeated construction involves the use of blocks or similar objects as post and beams for possibly supporting additional levels or "floors" of a structure. Trabeated construction occurs when a child demonstrates ideas about perpendicularity as a means of supporting a larger structure. These constructions occur, for example, when a child places four cylindrical or cubical blocks so they are equidistant (posts) and then places long blocks horizontally (lintels) to give the appearance of post-and-lintel construction (see figure 4.7). According to one architect, trabeated construction presents one of the most stable forms of foundation (Fairbanks, pers. comm.).

Posting refers to the use of objects used for supporting bridges, roadways, or track. Posting involves the arrangement of objects having vertical support or column and lintel construction. Children demonstrate posting when they build bridges, roadways, or train track from play blocks, particu-

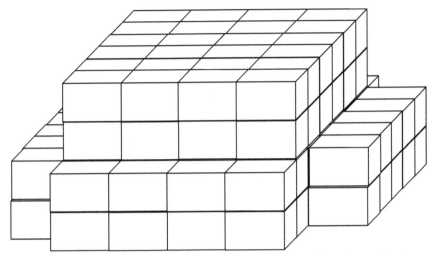

Figure 4.6.   Example of children's use of foundation as support for a larger structure

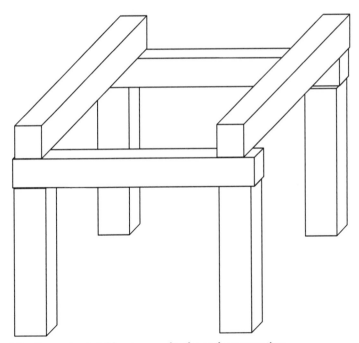

Figure 4.7.   Example of children's use of trabeated construction

larly when certain blocks are used as suspensions for longer pieces of block (see figure 4.8).

Engineering

Engineering describes a child demonstrating a sense of accuracy when arranging objects or a child's skillful or artful contrivance or manipulation of objects. Engineering can involve informal or formal measurement or estimation or the accuracy used in a construction. This can be based on length of objects or openings of enclosed structures for fitting objects. Engineering, which seems to engender the notion of precision, can also involve drawing figures.

Two different videotaped segments in chapter 3 illustrate the engineering activity. In one of them, Alejandro guides Harry in the construction of a garage made out of blocks. Given that blocks are less stable than snap pieces like Legos, they must be more attentive to precision to keep the large, hollow block structure erect. In the other, Andy, David, and Jimmy build another garage structure; however, in this case, the Lego structure has been mostly completed. According to Andy's specifications, however, changes need to be made to the space within the Lego structure where toy cars can be parked.

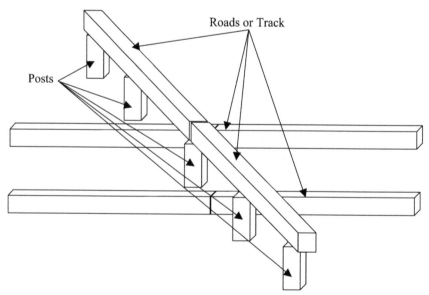

Figure 4.8. Example of children's use of posting

Proportional Reasoning

Proportional reasoning occurs when the child demonstrates knowledge of the ratio of a smaller model (e.g., toy car) to a larger one (e.g., garage constructed out of blocks) as being equal to the ratio between a smaller life-size object (e.g., car) and a larger life-size object (e.g., garage). It refers to a child's awareness of a smaller model with respect to its placement in or near a larger model (e.g., the placement of a Lego car inside a larger Lego garage). When referring to spatial, geometric, and architectural activity of four- and five-year-old children, proportional reasoning, then, deals with mathematical intuitions concerning space without the use of written number.

In the next section of this chapter, we examine young children's free play activities in order to determine the behaviors identified in the SPAGAR classification system. We present an overall picture of the spatial and geometric thinking and underlying architectural principles that may be manifest in children's everyday play. Empirical evidence showing the possible relationships between certain groups of children (based on age, gender, and social class) and spatial, geometric, and architectural ideas are also provided.

EMPIRICAL INVESTIGATION USING SPAGAR

One of the most startling results of our research in the area of preschoolers' everyday mathematical activities is the discovery that four- and five-year-old children are engaged in mathematical activity for nearly half the time during free play (Ginsburg, Pappas, and Seo 2001). Given this finding, we investigated the types of environments in which young children engaged in mathematical thinking more frequently. Our findings indicate that children are engaged in mathematical and scientific activity most often when the environment is conducive to pattern and shape activities. These activities seem to demonstrate their problem solving skills and challenges to given situations. The following section provides the results to our investigations using the SPAGAR system.

The results are divided into two sections. The first section examines all ninety four- and five-year-old children in terms of overall SPAGAR activity and the thirteen different types of spatial, geometric, and architectural activity. Age, gender, and social class comparisons are also considered. Surprisingly, sixty-four percent of the children in the sample are engaged in spatial, geometric, or architecturally related activity. Further generalizations concerning young children's SPAGAR activities are discussed. Second, are there any differences when examining children who are engaged in spatial, geometric, or architectural activity for a significant amount of time, namely at least one-third of their entire videotaped segment? In the second section, we examine only those children engaged in any one of these activities for five or more minutes.

Overall Findings of Spatial, Geometric, and Architectural Activity

The first question concerns the average percentage of time out of a total of fifteen minutes that children spend on spatial, geometric, and architectural activities. During free play, children were engaged in spatial, geometric, or architectural activities for almost one-third, or 29 percent, of the time. Based on the number of minutes, figure 4.9 presents the frequency of children engaged in different numbers of minutes of this activity. Of the ninety children, fifty-three were engaged in spatial, geometric, and architectural activity, while thirty-seven were not.

While observing the children more carefully as they were engaged in free play, we found that they spent a great deal of time in activities having to do with identifying shapes (figure identification), matching shapes to puzzles or impressions of three-dimensional figures (shape matching), navigational activities (direction/location), and activities having to do with symmetry (symmetric relations). Our findings suggest that children were engaged in spatial and geometric activities for twenty-six percent, a little over one-quarter, of the time. If we were to further separate the SPAGAR activities to include only the architecturally related codes, we would find that children are engaged in architecturally related activities for three percent of the time.

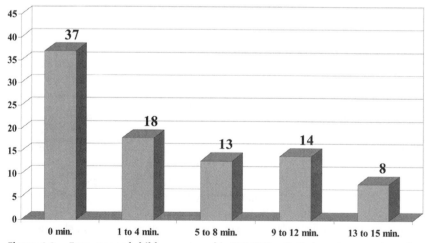

Figure 4.9. **Frequency of children engaged in SPAGAR activity based on number of minutes**

The relatively low percentage of time spent on architecture-related activity appears to be associated with a number of factors. Some of these factors include a child's selection of the type of play (play center), the objects with which the child plays, the overall resources of the preschool environment, and adult or peer intervention in terms of a particular free play activity.

Examined next are the frequencies of the different types of spatial, geometric, and architectural activities. What is the average percent of time out of a total of fifteen minutes that a child spends on the thirteen specific types of spatial, geometric, and architectural activities? The average percent of time spent on each spatial, geometric, and architectural activity, as well as groups of different activities, are provided in table 4.3. These percentages were determined by dividing the means of each activity by fifteen minutes. The most common activities (i.e., those activities in which children spend the most amount of time) are figure identification (twelve percent), shape matching (seven percent), plane symmetry (six percent), direction/location (five percent), and patterning (four percent).

In focusing our attention on the fifty-three children who did engage in SPAGAR activity, you will notice that the percentage of time these children are engaged in spatial, geometric, or architectural activity increases considerably. During free play, children engaged in spatial, geometric, or architectural activities spend nearly half (forty-nine percent) of the time on these activities. Children who engaged in spatial and geometric activities did so for forty-four percent of the time. This is an increase of nearly twenty percent when comparing these children with the group as a whole. Children who engaged in only architecturally related activities did so for an average of five percent of the time. The average percentages of time spent on each spatial, geometric, and architectural activity of the fifty-three children who engaged in SPAGAR activity are also provided in table 4.3. The most common activities (i.e., those activities in which children spend the most amount of time) are figure identification (twenty-one percent), shape matching (eleven percent), direction/location (nine percent), patterning (seven percent), and engineering (six percent).

Children Engaged for Five or More Minutes in SPAGAR

This section examines those children engaged in any one of the specific spatial, geometric, or architectural activities for five or more minutes within their fifteen-minute segment—that is, for at least one-third of the time engaged in free play activity. Here we look to see if there are any differences between the cognitive behaviors of the thirty-three children when compared to the entire sample. Referring to the frequency distributions alone may provide little, if any, justification for using the five-minute mark as a cut-off point when analyzing four- and five-year-old children engaged in

Table 4.3.   Percentage of time children engage in each activity

Category	Percentage of Time Spent on Each Activity			
	n = 90		n = 53	
Symmetric Relations				
Line Symmetry	2		4	
Plane Symmetry	6		3	
Rotational Symmetry	1		2	
Total		9		9
Patterning	4		7	
Total		4		7
Shapes				
Figure Identification	12		21	
Shape Matching	7		11	
Total		19		32
Direction/Location	5		9	
Total		5		9
Architectural Relations				
Enclosure	1		2	
Foundation	0.4		1	
Trabeated Construction	1		2	
Posting	1		1	
Engineering	3		6	
Proportional Reasoning	0.4		1	
Total		6.8		13

spatial, geometric, and architectural activity. People who have worked with preschool aged populations realize that children who are engaged in an activity for five minutes or longer demonstrate persistence, interest, motivation, and somewhat greater concentration than those who do not spend as much time. The main explanation here is that using five minutes as a cutoff seems valid from a psychological standpoint, given that a five-minute attention span for young children in voluntary activity, specifically during free play, is rather high if no distraction exists (McCune and Zanes 2001).

The first question in this section concerns the number of children actually involved in any one spatial, geometric, and architectural activity for five or more minutes. Results indicate that a total of thirty-three children out of ninety are engaged (for at least five minutes of their fifteen-minute segment) in any one of the thirteen activities. We have found that the children spend over two-thirds, or an average of sixty-nine percent, of the time on these activities. Again, if one considers the percentage of time children are engaged in only symmetric relations, patterning, figure identification, shape matching, or direction/location activities, our findings show that children spend over 61 percent of their free play time engaged in these activities. In addition, among this group, children are engaged in only architecturally related activities for eight percent of the time. When considering the thirty-three children engaged in SPAGAR activities for five or more minutes, the average percentages of time spent on each spatial, geometric, and architectural activity are given in table 4.4. The most common activities (i.e. those activities in which children spend the most amount of time) are figure identification (thirty-two percent), shape matching (fifteen percent), direction/location (eleven percent), patterning (eleven percent), and engineering (nine percent).

SUMMARY AND IMPLICATIONS

The results from this empirical investigation show that young children have a natural inclination toward both mathematically and scientifically related everyday, spontaneous activities. More specifically, our analysis of young

Table 4.4.   Percentage of time children engage in each activity

Category	Percentage of Time Spent on Each Activity	
Symmetric Relations		
Line Symmetry	6	
Plane Symmetry	4	
Rotational Symmetry	2	
Total		12
Patterning	11	
Total		11
Figure Identification	32	
Shape Matching	15	
Total		47
Direction/Location	11	
Total		11
Architectural Relations		
Enclosure	3	
Foundation	1	
Trabeated Construction	3	
Posting	1	
Engineering	9	
Proportional Reasoning	1	
Total		18
TOTAL		100

children in the free play environment suggests that the mathematic and scientific behaviors exhibited by the children we observed tend toward spatial and geometric thinking activities in particular. The results of these findings highlight the intrinsic motivations of young children to participate in the inquiry skills that are associated with mathematics and science. Although the types of activities and percentages of time that children are engaged in these activities are worthy of note, we find that the greatest benefit is placing the results in larger psychological and educational contexts. Based on our findings, we suggest that curriculum specialists, teachers, childcare educators, and parents will recognize the need to generate opportunities for young children to experience informal mathematics-related activities in ways that will bridge the gap between everyday experiences and scientific concepts. In discussion with numerous childhood educators, we are often surprised that many individuals are unaware that infants and young children engage in mathematically and scientifically related behaviors (Gattegno 1973; Gopnik, Meltzoff, and Kuhl 2001). In corroboration with recent research, our investigation demonstrates that young children are by no means as devoid of spatial, geometric, and architectural ideas as many adults may be led to believe. The following sections elaborate on both psychological and educational implications of these results.

Psychological Implications

The results of our investigation yield a number of implications in the area of developmental and cognitive psychology. First, it is evident, as much of the research suggests, that children possess a powerful intellectual capacity well before they enter formal schooling (Flavell 1982; Siegler 1996), and a great deal of this competence has to do with mathematical thinking (Fennema et al. 1997; Geary 1994; Ginsburg 1989; Resnick 1989). However, early mathematical thinking is not comprised of number concepts or activities alone. As the results indicate, young children are clearly involved in spontaneous spatial, geometric, and even architectural activity.

Next, it should be noted that SPAGAR does not seem to reflect Piaget's topological primacy thesis in terms of the types of spatial, geometric, and architectural activities in which four- and five-year-old children are involved. Recalling chapter 2 of this text, Piaget and Inhelder (1967) demonstrate how young children's spatial thinking engenders topological notions; that is, they generally think of geometric shapes and solids in an elastic way—one which lacks rigidity or the notion of lines and angles that would be present in the Euclidean system. Moreover, topological primacy is said to be present well into the fourth or fifth year. In contrast to Piaget's well-known theory on young children's conception of space, most of the

SPAGAR activities are not topological at all. In fact, they involve notions of the distinctions between more or less curvilinear and rectilinear shapes, as well as properties of shapes involving parallel and perpendicular lines. This finding parallels Huttenlocher, Newcombe, and Sandberg's (1994) conclusion that children as young as sixteen months are able to identify the location of a toy hidden in a sandbox by use of Euclidean, or metric, modes of problem solving, not topological ones.

In sum, the SPAGAR codes demonstrate that four- and five-year-old children are engaged in activities that deal with a great number of Euclidean concepts, not topological ones proposed by Piaget and Inhelder. With the sole exception of the enclosure code, the spatial, geometric, and architectural activities in which young children engage themselves involve Euclidean principles of linearity through identifying shape and creating architectural foundations, which mostly deal with parallel and perpendicular concepts. It can be concluded, then, that contextual observation methodology does not reveal extensive use of topological notions.

Educational Implications

The findings of this empirical investigation yield educational implications as well. An important question, then, is the following: Would an integrated mathematics and science curriculum—one that includes spatial and geometric concepts as well as architectural principles—enhance preschool education? Indeed, this would depend on the type of mathematics curriculum offered. First, Ginsburg, Inoue, and Seo (1999) conclude that four- and five-year-old children possess a rich understanding of mathematical concepts that will enable them to succeed in formal mathematical ideas upon entrance to elementary school. This investigation corroborates the Ginsburg et al. study (2003), which found that young children also possess sophisticated knowledge of spatial and geometric concepts in their everyday free play. One argument, then, would be that the creation of a preschool integrated mathematics and science curriculum based on young children's spontaneous mathematical knowledge in the everyday context may contribute to a broader understanding of more complex mathematical ideas in later years. This is not to say, however, that any preschool integrated mathematics and science curriculum is beneficial for success in later grades; clearly, curricula that focus on mathematical topics emphasizing rote, mechanical skills and written symbolism may hamper, not further, young children's mathematical understanding (Ginsburg 1989).

Second, a great deal of evidence suggests that children develop important mathematical skills on their own: counting (Gelman and Gallistel 1978; Wynn 1995), important arithmetic concepts (Baroody and Wilkins 1999), addition and subtraction concepts (Brush 1978), and arithmetic procedures (Carpenter, Moser, and Romberg 1982).

But what about conceptual knowledge and skills in ideas regarding space and geometry? Despite its importance in the curriculum, the teaching of spatial and geometric concepts is lacking in many school districts across the country (Porter 1989; Thomas 1982). With the exception of Clements and his colleagues (Clements and Battista 1989, 1992; Clements 1999; Clements et al. 1999), little, if any, research has been devoted to this topic or has informed teachers and other mathematics educators. Mathematics curricula in the early grades, then, place a great deal of emphasis on number at the expense of other important mathematical areas.

Unlike earlier studies devoted to spatial and geometric thinking, the results from this investigation can inform educators in several ways. First, it shows that the greatest amount of young children's spontaneous everyday mathematics deals with spatial and geometric activities. Given that young children are engaged in spatial, geometric, and architectural activity for nearly one-third of their free play time, mathematics curricula in the early grades may benefit by broadening their scope and focus by including spatial and geometric concepts as well.

Third, the children in this investigation were not taught specific spatial or geometric concepts; they performed them without any formal mathematics or science training. This very notion hinges on the psychological and educational research that demonstrates young children building on their prior experience with, and understanding of, shapes and other spatial and geometric properties. That is, young children do not view shapes passively; they explore with them through drawing, manipulation of objects (as in their block play), and even through language or explanation. Educators, then, can develop geometry curriculum with the understanding that prior to formal school entrance, young children possess a wealth of knowledge in spatial and geometric concepts.

Fourth, a rather large part of the spatial and geometric activity of four- and five-year-old children deals with architectural principles, particularly when working with Lego- and block-related materials. Based on the results above, the inclusion of basic architectural principles within a preschool geometry curriculum can enhance young children's understanding of geometric concepts that are introduced in formal schooling.

Since young children, who often focus on properties of geometric shapes, seem adept in these areas, spatial, geometric, and architecturally related curricula in preschool and the early grades may foster young children's understanding in these areas by emphasizing not solely the visual aspects of shape (as defined in Van Hiele's first level of geometric thinking), but their properties as well. Further, it is important to note that the process or inquiry skills that young children exhibit in their everyday free play activities demonstrate the inextricable link between the study of mathematics and science during the preschool ages.

In the next chapter, we examine young children's activities that exhibit spatial, geometric, and architectural thinking from the perspective of age, gender, and socioeconomic class.

CHAPTER TOPICS FOR DISCUSSION

1. Identify different methodological approaches for studying young children's cognitive processes and determine whether the contextual observation approach used in this volume is the most viable for tapping young children's spontaneous spatial, geometric, and architectural knowledge.
2. We argued that "formal" thinking is a grossly overgeneralized term. Donaldson (1978) refers to "formal" thinking, not as thinking that takes place in the school environment or when working with so-called formal learning (e.g., written forms of mathematical or scientific terms and concepts), but rather as "disembedded thinking" (i.e., the lack of context). Donaldson presents the topic of formal logic as an example. Identify a concept, either in mathematics or science (other than Donaldson's example), that is often introduced through disembedded thinking. Next, identify at least one way in which the concept can be presented through embedded thinking.
3. Identify and explain at least five ways in which careful analysis of a young child's use of language can help in determining the child's emergent spatial, geometric, or architectural knowledge.
4. Suppose you were hired to create and develop early childhood mathematics curriculum. Identify and explain how you would go about developing a curriculum on spatial and geometric concepts through the presentation of architectural principles that seem to be inherent in children's minds during free play.
5. We have provided educational implications as they relate to young children's spatial, geometric, and architectural activities. What may be some possible implications of the research presented in this chapter that relate to the teaching and learning of geometric concepts in the upper elementary level grades?

NOTES

1. Of course, one must embrace the position that young children's actions, habits, and particularly cognitive functioning in everyday life is intrinsically different from that of adults.

5

Age, Gender, and Socioeconomic Status Factors in Spatial, Geometric, and Architectural Thinking

> ... one needs to understand and acknowledge inevitable preferences in order to know their influence—so that fair treatment of data and arguments can be obtained!
>
> Stephen Jay Gould (1996, 36)

The data in the previous chapter indicated that young children engage in spatial, geometric, and architectural thinking during nearly one-third of free play time. These results are very encouraging for both cognitive development and education specialists. But what can we confirm, if anything, about the role of age, gender, or socioeconomic status (SES) with regard to spatial, geometric, and architectural thinking? More specifically, does age influence the numbers of minutes in which children engage in spatial, geometric, and architecturally related activities? How do girls fare in comparison with boys in terms of spatial, geometric, and architecturally related activities? Does one's socioeconomic status have an effect on how much time one spends on spatial, geometric, and architecturally related activities?

These questions form the basis of the present chapter. This chapter is divided into three sections. The first has to do with the role of age and time spent on spatial, geometric, and architectural activities. The second section deals with gender and its possible influence on time spent on spatial, geometric, and architectural activities. Finally, the third section examines whether socioeconomic class affects the amount of time a child is engaged in spatial, geometric, and architectural activities.

AGE RELATIONSHIPS BETWEEN FOUR- AND
FIVE-YEAR-OLD CHILDREN

Numerous studies have been designed to examine the effects of age on cognitive development. Topics involving children's intuitive physics (Anderson and Wilkening 1991; McCloskey 1983; Siegler 1995), spatial thinking (Landau, Gleitman, and Spelke 1981; White, Green, and Steiner 1995), and the development of scientific thinking (Flavell 1999; Kuhn 2002) have all examined whether specified cognitive domains are innate, environmentally dependent, a function of age and maturity, or some type of interaction among these variables. Nearly all of the work in these areas has emanated from the seminal works of Piaget.

The specific question of age with respect to cognitive and intellectual development in general and spatial thinking in particular has been debated since Piaget expounded on his topological primacy thesis with regard to children's conception of space and geometry prior to the age of five years. Since then, a number of schools of thought have emerged and challenged the Piagetian topological argument. One such group consists of researchers who espouse the nativist perspective (see chapter 2). These researchers agree that spatial thinking (as well as other cognitive domains of intellectual development) is one of numerous heritable characteristics of cognitive development and suggest that Euclidean concepts are present shortly after birth (Landau, Gleitman, and Spelke 1981; Landau, Spelke, and Gleitman 1984; Mandler 1988; Spelke and Newport 1998). Landau, Gleitman, and Spelke (1981), for example, base their position on the study of one blind preschool-aged child who is able to calculate distances and reference points—Euclidean-based concepts—in locating a target or terminal point in a given task. They then conclude that preschool children in general have an innate ability to carry out tasks involving navigation or the location of objects metrically, not topologically.

Later in his career, Piaget renamed the terms associated with the topological-projective-Euclidean chronology by referring to them as "intrafigural," "interfigural," and "transfigural" relations, respectively (Piaget and Garcia 1989). Piaget's renaming of terms implies his modification of perspective and subsequent recognition that infants' and young children's spatial thinking is not as plastic (i.e., topological) as he had originally posited (see Piaget and Inhelder 1956/1967; Piaget, Inhelder, and Szeminska 1960). The general argument, then, is that the topological primacy thesis may not necessarily be indicative of progressions of spatial development between four- and five-year-old children.

Moreover, little empirical investigation has been conducted dealing with spatial development and the progression of spatial thinking from one age to the next. Studies that have been conducted in this fashion ask participants (young children) to engage in particular tasks. These studies, too, challenge the Piagetian notion of topological primacy. For example, two related studies deal with infants' and young children's perceptions of the placement of objects in continuous substances or matter, like sand in a sandbox (Huttenlocher, Newcombe, and Sandberg 1994; Huttenlocher, Newcombe, and Vasilyeva 1999). These studies, through the implementation of "inspection time" or "looking time" methodology, have concluded that even young infants spend a longer amount of time looking in the location where an object was buried in a sandbox even though the object reappeared in another location, demonstrating metric Euclidean thinking. As Liben (2002) has indicated, however, Piaget would argue that continuous space studies using sand or liquid may demonstrate infants' and young children's perceptions of space and not conceptions of space. That is to say, the studies conclude what infants and young children see and not what they can show regarding the displacement of the object in a metric or representational fashion. Piaget, according to Liben, would also question the role of infants' and young children's accuracy in defining the original location of an object, as well as the constrained environment associated with the contrived rectangular features of the sandboxes.

Fortunately, the study of young children's spatial thinking in the everyday free play of the preschool setting seems to resolve the problem of the constrained environment. In conducting our empirical investigation, we did not initially anticipate major differences between the number of minutes engaged in spatial, geometric, and architecturally related activities between four-year-old and five-year-old children. Our findings, however, demonstrate that age differences are not statistically significant in some cases and are significant in others.

In our analyses, we found it helpful to compare and contrast the young children's observed behaviors in a number of ways. First, each analysis examines the variables of age, gender, and socioeconomic class in order to determine if a relationship exists among these factors with time. In this investigation, time is a proxy variable. It can be argued that time in young children's free play represents other attributes that can be labeled as motivation, interest, or persistence. The time engaged in spatial, geometric, and architecturally related activities demonstrates samples of behavior linking abstract concepts with concrete measures. The first part of our analysis is set against the entire sample of ninety preschool children. Taken together, these children represent a heterogeneous sample that would look like most preschool class environments. The children range in age from four to six years, represent different levels of socioeconomic status, and are balanced by gender and ability levels.

The second part of the analysis examines two subgroups of children taken from the original sample of ninety preschool children. The first subgroup includes fifty-three children who are engaged in spatial, geometric, and architecturally related activities, and the second subgroup includes thirty-three children who are engaged in spatial, geometric, and architecturally related activities for at least five or more minutes during each fifteen-minute videotaped segment. Figure 5.1 outlines our analysis of the entire sample and those of the subgroups of fifty-three children and thirty-three children, respectively. With these subgroups, we ask the same questions we asked with the entire sample. In addition, we compare and contrast the behaviors among and within the various groups of children.

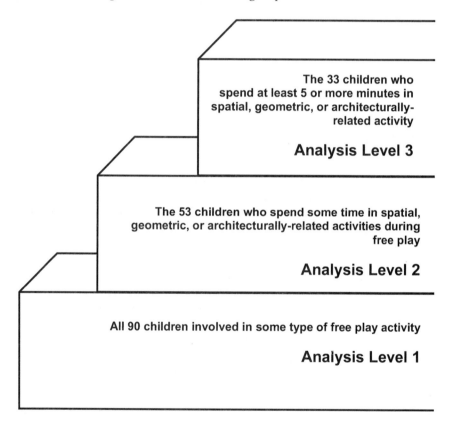

*An analysis was conducted at each level by age, gender, and socioeconomic class.

Figure 5.1.   How young children spend their time during free play*

OUR QUESTIONS ABOUT AGE AND SPATIAL, GEOMETRIC, AND ARCHITECTURAL ACTIVITY

Correlational analysis revealed that there is a significant relationship between age and overall spatial, geometric, and architectural activities ($r = .34$, $p < 0.01$). This means that the older the preschool child, the more likely they are to be engaged in spatial, geometric, and architectural activities. The older children in the sample demonstrated their emergent spatial, geometric, or architectural propensities in a number of ways. These include a greater amount of time spent on navigational or locative tasks, more precise descriptions involving direction or the identification of Euclidean figures (i.e., geometric shapes), more elaborate uses of symmetry, and greater precision in matching of both rectilinear and curvilinear figures.

Next, age was tested to determine whether it correlates with spatial and geometric activity alone. Correlational analysis indicates that there is a significant relationship when comparing age with only spatial and geometric activities ($r = .38$, significant at the 0.01 level). Spatial and geometric codes include point, line, and rotational symmetries; patterning; figure identification; shape matching; and direction/location. In examining these codes, most educators would agree that these activities fall under the "Geometry" standard in the *Principles and Standards for School Mathematics* (NCTM 2000) and the National Science Content Standard B, "Properties of Objects and Materials" and "The Position and Motion of Objects" (National Research Council 1996). The symmetries and patterning lead to transformational concepts, figure identification and shape matching deal with recognizing previously known and learning new geometric shapes, and direction/location may lead to the study of coordinate systems and the location of points.

The architecture codes (enclosure, foundations, trabeated construction, posting, engineering, and proportional reasoning) also suggest geometric behaviors. Unlike the spatial and geometric codes, the architecture codes may not necessarily reveal explicit geometric concepts at the elementary school level. They do, however, reveal notions of more advanced geometric concepts that may be encountered later in school. These concepts may include angle measurements (trabeated construction), geometric similarity (proportional reasoning), or circle measure (some types of enclosure). Our findings revealed no statistically significant differences that existed between the different groups for age and architecturally related behaviors.

Our next set of questions and observations focus on the ways in which the fifty-three children who spent some period of time of their free play engaged in spatial, geometric, and architectural activities compare in terms of age. Table 5.1 presents the means and standard deviations regarding four-year-old children and five-year-old children who are involved in spa-

Table 5.1. Percentage of time children engage in SPAGAR activities by age

Age	N	Mean	Standard Deviation
Four-year-olds	23	6.78	4.70
Five-year-olds	30	7.87	4.29
Total	53	7.33	4.50

tial, geometric, and architectural activity at least some of their free play time. These results show that there is in fact a significant relationship between age and overall spatial, geometric, and architectural activities ($r = .37, p < 0.01$).

We return to the question of age and its correlation with only spatial and geometric activity. Correlational analyses have shown that there is a significant relationship when comparing age with only spatial and geometric activities ($r = .43$, significant at the 0.01 level). When looking specifically at a possible correlation between age and architecturally related activity, we found no significant differences.

In the group of thirty-five children who engaged in spatial, geometric, and architecturally related activities for at least five minutes or more during their fifteen-minute free play period, correlational analysis shows no relationship between age and spatial, geometric, and architectural activity ($r = .21$). As seen in table 5.2 below, the means of the four-year-old children when compared to those of the five-year-old children are close. Given these close means, a t-test was performed, which, in corroboration with the correlational analysis, yields no significant differences.

Next, to determine if age is correlated with spatial and geometric activity during Lego and block play both correlational analysis and a t-test were performed using the group of thirty-five children. A significant correlation exists between age and any one spatial and geometric activity ($r = .34$). The means and standard deviations are presented in table 5.3.

Do the thirty-five four- and five-year-old children engage in different amounts of architecturally related activities? Chi-square tests were used in this case, since the number of children doing architecturally related activities is so low. Like the two previous sections examining architecturally

Table 5.2. Percentage of time children engage in SPAGAR activities for at least five minutes, by age

Age	N	Mean	Standard Deviation
Four-year-olds	13	10.46	2.47
Five-year-olds	20	10.20	3.05
Total	33	10.33	2.76

Table 5.3. Percentage of time children by age engage in SPAGAR activities alone for at least five minutes

Age	N	Mean	Standard Deviation
Four-year-olds	13	8.46	4.12
Five-year-olds	20	9.60	3.44
Total	33	9.03	3.78

related activity, children were compared based on their age as follows: four years zero months to four years eleven months in one group and five years zero months to six years zero months in the other. Presence or absence of this activity is given in table 5.4. Significant differences do exist when comparing age with architecturally related activity ($\chi^2 = 3.85$, df $= 1$, $p < 0.05$) in favor of younger children; that is, the four–year-old children were engaged in architecturally related activity twice the amount of time as the older children.

IMPLICATIONS OF AGE AND DEVELOPMENT IN TERMS OF TIME ENGAGED IN SPATIAL, GEOMETRIC, AND ARCHITECTURAL ACTIVITIES

Our findings suggest that age does have some role in the amount of time children engage in cognitive tasks related to spatial, geometric, and architectural activities. The last finding (the relationship between age and architecturally related activities alone) might seem counterintuitive. How is it that the four-year-old children will engage in architecturally related activities a greater amount of time than their five-year-old peers? Our finding of developmental discrepancies regarding age is not as unusual as it may first appear. One also has to look at the difference between implicit and explicit knowledge of a particular topic of study. Implicit knowledge is what is conveyed in our empirical investigation—our interpretations of young children's time spent on spatial, geometric, and architectural activities. Explicit knowledge can only be examined by the child's use of language and their verbal descriptions of what occurs from both a mathematical and scientific standpoint.

Table 5.4. Presence or absence of only architecturally related activity by age

Age	Absence	Presence	Total
4 years to 4 years 11 months	7	6	13
5 years to 6 years 0 months	17	3	20
Total	24	9	33

First, we note that although the four-year-old children engaged in what we classify as architecturally related activities for a greater amount of time, these activities are not necessarily more complex or elaborate in construction. For example, the four-year-old children were often observed constructing posts and beams with blocks or generic towers with either Legos or blocks (architectural principles), whereas the five-year-old children spent a greater amount of time paying more attention to symmetric characteristics, more elaborate patterns, and concentration on physical science principles such as balance and form.

Second, this finding is supported by the study of children's intuitive physics by Karmiloff-Smith and Inhelder (1974), who demonstrate that four-year-old and eight-year-old children outperformed six-year-olds in their knowledge of force and weight in using a balance. The six-year-old children responded according to the naïve theories that they developed regarding the physical properties of objects and how they can be balanced. In contrast, the eight-year-old children had already developed more advanced theories that took into account the physical interaction with the objects and their cognitive awareness of how the objects would behave. Thus, they were able to successfully complete the task. The four-year-olds, however, were working from experiential knowledge. They demonstrated a hands-on interaction with the objects and relied on observation and sensory feedback. Their interaction with the objects was based less on their perceptions of physical reality and more on their sensory experience.

It should be noted that many of the studies within this field have been critiqued for methodological inconsistencies and interpretations of the children's actions. Due to the methodological problems that arise in the analysis of young children's cognitive processes, case study analyses are an important complement to empirical studies to help flesh out the possible explanations of the children's actions (see case studies in chapters 6 and 7).

GENDER-RELATED ASPECTS OF SPATIAL AND GEOMETRIC THINKING

Without question, the issue of gender differences in spatial skills and in geometry has been researched extensively. Some studies in this area, primarily those that focus on in-school spatial skills and geometric concepts, suggest that males outperform females in most spatial and geometric tasks (Benbow and Stanley 1992; Bock and Kolakowski 1973; Chiang and Atkinson 1976; Stafford 1961). Although research on sex differences in spatial thinking of young children is abundant, the methods of nearly all these studies use standardized testing measures and other similar psychometric designs that may not necessarily paint an accurate picture about a certain sex's cognitive ability when compared with the other. Nevertheless, research in this area spans from those who study genetic and hormonal differences (McGee 1979) to those who focus on developmental aspects of gender differences in spatial thinking (Bem 1981).

One major group of researchers on sex differences in spatial thinking bases their studies on genetic or biological factors. Much of the existing research on genetic explanations of sex differences regarding spatial thinking usually favors male dominance. Benbow and Stanley (1992) posit that males perform, on the whole, better than females in mathematical problem solving; this may have to do with some of the research that demonstrates males' overall high performance on activities that require spatial tasks. As Benbow and Stanley argue: "sex differences in achievement in . . . mathematics result from superior male mathematical ability, which may in turn be related to greater male ability in spatial tasks" (1992, 109).

Another hypothesis is that a major X-linked gene determines spatial (and geometric) abilities in humans (Stafford 1961; Bock and Kolakowski 1973) and that this gene accounts for better (or worse) performance in terms of spatial ability (Chiang and Atkinson 1976; Waber 1977). The idea is that the dominant form of this X-linked gene lowers one's level of spatial ability, while the recessive allele is said to raise the level of spatial ability. So, since males have only one X chromosome, proponents of this hypothesis believe that males will more likely inherit higher levels of spatial ability than females, who have two X chromosomes. Boles (1980), on the other hand, has countered this position by arguing that nearly all the empirical studies in this area failed to find significant sex differences in spatial ability.

Some researchers have argued that sex differences are a result of specific biological or physiological conditions related to brain functioning. It did not take long, however, for researchers to examine sex differences in spatial thinking abilities in terms of left-right brain operations. Waber (1979) found that when asked to draw a complex figure, young girls between the ages of five and thirteen tended to focus more attention on individual parts of the figure, while boys of the same age tended to replicate the complex figure in such a way that emphasized external and more broad or extensive characteristics. Both Waber (1979) and Harris (1981) conclude that boys display more right-brain (spatial relations) characteristics, while girls seem to display more left-brain features. Springer and Deutsch (1981) conclude that females demonstrate more bilateralization than do males and that greater lateralization toward one hemisphere of the brain, more common among males, increases one's abilities in spatial relations activities.

Unlike those who have examined the biological attributes of spatial differences between males and females, several researchers have also investigated this area from the perspective of cognition and development. Siegel and Schadler (1977) investigated preschool children's spatial representations of their classroom environment. There were thirty subjects, fifteen boys and fifteen girls in their study. Children were asked to construct a three-dimensional model of their classrooms. Models were scored by three criteria of accuracy: absolute accuracy, local relational accuracy, and global relational accuracy. Their results indicate that the accuracy of boys was far greater than the accuracy of the girls.

Liben and Golbeck (1980) examine the differences among males and females concerning specific Piagetian spatial tasks, namely, those related to the understanding of horizontality and verticality. They conclude that correlations between both horizontal and vertical scores were strong among males but weak among females. In comparing boys and girls in terms of verbal usage associated with spatial and geometric thinking, Clements (1983) found that girls tend to use verbal descriptions while boys do not. Baenninger and Newcombe (1989), however, argue that no correlation exists between a child's involvement in spatial activities and their abilities in spatial thinking. They also claim that neither males nor females differ in terms of their involvement in spatial activity and their improvement in spatial ability. Fennema and Carpenter (1981, 1998) have argued that the gender gap concerning spatial and geometric abilities is a result of differences in spatial visualization. In another study, Fennema and Tartre (1985) conclude that there is a rather high correlation between mathematical ability and spatial visualization (between .30 and .60), and males fall in the upper end of this range while females score lower.

Within the last two decades, a number of studies have questioned male superiority in spatial thinking skills. Both Linn and Hyde (1989) and Feingold (1988) argue that the gender gap in spatial activities or abilities is closing. Halpern (1989) suggests that male dominance in spatial relations seen in the research corpus on gender differences in spatial thinking is a result of biased testing instruments, methodological approaches, schooling, teacher bias, and changes that are occurring in various populations. However, it is not indicated how these biases occur. Nevertheless, Halpern's conclusions hinge on the notion that the examination of gender differences using alternative testing instruments, namely, the clinical interview or naturalistic observation, is severely lacking. Further, most studies examining gender differences in terms of spatial or geometric knowledge focus on in-school activities (e.g. Fennema and Sherman 1977; E. S. Johnson and Meade 1987; Linn and Hyde 1989; Tartre 1990) and overlook spatial or geometric competencies that occur in the out-of-school context.

Of course, as we have described in the previous chapter, we use contextual observation methodology (along with case study analyses in chapters

6 and 7) to help ameliorate the problem of comparing spatial, geometric, and architecturally related activities in the everyday context between boys and girls.

OUR QUESTIONS ABOUT GENDER AND SPATIAL GEOMETRIC, AND ARCHITECTURAL ACTIVITY

Does gender influence the amount of time young children are engaged in spatial, geometric, and architecturally related activity? More specifically, do boys and girls differ in the presence or absence of spatial, geometric, and architectural activity? Our results indicate that there is no significant difference between boys and girls in the amount of time spent in these activities. It is important to note that none of the materials at this age are seen as gender specific. If we look at spatial and geometric activities alone, we ask whether boys and girls differ in the presence or absence of spatial and geometric activities. Again, no significant differences exist between gender and the presence and absence of only spatial and geometric activity. Do boys and girls differ in the presence or absence of architecturally related activities? Still, no significant differences exist between gender and the presence and absence of architecturally related activities.

We again turn to the fifty-three children who spent some period of time of their free play engaged in spatial, geometric, and architectural activities and determine if differences exist in terms of gender. First, how do the thirty boys and twenty-three girls within the sample of fifty-three compare in terms of time engaged in different amounts of spatial, geometric, and architectural activity? Table 5.5 presents the means and standard deviations regarding boys' and girls' involvement in these activities. Results from a t-test demonstrate no significant differences between boys and girls and overall spatial, geometric, and architectural activities.

The next analysis examines whether the thirty boys and the twenty-three girls engage in different amounts of spatial and geometric activities alone. Again, means and standard deviations are provided in table 5.6. Results

Table 5.5. Difference in SPAGAR activity by gender

Gender	N	Mean	Standard Deviation
Boys	30	7.33	4.63
Girls	23	7.48	4.33
Total	53	7.40	4.48

Table 5.6. Difference of spatial and geometric activity by gender

Gender	N	Mean	Standard Deviation
Boys	30	6.50	4.69
Girls	23	6.78	4.23
Total	53	6.64	4.46

from a t-test still show no significant differences between gender and only spatial and geometric activities.

Next, do the thirty boys and the twenty-three girls differ in the presence or absence of architecturally related activities? Once again, no significant differences exist between gender and the presence and absence of architecturally related activities.

Next, are there any gender differences with the thirty-three children who spend one-third or more of their time (five or more minutes) engaged in spatial, geometric, and architectural activity? To answer this question, we consider how the eighteen boys and fifteen girls may differ, if at all, in terms of time engaged in different amounts of spatial, geometric, and architectural activity. As table 5.7 indicates, comparing the means of the boys and the girls shows similar results—namely, over ten minutes of time engaged in spatial, geometric, and architectural activity. A t-test demonstrates no significant differences between gender and overall spatial, geometric, and architectural activities.

In examining the amount of time engaged in spatial and geometric activities alone and architecturally related activities alone, t-test results showed no significant differences exist between boys and girls (see table 5.8 for means and standard deviations).

Table 5.7. Percentage of time children engage in SPAGAR activities for at least five minutes, by gender

Gender	N	Mean	Standard Deviation
Boys	18	10.50	2.94
Girls	15	10.06	2.71
Total	33	10.28	2.83

Table 5.8. Percentage of time children engage in spatial and geometric activities alone for at least five minutes, by gender

Gender	N	Mean	Standard Deviation
Boys	18	9.16	4.20
Girls	15	9.13	3.14
Total	33	9.15	3.67

IMPLICATIONS OF GENDER AND TIME ENGAGED IN SPATIAL, GEOMETRIC, AND ARCHITECTURAL ACTIVITIES

The results indicate no significant difference in spatial, geometric, and architecturally related activities between boys and girls. This is encouraging in contrast to the plethora of research that supports gender differences in mathematics and science commencing in the early years of elementary school. The spatial, geometric, and architectural codes may be seen as protomathematical and protoscientific concepts and skills that may relate to future achievement in mathematics and science. If young children do not exhibit any gender-related differences in the type of activity and the amount of time engaged in a particular cognitive activity in the early ages, then what reasons can explain the differences that emerge in the elementary school years?

One explanation is that the quality of the early experiences of children has been documented as extremely important to their later development. Some of the differences that emerge in the later elementary years can be attributed to the quality of the experience in an early childhood program. Studies indicate that there are substantial quantitative and qualitative differences in the input and outcomes of pre-kindergarten programs. In general, early intervention strategies like Head Start were designed to increase achievement of socially disadvantaged children by providing an enriched environment (Ceglowski 1998; Soar and Soar 1972).

A closer review of the research suggests that only high-quality programs have lasting effects on poor children (Schweinhart 1994). The Perry Preschool Program in Michigan is one example. Longitudinal data from the Perry Preschool Program provide encouraging results of long-term academic, social, and economic benefits of early educational intervention. The program design required one fully qualified and certified teacher for approximately seven students who was required to conduct weekly home visitations. These data demonstrate increased IQ scores eight to ten times beyond increases reported by other Head Start–like programs, reduction in special education services by forty-three percent, and a twenty-four percent reduction in the dropout rate (Schweinhart et al. 2005; Barnett 1996; Schweinhart, Barnes, and Weikart 1993). The data from exemplary pre-kindergarten programs reveal a correlation among the variables of advanced level of teacher preparation, small class sizes, and lasting educational benefits.

A second explanation for the emergence of gender differences in mathematics and science later in childhood has to do with the achievement-related choices that are influenced by stereotypical gender-expected behaviors. The importance of gender-role formation and its influence on educational and vocational choices have been investigated by Bem (1981), Eccles (1985), Fox and Cohn (1980), Hollinger (1991), and Nash (1979). Each of these investigators paid special attention to the way gender-role socialization may affect girls' educational and occupational choices. The research indicates that certain childhood experiences may have an influence on the formation of future personality traits. In turn, these early experiences foster the development of attributes that are theorized to be better suited to the pursuit of interest and achievement in mathematics and science.

It has been suggested that through an interaction of socialization processes and environmental influences, gender differences in course taking occur in science and mathematics (Eccles Parsons 1984; Eccles 1985; Farenga and Joyce 1999a, 1999b). This may be the direct result of the gender-role socialization process. Research indicates that differences in the socialization process of elementary school–aged children appear to favor boys' achievement, interest, and attitude toward science (Kahle 1990).

The results of our work lead us toward an interactionist explanation for behaviors exhibited by girls and boys. The importance of examining different patterns of socialization, interaction, and interpersonal experiences has been cited in numerous studies (Archer and Lloyd 1982; Bem 1981; Block 1983; Culp, Crook, and Housley 1983; Markus and Oyserman 1989; Smith and Lloyd 1978; Wolf 1966). All of these studies identify how parents of young children handle and treat children differently based on the sex of the child. Interestingly, mothers reacted differently to the same baby depending upon whether it was presented as a boy or a girl. As indicated earlier, our children demonstrated no preference of materials or length of time engaged in spatial, geometric, and architectural activities. However, some negative social implications regarding the appropriateness of these types of demonstrated behaviors may not yet have been learned.

The finding that mothers in the studies are unaware of their actions highlights the importance of the process of unconscious socialization (Nisbett and Wilson 1977). These early experiences of boys and girls aid in the construction of self concept and result in thought processes or schemata that are different in content and form for women and men (Bem 1981; Markus and Oyserman 1989; Neisser 1976). Hollinger states, "of all the existing barriers, sex-role socialization's impact on the child's developing self-belief system is the most pervasive and limiting" (1991, 136).

The empirically-based research of Bakker (1990) has shown that certain behaviors stimulate specific areas of the brain, causing increased acquisition of knowledge. A question that arises is whether certain behaviors shape cognitive style and to what degree it is mutable. Is the brain a "dependent variable," whereby long-term exposure to a variety of early experiences develops the brain to be more receptive and create a positive perception to certain types of learning? If this is the case, the importance of the spatial, geometric, and architecturally related activities in preschool cannot be underestimated for possibly priming students' mathematical readiness.

Archer and Lloyd state, "in older children that there is a clear relationship between high spatial performance and experience with three-dimensional forms—for example, wood working, model making, or toys such as Lego and Meccano" (1982, 236). Siann (1977) suggests that certain activities that are linked to spatial ability are also considered traditionally masculine or feminine and may only be encountered if appropriate to one's gender. As noted by Johnson (1984), if the science curriculum is built around interest, attitudes, and experiences that are present for one sex and not the other, identical treatment of the sexes will only accentuate the inequity. The same holds true for the mathematics curriculum as well.

Research embodying social orientations between the sexes has found dis-similarities in a number of areas. Discussions that include play (Hughes 1999; Lever 1976), friendship or social patterns (Gilligan 1982; Hoffman 1977; Lansky et al. 1961), course selection (Farenga and Joyce 1998, 1999a, 1999b), nurturing behavior (Feldman and Nash 1977; Goldberg, Blumberg, and Kriger 1982), moral development (Gilligan 1982; Kohlberg 1966, 1978), or social connectiveness (Block 1973; Chodorow 1978, 1989) all conclude that clear differences exist between the sexes and their view of the world. In short, what these studies show is that one's inclinations toward a specific cognitive domain may be affected by socialization processes. Often, this relationship is based on anticipated or stereotypical gender roles.

SOCIOECONOMIC CLASS COMPARISONS IN SPATIAL AND GEOMETRIC THINKING

To date, the literature on mathematical thinking—regardless of context—is in need of research devoted to issues of social class. This is clearly evident from the research showing the growing inequality among different social class groups (Natriello, McDill, and Pallas 1990; Oakes 1990). Existing research that considers socioeconomic class in terms of young children in the everyday context is limited (Ginsburg, Inoue, and Seo 1999; Ginsburg, Pappas, and Seo 2001). The earlier study (1999) shows that children of low-income households are engaged in mathematical activity nearly half the time (46 percent) during free play. The results of the latter study (2001) show that, although low-income children differ from middle- and upper-income children in terms of the type of mathematical activity in which they are involved, there are no significant differences in terms of the amount of time children of different social classes are engaged in mathematical activity.

Aside from the amount of time engaged in mathematical activity, Ginsburg, Pappas, and Seo (2001) found that the relative frequency of children's free-play activity involving pattern and shape (twenty-five percent) was nearly double that of activities involving magnitude comparison—the second most popular mathematical activity (thirteen percent). Given that pattern and shape activity involves spatial and geometric thinking, an investigation of the different types of spatial and geometric concepts in which children of different social classes engage during free play is necessary.

In addition to the paucity of studies on mathematical thinking and social class, we know very little about the ways different social classes compare in terms of spatial and geometric thinking in general. Moreover, we know next to nothing about how four- and five-year-old children of different social classes vary in terms of the amount of time spent on mathematical activity involving spatial and geometric thinking or the types of spatial and geometric ideas and architectural principles children employ during free play.

OUR QUESTIONS ABOUT SOCIOECONOMIC CLASS AND SPATIAL, GEOMETRIC, AND ARCHITECTURAL ACTIVITY

Does socioeconomic class influence the amount of time young children are engaged in spatial, geometric, and architecturally related activity? Do children from different social class groups differ in the presence or absence of spatial, geometric, and architectural activities?

As discussed in the previous chapter, the entire sample of ninety four- and five-year-old children was divided evenly between the three socioeconomic classes (i.e., one-third lower SES, one-third middle SES, and one-third upper SES). Social class was determined by city and state subsidies toward preschool programs as outlined by the Agency for Child Development Services (Ness 2001). Social class differences in terms of the relative frequency of different types of spatial, geometric, and architectural activity are shown in figure 5.2. Categories have been combined, since the frequencies of each of the thirteen categories are relatively low. A Pearson chi-square test shows no significant differences among social class groups in the presence or absence of spatial, geometric, and architectural activity.

We ask whether children from different social class groups differ in the presence or absence of spatial and geometric activity alone. Given a somewhat skewed distribution—that is, a large number of the entire sample not performing spatial and geometric activity—Pearson's chi-square test was performed and indicated no significant differences among social class groups in terms of the presence or absence of spatial and geometric activity alone. Children from different social class groups were compared based on

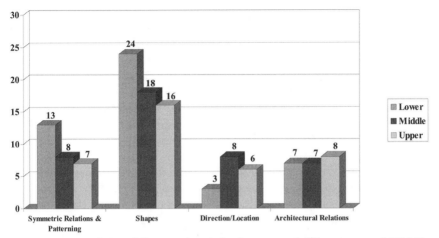

Figure 5.2. **Social class differences in relative frequency of different types of SPAGAR activity**

the presence or absence of architecturally related activity alone. Once again, Pearson's chi-square test shows no significant differences among social class groups in the presence or absence of architecturally related activity.

Like the previous investigations with age and gender, we examined the fifty-three children who spent some period of time of their free play engaged in spatial, geometric, and architectural activities to determine the existence of socioeconomic class differences. Fortunately, the number of children in each of the three socioeconomic groups was almost the same (eighteen low-income, eighteen middle-income, and seventeen upper-income children). We asked whether children from different social class groups engage in different amounts of spatial, geometric, and architectural activities. Table 5.9 provides descriptive statistics regarding children's involvement in these activities based on socioeconomic status. A one-way analysis of variance (ANOVA) for independent means shows no significant differences between social class and overall spatial, geometric, and architectural activities.

If we examine spatial and geometric activity alone, do children from dif-

Table 5.9. **SPAGAR activity among children by SES**

SES	N	Mean	Standard Deviation
Low Income	18	8.28	5.38
Middle Income	18	7.05	3.84
Upper Income	17	6.82	4.11
Total	53	7.40	4.46

ferent social class groups engage in different amounts of activity? Table 5.10 provides means and standard deviations based on socioeconomic class. As in the overall case with all ninety children, a one-way analysis of variance (ANOVA) for independent means yielded no significant differences between social class and only spatial and geometric activities.

We next consider whether children from different social class groups differ in terms of the presence or absence of architecturally related activity. Again, Pearson's chi-square test shows no significant differences among social class groups in the presence or absence of architecturally related activity.

Finally, as in the analyses of age and gender, we determine if there are differences with regard to socioeconomic class with the thirty-three children who spend one-third or more of their time (five or more minutes) engaged in spatial, geometric, and architectural activity. Like the sample of fifty-three mentioned earlier, the numbers of children among the socioeconomic groups are not skewed: Of the thirty-three children, there are twelve low-income children, eleven middle-income children, and ten upper income children. We now consider how the socioeconomic groups may differ, if at all, in terms of time engaged in different amounts of spatial, geometric, and architectural activity. Means and standard deviations of children of different social class groups engaged in spatial, geometric, and architectural activities are given in table 5.11. When comparing social class differences, the low-income group shows a slightly higher mean (11.67) than their middle- and upper-income peers (9.45 and 9.60, respectively). A one-way analysis of variance (ANOVA) for independent means demon-

Table 5.10. Percentage of time children engage in spatial and geometric activities alone by SES

SES	N	Mean	Standard Deviation
Low Income	18	7.67	5.41
Middle Income	18	6.28	3.97
Upper Income	17	5.88	3.85
Total	53	6.62	4.46

Table 5.11. Percentage of time children engage in SPAGAR activities for at least five minutes, by SES

SES	N	Mean	Standard Deviation
Lower Income	12	11.67	2.64
Middle Income	11	9.45	2.51
Upper Income	10	9.60	2.91
Total	33	10.30	2.80

strated no significant differences between social class and spatial, geometric, and architectural activity.

Do children from different social class groups engage in different amounts of spatial and geometric activities alone? The fairly similar means and standard deviations indicate few if any differences (see table 5.12). A one-way analysis of variance (ANOVA) for independent means confirms this and demonstrates no significant differences between social class and any one spatial and geometric activity.

And last, do children from different social class groups differ in the presence or absence of architecturally related activity alone? Once again, no significant differences among social class groups in the presence or absence of architecturally related activity. In sum, these findings generally conclude that there is little, if any, relationship between one's socioeconomic class and overt spatial, geometric, and architectural activities in our analysis of young four- and five-year-old children during free play.

IMPLICATIONS OF SOCIOECONOMIC CLASS AND TIME ENGAGED IN SPATIAL, GEOMETRIC, AND ARCHITECTURAL ACTIVITIES

When examining the social class differences in relative frequency of different types of spatial, geometric, and architectural activity (see figure 5.2), we find that children of low-income households engage in symmetric relations and patterning a great deal longer (nearly forty percent more) than children of middle-income households and almost double the amount of time (forty-six percent) as children of upper-income households. We find very similar results in terms of the time engaged in shape activities—low-income children spent more time engaged in figure identification and shape matching activities than did their middle-income (twenty-five percent more time) and upper-income (thirty-three percent more time) peers. In examining the mean scores among the SES groups, the lower SES group appeared to engage in a greater amount of activity with regard to symmetric relations and shape activities. Although these differences are not significant, one pos-

Table 5.12. Percentage of time children engage in spatial and geometric activities alone for at least five minutes, by SES

SES	N	Mean	Standard Deviation
Lower Income	12	10.75	3.74
Middle Income	11	8.27	3.66
Upper Income	10	8.20	3.36
Total	33	9.15	3.70

sible explanation is that children of the lower SES group may have less of an opportunity to engage in these activities with Lego and block-related materials outside of the preschool environment, whereas children of the middle and upper SES groups appear to be more likely to be exposed to these materials at home (Roth et al. 2003).

The middle-income children spent a greater amount of time with direction/location activities, and the number of children in each socioeconomic group who spent time in architecturally related activities was approximately the same. Although these descriptive statistics reveal a slight edge with low-income children spending time on symmetric and shape activities, we clarify that, as our results earlier have indicated, no significant differences exist on the number of minutes engaged in these activities in terms of socioeconomic class. We also emphasize that all of the preschool environments in this investigation have provided ample opportunities and more than sufficient play materials, regardless of social class. Further, even the low-income group does not reflect conditions that are reported in the research examining cognitive abilities of children in abject or severe poverty whose opportunities are extremely limited.

Nevertheless, our results on socioeconomic status show that low-income children have a great deal of potential in activities involving spatial and geometric cognition. Findings in earlier studies are inconclusive, however. While Starkey and Klein (1992) show that low-income children have major deficiencies in mathematical ability when compared to other children, other studies (Carraher, Carraher, and Schliemann 1985; Ginsburg, Pappas, and Seo 2001; Ginsburg et al. 2003; Petitto and Ginsburg 1982; Saxe 1991) present a different picture—mathematical ability and time engaged in mathematically related activities (SPAGAR activities in particular) is not based on one's socioeconomic status or on cultural differences having to do with nationality or geographic area (e.g., individuals from illiterate societies versus those from literate societies). The contextual observation methodology used here has demonstrated little, if any, differences in cognitive-based activities among social class groups.

We discussed above an important finding in our analyses, namely that evidence of spatial, geometric, and architectural thinking appears across social class boundaries. We also identified Starkey and Klein's study (1992), which concludes that children of low-income families are deficient in mathematical tasks when compared to their middle-income and upper-income peers. One may wonder whether these contrasting conclusions can be reconciled. In corroboration with Starkey and Klein, McLoyd (1997, 1998) studied children in poverty and noticed that poverty impacts families' lives in negative ways by increasing stressors, thereby reducing the chances of providing conducive environments for intellectual and cognitive development. McLoyd (1998) also noticed that parenting in households under the poverty line was more punitive and involved much more corporal punishment than did parenting practices in families who were never poor. Parents in poverty are often stressed single-parent mothers working two or more minimum-wage jobs. In agreement with Starkey and Klein (1992) and McLoyd (1997, 1998), other researchers have posited that children whose families are in chronic poverty perform more poorly than those whose families were in poverty for a brief period (or periods) of time (Bolger et al. 1995; Duncan and Brooks-Gunn 1997; Johnson et al. 2005; McLeod and Nonnemaker 2000).

More recently, the National Institute of Child Health and Human Development Early Child Care Research Network (2005) conducted a longitudinal study spanning approximately ten years from 1991 to 2001, which investigated the cognitive and social development of children from birth through age nine. The group based their investigation on four criteria: children whose families never fell below the poverty line, children whose families were poor during the infancy years (birth through three years) but not later, children whose families were not poor during the infancy years but became poor later (ages four through nine), and children whose families were consistently below the poverty line. They conclude that children whose families experienced any period of poverty demonstrated more behavioral problems and scored lower on cognitive tasks than did those children whose families were never in poverty. They further conclude the existence of a positive correlation between children in poverty and both poor family situations and a lack of higher cognitive performance.

Findings in two of our more recent studies (Johnson et al. 2005, forthcoming) concur with the results in the NICHD study. Our investigations, however, show direct correlations between poverty and poor school performance and achievement. These studies examine children who are below the level of income that are in the present study and measure student achievement in a very traditional manner—i.e., high-stakes testing.

CONCLUSION

The results show that, with the sole exception of some cases with age, there were no significant differences in spatial, geometric, and architectural activity among four- and five-year-old children in terms of gender or socioeconomic class. Along with this important finding, however, it is necessary to introduce a caveat: the statistical results concerning the general lack of differences in spatial, geometric, and architectural activity among four- and five-year-old children in terms of gender and socioeconomic class are based on a relatively small number of children. That is, out of ninety four- and five-year-old children, fifty-three are engaged in some form of spatial, geometric, and architectural activity, while thirty-seven are not.

Nevertheless, aside from this issue, a case can be made for arguing the absence of *significant differences* in these areas. One way to do this is to consider the descriptive statistics when looking at age, gender, and socioeconomic class. Consider, for example, gender comparisons concerning overall activity among four- and five-year-old children who are engaged in some form of spatial, geometric, or architectural activity in the everyday context (i.e., engaged for at least one minute within the fifteen-minute segment). As the results suggest, no significant differences exist between boys and girls and overall SPAGAR activity. Of course, it can be argued that the sample size is too small to come to this conclusion. However, given the closeness of the means of SPAGAR activity among boys and girls, it can be concluded that there is very little difference between the amount of time boys spend on this activity when compared with the amount of time girls spend on this activity. Another reason to conclude the absence of significant differences is that other studies have confirmed similar findings with regard to gender and socioeconomic class (Ginsburg, Inoue, and Seo 1999; Ginsburg, Pappas, and Seo forthcoming) and comparison of two cultures—in the U.S. (New York City) and in Taiwan (Taipei)—in terms of spontaneous mathematical behavior in the everyday context (Lin and Ness 2000).

With respect to the case studies that follow in chapters 6 and 7, a word of caution is presented: It is important not to consider these children as anomalies—that is, children with exceptional talents in space, geometry, or architectural principles that others may not necessarily possess. Other children could just as easily have been chosen for analysis. Further, the analysis shows that certain social interactions are conducive to various types of spatial, geometric, and architectural activity. This can clearly be seen through Nat's episode in chapter 6: his brief skirmish with Darren may have prompted his construction of an elaborate roller coaster system. Types of play and social interactions are not the only factors that contribute to one's capturing of elaborate spatial, geometric, and architectural activity; certain objects, too, afford greater possibilities in young children's mathematical behavior. Some findings suggest that a child's involvement with Legos and blocks may contribute to a greater amount of mathematical activity (Archer and Lloyd 1982; Lin and Ness 2000).

CHAPTER TOPICS FOR DISCUSSION

1. One of our findings suggests that four-year-old children engage in more architecturally related activities than five-year-old children. Some possible causes have been suggested, but they are only interpre-

tations that are based on the outcomes of the study. Identify at least two additional explanations as to why the four-year-old children spent more time with architecture than the five-year-old children in our data set.

2. There are two somewhat conflicting outcomes with regard to the effects that socioeconomic class has on cognitive development. One group of researchers within the last twenty years has argued that preschool-aged children from low-income households perform less adequately than their middle- or upper-income peers from a cognitive standpoint, while another group has posited that there is no statistically significant difference in terms of cognitive development with regard to social class differences. Take a position with either group, and provide a rationale as to why you agree. Then, identify ways in which the other group can improve on possible shortcomings in their research or methodological approaches.

3. Based on your readings in this text, critique the following scenario:

> In her preschool class of five-year-old children, Ms. Rolle kept a restriction on the number of minutes that children were allowed to work uninterrupted in the block center of the play area. Children who engaged in activities within the block center worked with the blocks in different ways. Some were engaged in solitary play, others worked in parallel or collaborative play, and others engaged in competitive play. At the end of the free play period, Ms. Rolle would take photographs of each of the children's Lego or block constructions and post them on the bulletin board. In addition to this procedure, Ms. Rolle alternated the days in which boys and girls were allowed to work in the block center. Several parents approached Ms. Rolle with concerns that their children were not spending as much time in the block center as other children were, especially some of the parents of boys.

Take a position as to whether Ms. Rolle's restriction on time in the block center between boys and girls is valid and appropriate. Please support your position with evidence from what you have learned in the area of spatioscientific and geometric cognition and gender differences in mathematics and the physical sciences.

6

Constructing Alone: Cases 1 and 2

> Play is not the predominant feature of childhood but it is a leading factor in development.
>
> Lev Vygotsky (1978, 101)

Young children build big bridges. The use of the term *big bridges* is practical and metaphorical. Why practical? The following case studies demonstrate young children—between the ages of four years and five years eleven months—engaged in geometric (but not task-based) activity so that there is a basis for identifying young children's spontaneous and everyday geometric abilities. These children engage in their own activities during free play time in preschool or in their daycare setting that includes blocks and Legos. Moreover, these activities summon cognitive strengths in geometric knowledge impossible to gauge in a task-oriented environment (e.g., Piagetian interviews, performance-based assessment).

How is *big bridges* metaphorical? First, the notion of bridge building in the educational domain has far-reaching implications. We often use the phrase "connect the gap" referring to connecting what a child does not know or cannot do with what she does know or can do. At the elementary school level, we might think of "bridges" as objects or manipulatives constructed for the sole purpose of closing cognitive gaps and increasing understanding of knowledge in different domains. In the case studies that follow in this chapter and in the next, it is important to identify how the constructions serve as both practical and metaphorical bridges and how the cognitive behaviors of these children can inform adults about ways to connect informal and formal concepts.

CASE STUDY ANALYSES

The next two chapters present a different perspective on children's spatial, geometric, and architectural activity. Four children's spatial-geometric and scientific behaviors are examined in detail. Here we provide a general framework for case study with regard to individual children's mathematical activities in the everyday context. The central purpose of the case study is to gain an in-depth understanding of the individual child's everyday mathematics. These individual cases offer what Geertz (1973) refers to as a type of "thick description" of how preschool children's understanding of mathematical ideas, particularly spatial and geometric concepts, are revealed in their creation of physical structures. This thick description permits an in-depth interpretation, which takes into account the child's history, motives, intentions, personal meanings, social discourse and interactions, cultural forms and artifacts, and the like.

In conducting a case study, then, it is important to examine the dynamic interactions between individuals, physical settings, and sociocultural contexts and the mathematics that emerges through such interactions. The following components outlined in Seo (1998) help define the structure and strength of the case study method as it relates to individual young children's mathematical propensities. See Ginsburg, Inoue, and Seo (1999) for additional explanation of the case study approach (which they refer to as "deep analysis"):

HOW TO CONDUCT A CASE STUDY THROUGH CONTEXTUAL OBSERVATION

1. Give general information about the target child: This may include name, age, socioeconomic status, ethnicity, and gender.
2. Introduce the main theme of the case study: This includes a short introduction of what the child is doing. Also, identify the mathematical content that is central to what the child is doing. Provide a brief review of the literature concerning the mathematical content that you plan to discuss.
3. Describe the child's activity and setting: More specifically, describe how the room is arranged, where the child plays with peers, the kind of play in which the child engages, and so forth. Also, identify the length of time of the segment in which the child is engaged in mathematical free play.
4. The analysis should be divided into episodes: Use your best judgment in dividing the segment into episodes. In doing so, you may use a mathematical goal, a change in mathematical content, or

schema (i.e., the actual motor task in which the child is involved) as criteria for dividing videotaped segments into episodes.

5. Describe each episode: Describe the behaviors of the target child and her playmates (if there are any), and describe the essence of their discourse. Use brackets [like this] to describe a child's mood, interest, or disposition.

6. Analyze each episode: The analysis of each episode follows a description of that episode. Each episode may deal with each of the mathematical categories in different ways.

7. Mathematical content: This section details the mathematical activity that reveals the child's mathematical competence. Questions here might include the following: What kind of mathematical questions does the child spontaneously ask? What kind of solutions does the child implement to answer her mathematical questions? How would you characterize the child's mathematical activity?

8. Personal factors: This category concerns personal factors that enable or constrain the child's mathematical activity. What motivates the child to engage in a particular type of mathematical activity? What kind of mathematical goals does the child form? How do the child's mathematical goals shift over the course of the activity? We also discuss other personal factors such as the child's personality characteristics, interest, or persistence related to her mathematical activity.

9. Physical setting: This category concerns physical settings related to the child's mathematical activity. What kind of objects does the child play with? How does the object enable or constrain the child's mathematical activity? How is the classroom arranged? Where does the target child play? How is the physical arrangement related to the child's mathematical activity?

10. Sociocultural context: This category concerns social and cultural factors related to the child's mathematical activity. Does the child play alone or with her peers or her teacher? What kind of social interaction does the child engage in? What cultural values are embedded in particular types of social interaction? How do the particular types of social interaction enable and constrain the child's mathematical activity? How does the child's social interaction shift over the course of the activity? How is the child's shifting social interaction related to her mathematical activity? What cultural values are embedded in particular kinds of play objects or physical settings? How are those cultural values related to the child's mathematical activity? What kind of play activity does the child engage in? How is the particular type of play activity related to the child's mathematical activity? How does the child's play activity shift over the course of the activity?

How is the child's shifting play activity related to her mathematical activity?

11. Write a summary of the kinds of mathematical activity that have emerged as the child engaged in play and how the child's mathematical activity was related to personal factors, physical setting, and sociocultural contexts. Then discuss what general conclusions can be made about the mathematical competence of the child (Adapted from Seo, 1998).

Specifically, it was possible for us to enter the everyday endeavors of four preschoolers from three different preschool or daycare centers. Perhaps the most acute difference between these four children is socioeconomic class. The first child is a low-income male and the second child is an upper-income female. Described in the next chapter, the third child is a middle-income male, and the fourth child is a low-income male. Nevertheless, the primary reason for selecting a child for a case study had to do with the number of minutes a particular child spent on spatial, geometric, and architecturally related activities. In general, a child is often selected if she spends at least two-thirds of the total time (i.e., ten out of fifteen minutes of each videotaped excerpt) on these activities. Each child's personal characteristics are discussed and analyzed in their respective sections below and in the subsequent chapter.

CASE 1: NAT'S ROLLER COASTER SYSTEM

Nat is a male five years and one month old. As a child of a low-income household, Nat attends a preschool in New York City for both low- and middle-income families. He thus has the opportunity to interact with a diverse group of children and benefit from the many resources afforded by the preschool. From an initial viewing of the fifteen-minute video segment of Nat, it would not be difficult for one to determine, on the surface, that he certainly has his share of both confidantes and adversaries. But what makes Nat unique is that he is able to express his spatial and geometric ability and architectural prowess with minimal interaction with peers.

Episode 1

In episode 1, when the video cameraperson begins taping, Nat is seen on the floor, exploring symmetries with play logs. This toy, common in a number of preschools and daycare centers, comes in several shapes and sizes— medium to long cylindrical pieces of wood, usually about nine or ten inches in length, and triangular prisms, about four or five inches at the base (see figure 6.1). The progression of events is the following.

Nat puts the finishing touches on his square, made of six cylindrical logs and two triangular pieces. The triangular pieces, which form a symmetry, are removed. Nat attempts to add a seventh log to the square. One set of parallel sides is constructed of two logs while the other set is constructed of one. These logs seem to come in at least three forms: one with a single notch in the middle (figure 6.1A), one with two notches near both ends (figure 6.1B), and another with four notches on one side of the cylinder and two on the other approximately two inches from each end (figure 6.1C).

Nat then takes a seventh log (C), and it appears as if he wants to attach this log to the square. Initially, Nat places log 7 on one of the single-notched logs of the square; he is unsuccessful in attaching it. He subsequently places it on the notches of the two single-notched (parallel) logs by turning log 7 nearly ninety degrees. Log 7 seems to fit comfortably in this position; however, Nat does not seem completely pleased with this position of the log. Nat removes log 7 and places it on the floor.

Nat takes log 8 (also a C) and seems unsure where he wants to place it. Initially, he places it on the side with two double-notched logs (the side

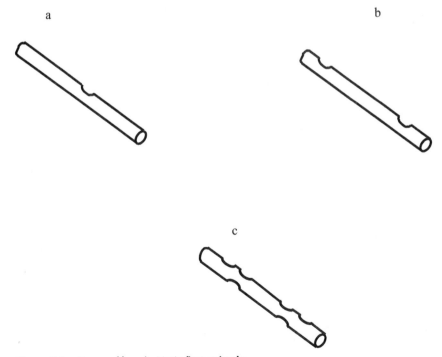

a

b

c

Figure 6.1. Types of logs in Nat's first episode

closest to him), with approximately one-third of it within the square (simi-lar to a cantilever position) and the remaining two-thirds hanging in the other direction. This position does not remain secure. So, Nat takes log 8 and attempts to attach it across the square, touching the parallel sides con-structed of double-notched logs. But this placement does not seem to please Nat either. Log 8 then is removed. As the first minute of the segment nears the end, Nat takes two triangular pieces and attaches them on the parallel single-notched logs so that they appear directly across (not diago-nal) from one another (see figure 6.2).

Analysis 1

Several observations can be made based on Nat's behavior in the first minute of his segment. First, the purpose of these logs is to build sides or angular roofs on miniature log cabins. But Nat did not use logs 7 and 8 for this purpose. Second, it is clear from the description that Nat has a plan in mind. However, it does not seem as if he is clear about how to proceed. This is evident through a number of trial-and-error situations associated with the placements of logs 7 and 8. Third, based on his removal of logs 7 and 8 from the square, Nat seems dissatisfied with the appearance of logs placed within the region of the square. Finally, Nat's intention was to build within the square structure, not outside of it. This is evident from the way Nat positioned logs 7 and 8—across the square with both ends leaning on the single-notched logs.

Nat exhibits a number of spatial and geometric behaviors and knowledge of architectural principles in this first episode. One mathematically related feature has to do with Nat's engineering abilities, particularly as it relates to empirical matching. Nat seems to use informal measurement, or magnitude comparison (particularly empirical matching) when attempting to attach logs 7 and 8 to the square. Empirical matching is a form of informal mea-surement that involves the child's ability to compare lengths of objects based on their appearance rather than on formal measuring procedures or techniques. The empirical matching is evident when Nat compares the lengths of logs 7 and 8 to the logs of the square in an attempt to attach them. Since the logs of the square are unable to support or attach to log 7, Nat compares the lengths of this log to the single-notched (perpendicular) logs by turning it ninety degrees. His informal measurement is accurate because log 7 fits comfortably on the single-notched logs. This is evident despite the fact that he suddenly moves log 7 from the structure.

Another mathematical feature evident in the first episode is Nat's demon-stration of symmetry. This feature is evident in two ways: Nat's temporary placement of log 7 on the notches of the single-notched logs and his reat-tachment of the two triangular pieces on single-notched logs (see figure

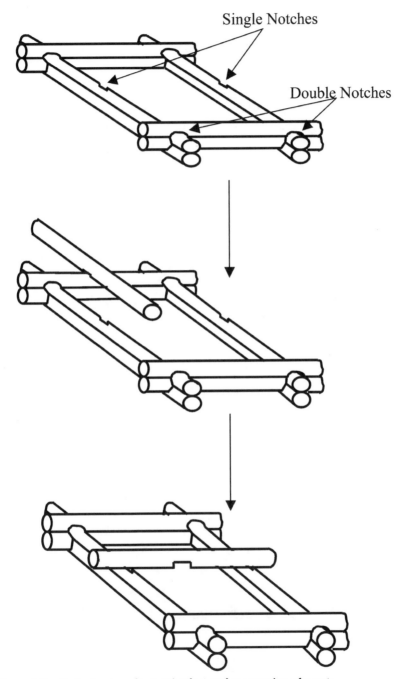

Single Notches

Double Notches

Figure 6.2.   Basic structure from episode 1 and progression of events

6.3). Nat places the triangular pieces so that they appear directly across (not diagonal) from one another. This is a clear example of plane bilateral symmetry in which one side of the square appears as a mirror image of the other.

A third mathematical concept demonstrated from this episode is the notion of parallelism and perpendicularity. Based on the ways the logs were manufactured, Nat seems to be quite aware that certain logs will fit on his structure only if they are placed parallel with, or perpendicular to, other logs.

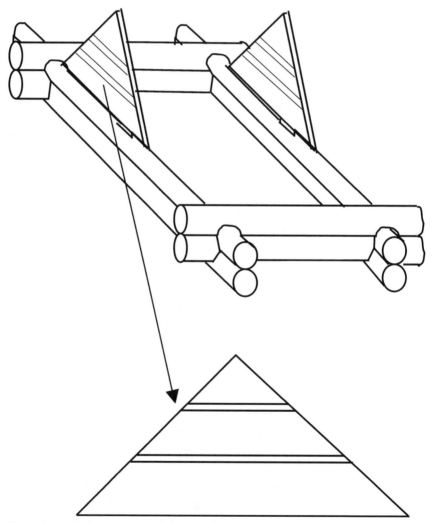

Figure 6.3. Nat's placement of triangular figures

It can be argued that the first episode ends as Nat stands and walks to the wall area to find additional pieces for the first activity. Not being able to find any, it is necessary for him to search in the cubby holes and bins holding blocks that are underneath the overhead play area.

Episode 2

Nat continues to look for more logs. He walks over to a milk case and is unsuccessful in finding them. Then, Nat continues his search for logs in other bins in the block area. Shortly thereafter, Darren, who was holding a wooden block, accidentally bumps Nat [lightly] on the forehead. Nat picks up a unit block from the block cabinet solely for the purpose of revenge. Nat, who appears quite angry at this point, hits Darren [lightly] on the back of the head. Antonio asks Nat to refrain from hitting Darren a second time. The teacher asks Antonio and Darren to participate in another project. The following dialogue clarifies this incident:

Darren: Antonio!
Antonio: Whoa, whoa, whoa! Ah! . . . [These interjections are due to a few blocks falling from a structure apparently built by Antonio and Darren.]
Darren: Do you like it? [Darren is asking Nat if he likes the structure that he and Antonio had built.]
Nat: Yeah!
Darren: [Darren hits Nat on the side of the forehead with one of the wooden blocks.] Sorry, Nat. Sorry.
Nat: "Sorry" doesn't work for me.
Darren: I didn't. . . . That wasn't that bad, was it Tony?
Antonio: No.
Nat: [Nat attempts to seek revenge by hitting Darren on the head with another wooden block.]
Darren: Didn't hurt! . . . . Don't do it again. I only did it to you once.
Antonio: Don't do it to him!
Teacher: Antonio . . . Darren . . .
Nat: Lourdes! [Antonio and Darren leave.]

Nat, who is alone at this point, appears to be become less restless and continues his search for logs. While looking for more logs in the bins, he stumbles upon two wooden pieces of railroad track. Although these pieces are attachable, Nat does not connect the pieces immediately. Through trial and error, Nat finally attaches the two pieces of track (see figure 6.5). He places this track on a section of the classroom floor where he can work.

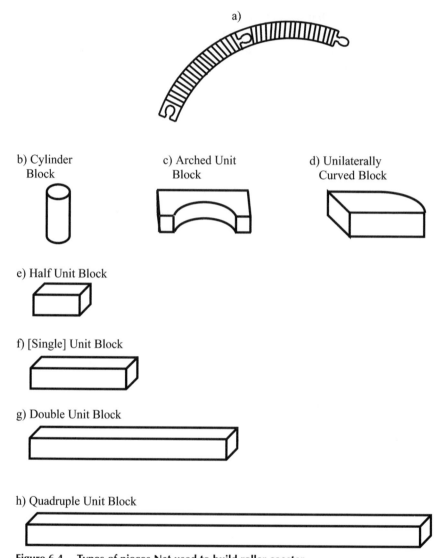

Figure 6.4.   **Types of pieces Nat used to build roller coaster**

Analysis 2

How did episode 2 come about? What were the necessary elements that may have contributed to episode 2? The final product of episode 2 is an elaborate roller coaster system that exhibits Nat's uncanny insight regarding geometric and architectural principles. Based on the scenario shortly after Antonio and Darren's exit, it seems as if it is possible to consider three inter-

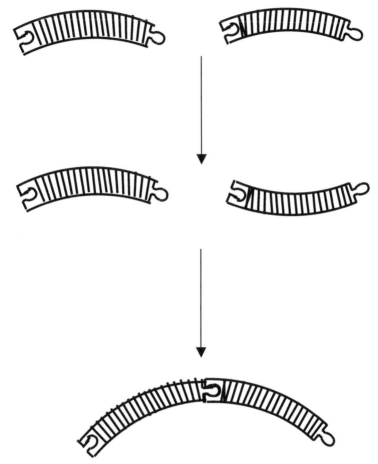

Figure 6.5.   Nat's encounter with the attachment of track through trial and error

pretations as to why Nat embarked on the construction of a roller coaster system.

The first interpretation is that Nat may have had an ulterior motive, or master plan, for the construction of the roller coaster system from the start, that is, before his brief skirmish with Darren. The second interpretation is that he was determined to build the roller coaster structure immediately after the incident with Darren and Antonio. The third, and seemingly most plausible of the three interpretations, is that while Nat's ill temper had diminished as he once again focused on play activity, he decided to put the wooden block (the one used to hit Darren) back into the cubby hole from where he had taken it and search for the toy logs (used in episode 1) in the bin. In doing so, he seemed to have stumbled upon two pieces of what appears to be toy wooden railroad track. Connecting these pieces may have led to his motivation to carry out the construction of the roller coaster track. Regardless of interpretation, however, one can say that, had it not been for the incident with Antonio and Darren, the roller coaster structure may have never come to fruition.

One important aspect of episode 2 is that it can also be interpreted as a second part of episode 1. How might this be possible? One major reason has to do with Nat's intention to continue searching for more logs for the structure he had built during episode 1. His encounter with Darren did not seem to affect his original plan to continue working on the log structure. Nat's intention to procure a unit block from a nearby cabinet had nothing to do with constructive play and nearly everything to do with using it for the sole purpose of revenge.

At the same time, Nat put this unit block back in its appropriate unit block cabinet. This is important for two reasons. First, it demonstrated Nat's ability to identify a common three-dimensional shape—a particular type of rectangular solid (figure identification). Second, it allowed Nat to search for more logs in bins that were located near the unit block cabinet. These same bins were where he had found the two pieces of track, the beginning stage of the roller coaster system.

Furthermore, Nat does not immediately attach the first two pieces of track. Through trial and error, Nat eventually attaches the two pieces after the third attempt. Figure 6.5 shows the progression from the first attempt to his third, and successful, attempt.

Episode 3

After placing the initial connected pieces of track on the floor, Nat returns to the block cabinets. He is stationary for approximately thirty seconds. It appears as if he is in deep thought. Instead of taking more pieces of track, Nat takes two cylinder blocks and two indented arch blocks and brings the four pieces to the floor area where he is about to work. Nat then picks up an undulated, hill-like, track piece that is lying on the floor near his work area and attaches it to the two initial pieces (tracks 1 and 2). Subsequently, he takes a small curvilinear piece of track (track 4) and attempts to attach it to the undulated track piece (track 3). Nat says "Hi" to Jose, one of the teachers' aides. Given that one end of the unfinished track system is left suspended in midair, Nat takes a unit block that had been also lying nearby, places it under the suspended track, and uses the unit block as a support, or foundation, for the suspended part of the track system. Initially, he is unsuccessful in supporting the track because the positioning of the unit block (large face down) left a gap and the track remained suspended.

Nat turns the unit block (medium-face down), and at this point, he success-fully supports the track (see figure 6.6).

Analysis 3

When returning to the block cabinet and bins, presumably for more pieces of track, Nat remains stationary, as if he is engaged in profound thought. This 30-second period of deep thought is important to consider because it is at this moment when Nat seems to think up a master plan for the creation of a roller coaster system—information which he withholds for

a)

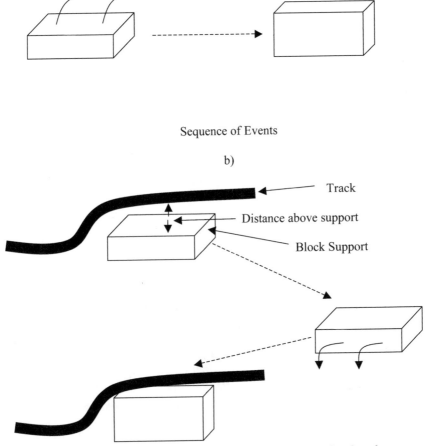

Sequence of Events

b)

Figure 6.6.　**Nat's positioning a unit block as a foundation for overhead track**

approximately five minutes. He initially divulges this information in the eighth minute of his segment. Two of the four pieces of block that Nat takes to the floor are used for foundational purposes.

As described in episode 3 above, after connecting the undulated piece of track, Nat connects the lower end of it firmly to track 2 so that the other side remains suspended in midair. He then connects a fourth, curved piece of track to the suspended part of track 3. At this point of the episode, Nat's understanding of foundation—one of several architectural principles—is made evident; in realizing that a support is needed to keep the suspended track pieces from falling, Nat takes a flat unit block and initially places it so that one of the largest faces is on the floor. A problem arises that forces Nat into another trial-and-error situation. Nat notices that the support (large-face down) does not reach the joints of tracks 3 and 4. In attempting to solve this problem, he uses one hand to secure the joint and the other hand to turn the supporting unit block so that the height of the block is adequate for supporting the track. He is successful in the second attempt, when he turns the block medium-face down (see figure 6.6).

Episode 4

Nat returns to the block cabinets and bins to search for more track. He pauses, again in deep thought, for approximately thirty seconds. Finally, he finds a fifth piece of track that is flat (track 5). Before he connects this flat track, he knows that he needs another support. Nat reaches into a nearby cabinet and does not find a block to his liking. He then finds a unit block nearby on the floor, which seems to work as a support. There is a problem, however: The space underneath the track does not allow the supporting block to be positioned in the direction he had intended—i.e., in the same direction of the track. So, Nat turns the supporting unit block approximately forty-five degrees so that it fits in the narrow space. In doing so, Nat attempts to support the joint between track 4 and track 5 using the unit block placed in a forty-five-degree position. He realizes however that the weight of track 5 will not be fully supported. Nat then pulls the unit block out. But this is only temporary because the real obstacle for Nat is the first of thirteen quadruple blocks that are touching and placed parallel to each other. The quadruple block is the longest piece in the standard block set. Other blocks include double unit blocks, unit blocks, and half unit blocks (see figure 6.4 and Kathryn's case study below for more elaborate descriptions of block sizes). This group of quadruple blocks is referred to here as the "landscape," for it serves as one part of structure's ground setting—the other being the floor.

Nat removes the first quadruple block, so that the supporting unit block can be positioned in the direction that he initially planned. The supporting unit block is placed in the original position, and track 5 is now attached and partially supported. Track 5 is not fully supported because part of it is suspended over the "landscape"—the remaining parallel touching quadruple blocks. To support the suspended track, Nat takes a one-quarter unit block, initially places it on the supporting unit block, but then realizes that this would prevent the continuation of track. He removes it and places the small one-fourth unit block in the correct location—on the landscape as a means of supporting the suspended part of track 5 (see figure 6.7). At this

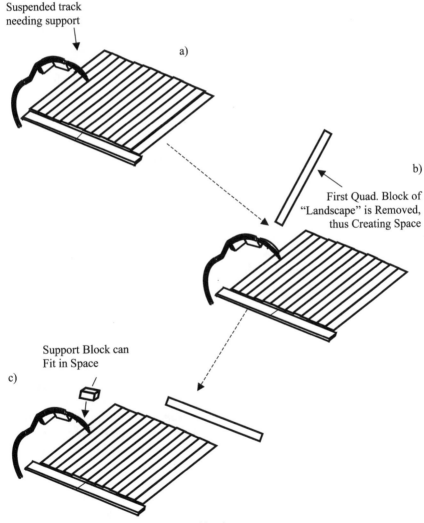

Suspended track needing support

a)

b)

First Quad. Block of "Landscape" is Removed, thus Creating Space

Support Block can Fit in Space

c)

Figure 6.7. Nat's removal of a piece of landscape

point, track 5 is successfully in place. Nat carefully inspects all the joints to ensure that they are secure. The episode ends as Nat tells one of the teachers that he is making a roller coaster: "Latucia, look [at] what I'm making! I'm making a roller coaster!"

Analysis 4

One major element of Nat's fourth episode has to do with the way in which the boy grapples with physical obstacles that seem to frustrate the continuation of the roller coaster system. The issue arises as Nat takes a unit block on the floor and attempts to use it as a means of supporting "overhead" track, particularly the joint that connects two pieces. He deals with this situation in two ways. In the first way, Nat deals with the oncoming wooden block landscape (which is approximately two or three inches above the floor landscape) by turning his material—the unit block support—so that overhead track can continue onto the wooden block landscape. This method of support could have been successful; yet Nat was still dissatisfied. He seemed wary about the positioning of the support. He then deals with the situation in a second way, one which involves the altering of the landscape. Nat's decision to alter the landscape for the continuation of the roller coaster system is one of the several unique aspects of this videotaped segment, one that clearly demonstrates the child's knowledge of architectural principles (see figure 6.7).

How does Nat deal with the landscape? Within the context of the preschool classroom, Nat's landscape is the floor area of the classroom that is surrounded by the area's block cabinets. This landscape includes the floor itself, as well as thirteen parallel, touching quadruple unit blocks whose ends are leveled by two quadruple blocks on one of the two sides (figure 6.7).

Two types of architectural principles are evident here. First, Nat clearly shows his understanding of support, that is, the notion that overhead constructions need a form of support in order to remain standing and not fall down. He creates support (through the use of unit blocks) in the form of posting, similar to the posts that support different types of bridges. Second, Nat's ability to employ techniques of engineering is exhibited in this part of the fourth episode, evident through his seemingly skillful manipulation of the landscape and his method of determining whether the support block will fit between another support block and the landscape as a means of sustaining overhead track (informal measurement).

Although Nat has removed a piece of the landscape, his problem of supporting the overhead track is not completely solved because the support for track 5 on the floor is taller than the distance from the floor to the surface of the wooden block landscape. Thus, track 5 remains partly suspended over the landscape. Nat seems to learn from past experience that a large unit block would be too large for supporting track suspended over the landscape; clearly, the suspended distance is less at this position than the suspended distance of overhead track on the floor. Accordingly, as a means of rectifying this situation, Nat takes a quarter unit block (approximately one-quarter the height of a unit block) and places it on the landscape for successful support.

Episode 5

Nat walks to the cabinet to search for more pieces of track and finds one piece (6). He attempts to attach this track but realizes he needs another support. To this end, he uses the indented arch block as a support. In the earlier episodes, supports were initially too low—that is, the block support had been initially placed large-face down and subsequently turned medium-face down. In this situation, the reverse happened—the support block is initially positioned medium-face down and subsequently large-face down. This procedure allows Nat to successfully support and connect track (track 6).

Analysis 5

Events in episode 5 show Nat's ability to learn from recent prior experiences. In earlier episodes, Nat's success in supporting overhead track was due to trial-and-error manipulation of unit blocks. In episode 5, however, Nat successfully positions a unit block (indented arch) support medium-face down, which allows the overhead track to fit comfortably on the supporting base. Nat seems to have learned from experiences in earlier episodes because he does not repeat any trial-and-error manipulations in subsequent events.

Episode 6

Nat searches for more track in a nearby bin and finds two pieces of track (tracks 7 and 8) and says "Two!" He places these two pieces down near the structure and walks to the bathroom. Nat returns from the bathroom, procures the indented arch block, and places it in the correct supporting position on the landscape so that the seventh track can be attached. Nat then grabs another block and successfully positions it so that the track is supported at the correct height. [The second supporting block is not the same shape as the previous two blocks, yet there was no trial and error at this point.]

Analysis 6

At this point, Nat clearly has a master plan for his roller coaster system. Furthermore, as evidenced from his subsequent behaviors, Nat's bathroom visit does not interfere with his plan to continue finishing the structure. Again, Nat successfully positions a block support appropriately so that track 7 connects with track 6 without difficulty but is not fully supported in the other end. A third time, Nat takes a unit block and successfully positions it to support tracks 7 and 8. Earlier trial-and-error experiences, then, seemed to have paid off for Nat, for he now seems to benefit from what he had learned in earlier episodes.

Episode 7

Again, Nat searches for more track. "I need more track." Brandon arrives and decides to share Nat's play space. Nat finds several pieces of track—this time, the pieces that Nat finds are longer and straight, unlike the previous pieces. Nat returns to the roller coaster structure. Nat seems to realize from previous experience that he needs support for the track. So he returns to the bin and finds a unit block. He carefully and correctly positions it on the landscape. Nat subsequently places the ninth piece of track on it. Though the track is longer, he does not consider that the support for the track (track 9) must also be longer. So, Nat removes the unit block support and searches for a longer supporting block.

Nat asks Brandon to hand him a specific type of block. Brandon says, "one of those?" [a single unit block].

Nat walks to the bin and says, "No, I need one of these!" [a double unit block.]

Analysis 7

Episode 7 is yet another example of Nat's learning from prior experience. What is important here is not solely the idea that Nat learns how to position support blocks from trial and error, but also that this learning actually suggests more efficient ways in which the boy engineers his structure. At this point (approximately ten minutes into the videotape segment), Nat's construction of the roller coaster system is proceeding at a much faster rate than at the early stages, which seems to be related to the boy learning more efficient strategies in tackling various problems—e.g. the height and placement of block supports, direction of track, and rearrangement of landscape.

Another important event of episode 7 has to do with another example of the boy's concern with appropriate support for a longer piece of track (track 9). Empirical matching is again evident here because Nat seems to know that the unit block, in comparison to the double unit block, is too short for supporting track 9. The boy's engineering knowledge is confirmed by his short dialogue with Brandon, who is unclear about Nat's intention— namely, to support a long piece of track with a longer block support.

Episode 8

Nat grabs an undulated track (track 10) and takes fifteen seconds to think about where it should be attached [he observes the entire structure]. He finally attaches it to the last piece (track 9). This tenth piece does not need support, and thus, the other end touches the landscape. Nat has two or three short pieces of track. He picks up a straight short piece (track 11) and attempts to attach it to the tenth piece (see figure 6.8).

At this point, Manny, another child, accidentally kicks the roller coaster system, and the initial track [the first five or six pieces of track] falls off the supporting blocks. Nat fulminates: "Yo, what's wrong with you Manny? Ms. Findlay, Manny broke my roller coaster!"

He subsequently spends time [almost two minutes] reconstructing the

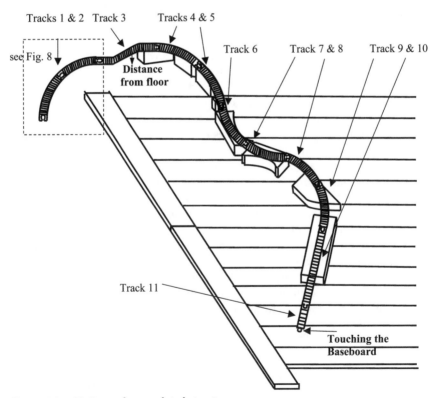

Figure 6.8. **Nat's nearly completed structure**

track and attempts to reconstruct it in its original form. Nat becomes more frustrated; nevertheless, he settles for a "modified" construction. Manny and Brandon offer their assistance, but Nat refuses their offer: "I know it's you Brandon, but you can't help!"

Nat detaches tracks 4 and 5. He reattaches tracks 1, 2, and 3, and attaches the latter to track 6. This is possible because track 3 undulates to the landscape. Tracks 4 and 5 are reconnected to track 1. Nat adds another long straight piece to track 4. The reconstruction is successful, and Nat subsequently takes a toy "roller coaster" [a toy car] and rolls it on his reconstructed track, thereby engaging himself in dramatic play: "Wee, wee, wee, wee . . . !" [as if feeling a sense of exhilaration while riding in a roller coaster].

Analysis 8

In the early part of episode 8, Nat seems as if he is in the homestretch in finishing his roller coaster system. Nat's attachment of undulated track 10 indicates that the boy does not want to end the structure on the support blocks. Instead, Nat puts "closure" to his structure by using an undulated track so that the roller coater track terminates on the landscape, not above it.

The high point of episode 8, however, occurs when Manny, another preschooler, accidentally kicks Nat's roller coaster system, forcing most of the track to fall off the block supports. This event sends Nat into a frenetic disposition. Nat, of course, becomes annoyed with Manny and refuses any help offered by other children. This incident differs from the earlier one with Darren in the sense that Nat does not resort to a new task. It is similar to Nat's encounter with Darren because Nat shows his cognitive abilities after he argues with Manny.

Nat is now faced with the task of reconstructing the entire system. He works through his frustration by reattaching tracks 4 and 5 to track 1. The first three original tracks, along with tracks 4 and 5, are turned so that track 1 attaches to track 6 and a twelfth piece (long track—now the first track in the system) is attached to track 4. In addition, Nat dispenses with the block supports on the floor and still manages to extend the system as he had done earlier. Nat's hard labor and use of his cognitive abilities in spatial and geometric concepts, as well as architectural principles (particularly engineering), seem to have paid off, for now he is able to engage himself in dramatic play—i.e., using the roller coaster system for the purpose of pretend play.

Discussion I

The case study of Nat is an example of a young boy exhibiting a great deal of geometric knowledge (bilateral symmetry, parallelism, and perpendicularity) and architectural principles in the everyday context (posting and engineering skills). But his cognitive ability in SPAGAR activity is not the only aspect demonstrated in this videotape segment.

Nat's ability to learn, too, is manifest throughout the segment, particularly after the third episode. Nat learns from prior actions to gain insight into more efficient strategies for solving difficult problems that involve both spatial-geometrical and architectural activities.

In addition to his cognitive abilities in mathematical thinking and his propensity to learn from prior experience, Nat does not seem to be a child who "lives for the moment." Nat is a planner; he shows clear signs of charting a course for constructing a large structure or system, i.e., a roller coaster system. It was not merely a whim or creation built on the spur of the moment. It was a well thought-out production that took place over a ten-minute period of time.

CASE 2: KATHRYN'S "HOUSE"

Kathryn is four years and eleven months old and attends a private upper-income preschool on the upper east side of Manhattan in New York City. This preschool has ample resources—there are more than enough play blocks for each child, and staff instituted a policy that both girls and boys receive equal amounts of play time with blocks. (At this particular preschool, boys tended to play with blocks for longer time periods than the girls.) Like many American preschools, this one has special centers for different types of activities.

This segment is unique in the sense that it demonstrates a young girl's (not boy's) rather sophisticated abilities in spatial and geometric concepts and understanding of fundamental architectural principles. As discussed in chapter 5, a great deal of research in spatial and geometric thinking examines the comparison of boys and girls in different spatial or geometrically related tasks, and much of this literature argues that boys display greater aptitude or abilities than do girls (Benbow and Stanley 1992; Waber 1979; Harris 1981). Yet few, if any, studies examine not only gender comparisons related to everyday mathematics but also case studies of both girls and boys and how they exhibit complex mathematical thinking in the everyday context.

Another phenomenon when examining individual cases of spatial and geometric thinking (and mathematical thinking in general) deals with social interaction. In the present situation, Kathryn exhibits these abilities having little or no interaction with other children. In her seven episodes within this fifteen-minute segment, Kathryn is involved in activities that employ the use of blocks. As examined below, much of what Kathryn does during her segment seems to run counter to Erikson's (1963) theory of infantile sexuality as it relates to spatial modalities between males and females. That is to say, Kathryn engages herself in the construction of very tall structures as opposed to low, semi-circular structures that, according to Erikson, are associated to the way girls play with blocks.

Similar to Nat's segment, Kathryn's is organized by a description of each episode followed by an analysis based on mathematical content, personal factors that may enable or constrain certain types of SPAGAR activity, the physical environment, and social and cultural factors that may either bring about or thwart mathematical activity.

Kathryn's behavior, which lasts for over ten minutes (the remainder of the segment), demonstrates her expertise in the area of spatial, geometric, and architectural concepts. This behavior is separated into seven episodes, showing a variety of aspects of spatial, geometric, and architectural knowledge.

Episode 1

Kathryn walks over to the block cabinet, looks into the video camera, takes three blocks—two half unit blocks and one double unit block—and carries them back to her area of the floor. Kathryn places the half unit blocks on the floor, at a distance of approximately one quadruple unit block between them. She then places one double unit block on the floor, parallel to the two half unit blocks, and pushes it in a back-and-forth motion. Kathryn then walks over to the block cabinet. Before doing so, however, Kathryn appears as if she is reaching for a unit block that is on the floor near her structure. Instead, she procures two more half unit blocks. Each of the two new blocks is then placed in an upright fashion on top of each of the half unit blocks that are already lying flat on the floor. Each of the two half unit blocks, then, forms an upside-down T as a base of a potentially large structure (see figure 6.9).

Kathryn subsequently makes a return trip to the block cabinet and selects a quadruple unit block. She takes this long block back to her upside-down

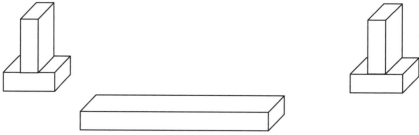

Figure 6.9.   Kathryn's upside-down T foundation and double unit block on the side

T base and places one end of the quadruple unit block on one of the bases. Since the distance between the bases is slightly longer than the length of the quadruple block, Kathryn moves the second upside-down T base closer, so it will support the other end of the quadruple unit block. At this point, the quadruple unit block is suspended by the two bases. Kathryn then takes a double unit block, which she had taken earlier from the cabinet, and places it in an upright fashion on one end of the quadruple beam that spans horizontally.

Analysis 1

Kathryn places the half unit blocks at the approximate length of a quadruple block—without initially procuring a quadruple block. It can be surmised from this event that Kathryn knew she wanted to create a base for a larger structure and that this base would initially support a quadruple block. If this is the case, then it is plausible to conclude that Kathryn has an adept sense of informal measurement.

After she returns from the block cabinet, it becomes evident that there is a clear purpose for the next two half unit blocks: they will serve as a support, or foundation, for a potentially larger structure. Initially, as mentioned above, each of the two new half unit blocks is placed vertically on the original horizontal half unit blocks. But there is more: Each new vertical block is placed on the original so that the subsequent structure includes two half unit blocks forming an upside-down T shape with a replica of this at a distance of the approximate length of a quadruple block—both pieces of the structure appearing symmetric (i.e., two upside-down Ts). Symmetry, too, is an important spatial characteristic necessary for architectural phenomena, like foundation and support (Blackwell 1984).

Kathryn does place a quadruple block on these upside-down T supports, with one end of the quadruple on one upside-down T and the other end of the quadruple on the second upside-down T. This event not only demonstrates Kathryn's mathematical behaviors regarding symmetry but also her engagement in empirical matching (engineering); she uses informal measurement by approximating the distance of the quadruple block when the two upside-down T supports were created earlier. Further, Kathryn takes a double unit and places it in an upright fashion, balancing on the quadruple block. It seems quite clear at this point that Kathryn's intention is to create a foundation for a larger tower structure, so the architectural principle of foundation is indubitably part of Kathryn's mathematical-architectural repertoire.

Episode 2

The second episode begins as Kathryn returns to the cabinet three more times to take one double unit block on each of these three occasions. Incidentally, while she returns to the cabinet, she turns her head back, looking at the unfinished structure she had just created. When Kathryn returns, she places the first of her three double unit blocks next to the one she had placed originally. She then places the second and third double unit blocks on the quadruple span. She readjusts the distance between each upright double unit block to ensure that there is an equal distance between each unit block. At this point, the structure consists of a base (two upside-down Ts), a quadruple span, and four upright, relatively equidistant double unit blocks (see figure 6.10).

Analysis 2

Three spatial and architectural activities seem to be present in Kathryn's second episode: attention to symmetry, ability to distinguish between different three-dimensional shapes (figure identification), and measurement and detail in terms of distance between the four double unit blocks (engineering). As soon as Kathryn places the first double unit block in an upright

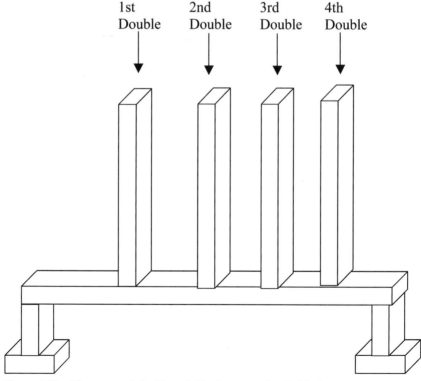

Figure 6.10.   Placement of double unit blocks on quadruple block

position on the base from episode 1, it becomes increasingly clear that her intention is to create a vertical tower structure.

It seems evident that Kathryn creates symmetry for the purpose of balancing a tower made of individual blocks above a fairly stable foundation. Symmetry is formed as Kathryn places the double unit blocks in an approximately equidistant fashion. How does figure identification play a role in this episode? Kathryn identifies the same block that she needs for the structure when she returns to the cabinet three times to obtain three more double unit blocks (obtaining one double unit block each time). And again (as in episode 1), the engineering principle is employed as Kathryn pays careful attention to the distance between each double unit block as a means of keeping her building erect.

Episode 3

In episode 3, Kathryn is reaching back, most likely to procure another block. While stretching back, she picks up a triangular, wedge-like block, which she then places on the left side of the quadruple block. This triangular block is wider than the width of the quadruple, so it hangs over both lateral edges of the quadruple block. This block is placed so that the downward slope is facing the fourth-placed upright double unit block. Again, Kathryn stretches her arms back, trying to reach for another block. Instead, one of the other children gives her a toy dolphin. Hoping that it remains stationary, Kathryn places the dolphin on the triangular block with little success; within a few seconds, the dolphin falls. Kathryn attempts to find a solution by taking the triangular block and placing it on the structure in some other position. She places it so that the descending slope is pointing upwards. Kathryn then places the dolphin on the triangular block successfully by having it lean against the fourth upright double unit block.

Analysis 3

Kathryn's ability to balance objects on a foundation seems to be the central theme of episode 3. Her manipulation of toy objects in this episode is an example of a trial-and-error situation. She manages to situate the wedge block so that the toy dolphin leans on the nearby fourth upright double unit block. Initially, Kathryn places the wedge so that the narrow vertex (with no base) points in a downward position. But she soon finds out through trial and error, that in order for the wedge to remain stationary and balance the toy dolphin, it cannot be situated with the vertex pointing downward. Kathryn rectifies the situation by putting the wedge on its base (which lies on the horizontal quadruple block), placing the dolphin on the vertex part of the wedge, and having it lean on the fourth double unit block. Trial and error pays off for Kathryn, for it seems as if she learned from her prior mistakes.

Episode 4

While looking at the video camera, Kathryn walks to the cabinet for three unit blocks. When she returns to her structure, Kathryn takes one of the unit blocks and places it horizontally on top of the first and second upright double unit blocks. Knowing that she is unable to fit the second unit block on top of the second and third upright double unit blocks, she moves the third upright double unit block closer to the second, and then the fourth double unit block closer to the third. When doing this, the toy dolphin falls from the triangular block. She now takes the second unit block and places it horizontally on top of the third and fourth upright double unit blocks. At this point, she picks up the toy dolphin and the third unit block from the floor.

Analysis 4

The fourth episode seems to explain why Kathryn initially places the upright double unit blocks so that they stand approximately equidistant from each other. Kathryn seems to deliberately place these upright blocks in this way because she wants to place the two unit blocks on the double unit blocks in a horizontal arrangement. The only way she is able to balance the horizontal unit blocks is to create a situation in which the upright double unit blocks are placed at the approximate distance of a horizontal unit block. Again, this is an example of Kathryn's artful contrivance of objects for the purpose of ensuring good form and function for her building—i.e., the engineering principle.

Episode 5

Kathryn takes the wedge from the structure, and in its place, she puts the third unit block. This block is placed upright very close to the fourth upright double unit block. Again, Kathryn walks to the cabinet to retrieve more blocks. This time, she gets a half unit block. When she returns, Kathryn places this half unit block on the upright unit block. But within seconds, the half unit block falls. Kathryn moves the upright unit block closer to the fourth double, almost touching. Again, she walks to the cabinet and retrieves another unit block. This second unit block is placed upright on the first unit block that is now almost touching the fourth upright double block. Kathryn takes the half unit block, which had fallen to the floor moments earlier, and places it horizontally on top of the fourth double unit block and the second upright (single) unit block. In short, Kathryn uses different size blocks to achieve a second level horizontal span—namely, the first two units plus the half unit block. Kathryn now takes the wedge shaped triangular block and places it on top of the horizontally placed half unit block. Kathryn then successfully places the dolphin on top of the triangular block.

Analysis 5

Episode 5 demonstrates further Kathryn's ability in artful manipulation of objects. At first, due to a lack of balance, the half unit block falls from the upright unit block that was placed close to the fourth upright double unit block. Why did she retrieve a second unit block from the cabinet? Because she eventually placed the half unit block horizontally, it seems evident that Kathryn needed a balance for the half unit block. For this reason, she placed the two unit blocks adjacent to the double unit block.

Why did she place two unit blocks one on top of the other and close to the fourth double unit block in an upright position? This action suggests that Kathryn understands the arithmetic concept of equality and the geometric concept of congruence—two identical rectangular solids are congruent to a single rectangular solid that is twice the size (or length) of the two original rectangular solids. In other words, the total length of two unit blocks is equal to the length of one double unit block. This is confirmed by the very fact that she places the original half unit block horizontally and balanced on top of the fourth double unit block and the upper of the two unit blocks; that is, the horizontal half unit block is level with the other two horizontal unit blocks that are supported by the first, second, and third upright double unit blocks (see figure 6.11). Subsequently, she is able to balance the wedge block and the toy dolphin.

Episode 6

Kathryn returns to the cabinet to take four half unit blocks. The first half unit block is placed in an upright fashion, to the immediate right of the triangular block. Kathryn then places the second half unit block at a right angle to the first half unit block. After it falls to the floor, Kathryn places this block next to, and flush with, the first half unit block. Kathryn attempts to put the third half unit block next to the second, but it doesn't seem to fit on the horizontal span. She then removes the second half unit block, and in its place, Kathryn puts another half unit block. This other half unit block is placed at a right angle, adjacent to the first half unit block. Unfortunately, this block also falls. But Kathryn is persistent—she picks up the fallen block and places it so that it touches the first block. Kathryn successfully places

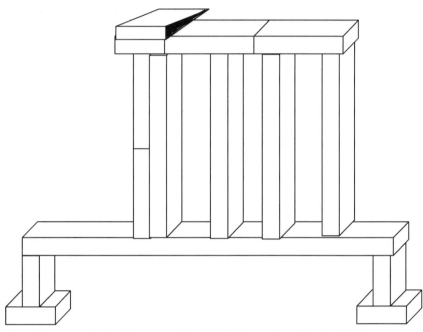

Figure 6.11.   Kathryn's placement of vertical, horizontal, and wedge blocks

this block at a right angle to the first block. She then places a third block on the beam so that it touches the first and second. A fourth unit block is then placed in a parallel position to the third block (at a right angle to the first and second blocks). Finally, Kathryn pushes the third and fourth half unit blocks toward the first two so that the four blocks form a rectangle.

Analysis 6

This episode essentially describes how Kathryn creates a distinct section or microcosm of her tower structure—a rectangular solid made of four half unit blocks. Its purpose becomes clear in episode 7, but the simple explanation for now is that it serves as a base for another mini-structure or toy—a base on top of a base. Kathryn knows that her rectangular solid (or structure within a structure) needs to be balanced and that the base—including the foundation and supporting blocks—needs to sustain the rectangular mini-structure.

Balance was only achieved through trial and error. Kathryn's second half unit block falls three times before she is able to structure all four half unit blocks. In terms of mathematical behavior, Kathryn seems to understand that in order to construct a rectangular solid out of four half unit blocks in such a constrained region, she must turn two of the blocks so that they are perpendicular to the first half unit block. She also seems to know that the widths of two half unit blocks are equal to the length of one single half unit block (see figure 6.12). Once again, Kathryn demonstrates her knowledge of congruence.

Episode 7

While glancing at the room, Kathryn walks over to a bin near one of the cabinets on the floor. She takes three toy cars. One of these toy cars is placed on top of the four half unit blocks that form a rectangle. This car covers nearly the entire surface area of the rectangle. Next, with no luck, Kathryn attempts to place a second car adjacent to the first. Knowing that it will not fit, she takes the second toy car and places it in the small area that is available in front of the first car. Unfortunately, the car falls, knocking over the dolphin, and both toys fall to the floor. Kathryn places the toy dolphin back onto the triangular wedge. The second car (which fell moments earlier) and the third car are placed on the section of the horizontal quadruple unit block containing free space (to the left)—that is, space that is unoccupied by the upright double blocks. Kathryn walks over to the bin a second time and procures another toy car, which is then placed next to the second and third cars on the horizontal quadruple beam. Again, Kathryn walks over to the bin. However, this time, she does not take anything from the bin. Instead, she walks to the block cabinet and procures a cone-shaped block and two other blocks. These two blocks are the same length as a unit block, but their height and width are one-half the size of the unit block, thus making it one-fourth the volume of the unit block.

Kathryn places the cone-shaped block to the right of the group of four half unit blocks (forming the rectangular solid) which are situated on one of the two horizontal (second level) unit blocks. The thinner unit blocks are then placed in an upright fashion to the right of the cone-shaped block, with the second thinner block balancing on top of the first. Kathryn walks to the cabinet for another block. She retrieves just one block—a triangular

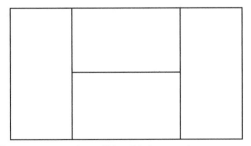

Figure 6.12.   Kathryn's rectangular solid: A bird's eye view

block (narrower than the first). Kathryn places this triangular block on top of the thinner unit blocks in such a way that its length appears horizontal, thus creating a balanced stack (see figure 6.13 for the finished structure). Kathryn, however, seems to anticipate an accident, since the placement of the triangular block in this manner will not balance the thinner stacked unit blocks. So she places it in a vertical position, with the descending slope facing upward. At this point, Kathryn no longer works on her structure, and walks to a group of children.

Analysis 7

Episode 7, the last episode in Kathryn's segment, demonstrates a young child's ability to balance numerous toys and blocks through principles of symmetry and foundation. Much of this last episode has to do with the extension of the structure. First, Kathryn undergoes several trial-and-error situations in trying to balance the toy cars and the toy dolphin. After she

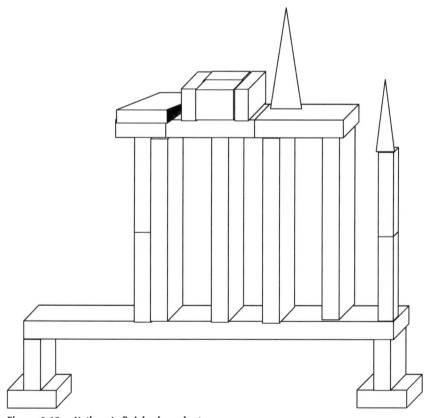

Figure 6.13.   Kathryn's finished product

succeeds in balancing these objects, she places a cone to the right of the rectangular box (constructed of four half unit blocks) and continues to extend the structure by balancing two thinner unit blocks. Had it not been for the overall symmetry of the structure, many of the upright, balancing blocks would not stay balanced or intact on the foundation blocks.

In the last part of episode 7, it seems as if Kathryn learned from prior experience; she does not place the large triangular block horizontally on the upper thinner unit block (which is balancing on another upright thinner unit block). Instead, she continues her balancing act by placing the triangular block on the higher of the two thin unit blocks vertically. The final scene shows a structure made of twenty-six blocks and toys, possessing a foundation, a second level, and a number of balancing pieces. Clearly, this is a creation that demonstrates a child's artful manipulation of play blocks and toys.

Discussion II

Based on the observation of the segment, Kathryn clearly has a master plan when in the process of constructing her tower. Unlike Nat, the notion that Kathryn has a master plan is not so easy to conclude from viewing the early parts of the segment. As time progresses, however, evidence mounts in favor of a plan or scheme in Kathryn's behavior. Unlike Kathryn, Nat immerses himself in periods of profound thought—several seconds at a time where it is clear to the observer that the boy has an agenda. Kathryn, too, has an agenda, but her agenda is only noticeable after the fact. Kathryn is surely involved in a thinking process; however, she does not spend several seconds at a time in deep thought as Nat does. Instead, the plan in her behavior is evident only after she places blocks at approximately the same distances apart. That is, an observer would realize Kathryn has a plan after the upright blocks are already situated and she returns and places additional blocks in a horizontal fashion on them. It is unclear as to what Kathryn has in mind to construct. Whatever the intention of the structure, Kathryn clearly has a blueprint, which is evident as time progresses.

Kathryn is engaged in numerous activities highlighting spatial and geometric concepts, architectural principles, and mathematical behavior in general. For one, she demonstrates informal knowledge of plane symmetry—her placement of the upside-down T supports and the equidistant upright double unit blocks are two examples. She is able to identify shapes, expressed through her three-time return to the cabinet to obtain double unit blocks. Furthermore, she demonstrates knowledge of foundation as she creates the upside-down T posts and scrupulously positions a quadruple block on them. Perhaps most evident is her skill at artful manipulation of objects, demonstrated through informal measurement techniques (empirical matching) and precise placement of different blocks to keep her building from falling on the floor. Finally, based on her placement of toy animals and toy cars, Kathryn seems to have a certain amount of understanding with regard to proportional reasoning; clearly, she creates the rectangular block figure for the purpose of fitting and supporting a toy car as a professional architect would do when designing a garage or parking lot.

In general, although it is certainly possible to distinguish between the different spatial, geometric, and architectural activities in which Kathryn is engaged, at the same time, a number of these activities are embedded in others or are symbiotically related and interdependent. For example, Kathryn's symmetry occurs based on her painstaking effort to ensure that the upright double unit blocks are equidistant; her ability to engineer, then, is an essential part in capturing her skills at symmetric relations.

Another aspect of the case study of Kathryn has to do with the way her engineering skills and knowledge of balance allow her to create an elaborate, ornamented structure. When viewing Kathryn's finished product, her placement of toy objects on the wooden structure and the way she balances smaller blocks on various levels of the structure suggest that she possesses the ability to combine the essential architectural aspects of aesthetic beauty with the "reality" of form and function.[1]

CHAPTER TOPICS FOR DISCUSSION

1. Discuss the strengths and weaknesses of case study analysis as a means of generalizing about young children's spatioscientific and architectural activities and intellectual development as a whole.

2. Based on your readings of the two case studies discussed and analyzed in this chapter, compare and contrast the spatial and architectural activities of Nat with those of Kathryn. Determine whether other factors—such as similarities or differences in social interaction, location or environment, play activity, or type of object—affect each child's engagement in mathematical activity.

3. Observe young children, preferably between the ages of three and six years, during free play. The setting should preferably be within the preschool, although observation of young children's free play outdoors will suffice. Then, select one of the case study children in this chapter, and compare that child with your observational analysis of the child (or children) you have observed in terms of each child's spatial and architectural propensities.

4. Both Nat and Kathryn work on their constructions in solitary play. In the first case study, however, one child joins Nat toward the end of the videotaped segment. Does the entrance of this child into the scene

alter the conditions in which the construction takes place? If so, how are the conditions altered?

5. Suppose another child, or more than one child, joined Kathryn during the construction process. How would the change from solitary play to group play affect the conditions of the construction? Would this social change affect the spatial and architectural activity? Please explain whether you believe that it would or would not have an effect and why.

NOTES

1. See O'Gorman (1998) with regard to the architectural principles of form, function, and aesthetics.

7

Constructing Interactively: Cases 3 and 4

> In anthropology, Clifford Geertz has argued for "thick description" of phenomena as a form of theoretical understanding. The same strategy may pay off for developmental psychology.
>
> Nora S. Newcombe and Janellen Huttenlocher (2003, 225)

This chapter complements the previous one in that it examines the role of free play in young children's intellectual development, particularly relating to spatial, geometric, and scientific activity. The underlying contexts are quite different however. The two cases in chapter 6 reveal the mathematical propensities of two four- and five-year-old children in two separate case studies, with both children working in mostly solitary play. This chapter identifies two target children in separate case studies who are engaged in mathematical activities with other children. They are not engaged in solitary play, but rather in other types of play that involve interaction with peers. Again, like the two cases in the previous chapter, it is important to consider the factors that contribute to each child's spatial and architectural activities.

CASE 3: YOUNG CHILDREN BUILDING SKYSCRAPERS—FERNANDO

Fernando is a four-year-old of middle-class background. He attends a preschool in New York City for children of middle income families. The entire length of the observation is eighteen minutes and twenty seconds. In this particular case, we describe and interpret the mathematical content of Fernando's activity and the contextual factors that influence it.

Although the cases in the previous chapter focused on solitary play, the children developed their structures near the company of others, who may have indirectly had influence on what was constructed. With this in mind, it seems logical to conclude that the emergence of preschool children's everyday mathematics is influenced by multiple factors, including individual, social, and cultural factors and the interaction between them. Contextual factors may affect the mathematical content of a child's set of play activities and contribute to the goals that the child constructs as she continues to play.

We seek to elaborate on this point through the analysis of videotape of Fernando's free play activity. We are interested in discovering the mathematical content of his play, what contextual factors shape and affect the content, and how his mathematical goals emerge from these interactions. In particular, we are interested in the association between Fernando's social interactions with his peers and his spontaneous mathematics.

The observation begins with Fernando, Ronny, and Gabe sitting in the block area of the classroom, each working on his own Lego structure. Fernando is stacking more Legos on top of the Lego tower he has been constructing. Fernando also has a rectangular piece of wood sitting on the top, balanced on a Lego that extends out from the rest of the structure. Gabe has created an asymmetrical structure with Legos extending off to the sides without any apparent pattern. He is holding a stacked tower of Legos in one hand.

Episode 1, Part 1

Fernando goes over to the Lego bin and picks up two square Legos, one red and one yellow. As he returns to his structure with his Legos, Gabe drops a tower of blocks onto his construction and says, "It broke my structure."

Fernando adds the two Legos to the yellow one already on top of the beam and says, "Look. Look at mine. Look it, Gabe." As Fernando says this, he hits down on one end of the piece of wood and flips the Legos and the piece of wood off the top of his construction, accompanying this action with some kind of noise. The Legos fall to the floor, and he mumbles something to Gabe as he picks them back up.

Gabe says, "Can I do that?"

Fernando replies, "Yeah."

Gabe says, "Let me try my [unintelligible] my structure." Gabe then accidentally knocks over his construction.

Fernando looks at Gabe's fallen structure and shrugs his shoulders and says, "See. Look. Look at mine. My . . . my . . . mine's not breaking. You see mine? Mine's not breaking."

Fernando places the piece of wood back on top of his tower in the same position as before. He says, "Look. Look, Gabe." He again flips the Legos and stick off the tower accompanied by the same sound effect as before. He starts to laugh and point at some Legos on the floor and says, "Oh, your structure. I didn't . . ."

Gabe says, "I broke my structure." They both pick up pieces off the floor.

Analysis 1, Part 1

When the observation begins, Fernando has already built his structure and placed the beam on top. Because this is already in place, we cannot say what his primary motivation is or how he discovered this activity of flipping the Legos off the top of a structure and onto the floor. It is clear, however, that he is very interested in exploring the process of what happens when he flips the Legos off. Gabe, too, seems to be interested in exploring processes. As Fernando experiments with flipping, Gabe seems to be interested in the destruction of his structure as he drops a stack of Legos onto the larger, asymmetrical structure he created before the observation began.

One of the more interesting aspects of their play is the way in which they are playing with the Lego blocks. As a cultural artifact, Legos are intended to be played with as a means to construct and create patterns and specific structures. One can go to a toy store and purchase a Lego kit to make a house, bus, or airplane. In this episode, however, Gabe and Fernando are not interested in constructing or creating something out of the Lego blocks but rather using the structures to explore processes and relationships. Fernando is concerned with the dynamics of what occurs when he flips the beam with the Legos on it, and Gabe is interested in observing the destruction of his structure.

Although we do not know how Fernando became interested in playing with the Legos in this manner, it does seem as if it is still a fairly new activity to him. Throughout this episode, Fernando is interested in exploring the flipping process, and he tries a number of different ways to do it. For the first two observed trials, Fernando places three square Lego blocks, two yellow and one red, on a piece of wood which is balanced on the top of a structure he previously created. Interestingly, each time he flips the beam, he pushes on the end on which the red Lego is placed. This trend does not continue, however, in the other trials.

Episode 1, Part 2

Fernando again places the piece of wood in its same place on top of his structure. Ronny comes over with his tower of Legos and tries to pick up one of the pieces of wood lying on the floor next to Fernando's structure. Fernando looks up and says, "Ronny. Why you make that robot, Ronny?" Ronny mumbles something about his robot as Fernando continues to pick up pieces that he knocked off his tower in his previous trial of flipping the Legos. He asks again, "Why you make that?" not really looking to Ronny as he asks the question.

He accidentally knocks his piece of wood off his structure at the same time that Gabe bumps into his own structure and accidentally knocks it over. Gabe says, "Oh, you . . . who broke my structure?"

Fernando says, "Not me," and shrugs his shoulders. Fernando then places two pieces of wood on each side of the top of his structure, parallel to one another and parallel to the long side of the rectangular Legos that comprise the structure. He says, "Oh, you saw this. Gabe! Gabe! Look. Look." He places one Lego on the end of each lever. "Look, Gabe. Gabe. Look over. Gabe. Gabe. Look at it . . ." He then flips the pieces of wood from the ends with the Legos on them . . .

Gabe says "Wow!" [showing fascination]. He asks Fernando to watch him as he builds onto his structure. Fernando doesn't look over but continues to play with his structure.

Analysis 1, Part 2

After exploring what happens when he flips one piece of wood with three Legos on it, Fernando places two pieces of wood, parallel to one another, on top of the structure. He again wants Gabe to watch what he is about to try, and Gabe seems to be an appreciative audience. It seems that after conducting a couple of trials with the one beam, Fernando now wants to try to see what happens when he flips two beams at once. He seems to be fascinated by this process of flipping the Lego blocks. One might wonder what his impetus was to play with these beams in this manner.

As interested in this as he is, Ronny's robot manages to provide a brief distraction. As Gabe and Fernando talk to each other and play with their structures in different ways, Ronny sits next to the Lego bin and continues to work on stacking Legos and creating his robot. When Ronny brings his robot over to see if it is as tall as the structure that Fernando created prior to the onset of the observation, Fernando seems almost surprised that Ronny is still concerned with construction. It is almost as if he expects Ronny to be playing with the Legos like he and Gabe are rather than continuing to construct something. The distraction, however, is only temporary, as it appears Ronny is only a minor player in this interaction. Fernando returns to flipping the two beams and trying to share the experience with Gabe (see structure in figure 7.1).

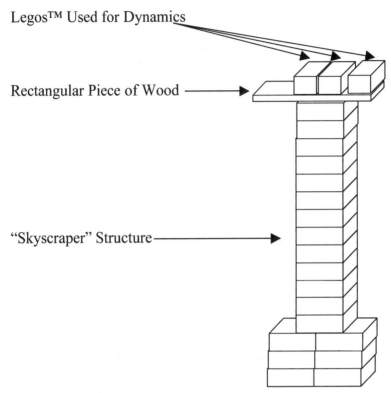

Legos™ Used for Dynamics

Rectangular Piece of Wood ————▶

"Skyscraper" Structure————————————▶

Figure 7.1.   Fernando's structure and the flipping of Legos

Fernando seems very proud of his discovery, as he is continuously asking Gabe to look over and watch him flip the Legos. It is interesting to note that, unlike Ronny who seems content to build and play with the Legos as they seem to be intended to be used, Gabe and Fernando are interested in playing with them an entirely different way.

Episode 1, Part 3

Fernando picks the two pieces of wood back up and returns them to the top of the structure. Then, he takes one of the pieces of wood off and begins to move the other piece of wood around, looking for a different place to rest it upon the structure. He puts it down, begins to pick up the other piece he had previously taken off, but then notices a part of Gabe's structure lying on the floor and decides to pick that up and put it on top of Gabe's structure. He says, "I'm going to put yours over here. It's nice. Look. Look at yours."

Analysis 1, Part 3

After Fernando tries flipping the two beams at once, he begins to place them back where they were but seems to decide against it. It appears that he wants to try another place and position from which to flip the Legos, but after looking at a couple of different ones, it seems he cannot find a good place to explore. He looks down and notices some Lego pieces of Gabe's fallen structure on the floor and decides to stop what he is doing and help Gabe rebuild his structure.

Episode 2

As Fernando is helping Gabe with his structure, Ronny comes over with his structure and again places it next to Fernando's. It seems that Ronny is comparing their heights. Fernando notices this and looks at his structure then over at Gabe's. Fernando picks his up and moves it next to Gabe's and says: "Gabe, why you make that? You know I'm bigger. You know I'm bigger."

Fernando picks up his structure and hands it to Gabe saying: "But Gabe. Hold . . . hold . . . hold my structure." Fernando then begins to add Legos to the bottom of his structure, and says: "Gabe, look it. I did this over there and I put over there and I put over there. That's it." Fernando says this as he continues to add more Legos to the bottom of the structure.

> Gabe: How about another one? That's all it is? It's finished?
> Fernando: No.
> Gabe: You need yellow?
> Fernando: No, I need red.
> Gabe: That's all it is? Is it finished?
> Fernando: Uh-huh.
> Gabe: Yeah?
> Fernando: Yeah.

Fernando then puts his structure down on the floor next to Gabe's to compare the heights and observes that his is still shorter than Gabe's is. Fernando says, "Hey! What are you doing up there?"

Gabe replies, "I'm doing working on my plane." They then ask Ms. Rendon, one of the preschool teachers, to look at each of their structures.

Ms. Rendon says, "Wow! Those are really neat!"

Fernando then turns to Gabe and asks him to hold his structure again. Gabe plays like he is going to crash the structure. Fernando continues to add to the bottom of the structure. Ronny moves in to play, and Gabe says, "No, you're going to break my structure."

Fernando says, "He . . . he . . . he not break it." Fernando takes his structure and moves it back to an upright position so he can again compare the heights of the two structures. As he takes it away from Gabe, Gabe asks: "Now it's finished?"

Fernando does not respond as he moves his structure next to Gabe's. Seeing that his is still not as tall, Fernando says: "Hey! What are you doing up there?"

Gabe says, "Hey, you need some more." He begins to grab Legos to add to Fernando's structure while Fernando holds it.

Fernando says, "More." Fernando directs Gabe to pick up certain Legos off the floor saying, "Take there and there."

Gabe says, "No, this was mine, I had it first."

Fernando says, "Take that one . . . on the floor."

Gabe says, "Here we go and here we go" as he adds blocks to the bottom. Then, he says, "Let's see how it is." Fernando moves it over next to Gabe's, and the two structures are now the exact same height. Gabe says, "Yours is crazy. Yours is crazy. Yours is crazy."

Analysis 2

This episode contains a series of height comparisons as Fernando strives to make his and Gabe's structures the same height. Fernando's interests shift as he is no longer interested in exploring the process of flipping but is now concerned with the magnitude of their structures. Initially, he is helping Gabe in rebuilding his structure, but he is distracted when he sees Ronny come over and put his structure next to Fernando's to compare their heights. Although Ronny is mostly a peripheral player in this observation, he is the impetus for Fernando's change in interest and goals. However, while Ronny is interested in how his structure measures up to Fernando's, Fernando is in turn interested in comparing his to Gabe's structure.

It would seem that the process of comparison is by nature a competitive activity, but that is clearly not the case here. Although it is evident that Fernando is concerned with the differences in the heights of their structures, his goal is not to be "bigger," as it may initially seem, but rather to be the exact same height as Gabe's. Gabe seems to understand this and allows Fernando to enlist him for help. Although Fernando never explicitly states his goal, Gabe seems to understand it. In fact, Gabe seems to share the goal, as he becomes an equal participant in the activity. He not only holds the structure for Fernando for the first two trials, but he eventually takes over and adds them on while Fernando holds the structure and tells him which Legos to add.

Based on his actions and his seeming disbelief when Fernando says the structure is going to be the same height, it appears that Gabe knows it is not going to be. Although Fernando needs to go through a process of trial and error in order to achieve his goal of being the same height, Gabe might be able to tell without direct comparison whether or not enough Legos have been added to make the structures exactly even. Once the structures are the same height and their goal has been achieved, Fernando and Gabe return to working on their own individual structures.

Episode 3

Gabe returns to working on his structure, which is distinctly different from Fernando's. Whereas Fernando has simply stacked the Legos one on top of the other to create a tall tower-like structure, Gabe's is asymmetrical, with blocks extending off to the sides without any apparent pattern. He continues to add to the top of his structure as he sings a little song about being "wacky." Fernando now begins to add Legos to the top of his structure. Suddenly, as Gabe is adding to his structure, his crashes to the floor as if he applied to much pressure while he was putting the Lego on top. He says, "You see? See what happens? See what happens when I do that?"

Fernando says, "Yeah. I'm not . . . I'm not breaking mine."

Gabe returns to rebuilding his and singing his little made-up song and Fernando continues to work with the top of his structure. At one point, Fernando almost tips over his structure, but he manages to catch it before it falls. He begins again to try to add to the top, but this time when it starts to fall he does not catch it as it hits the floor. Only a few pieces break off.

Fernando says, "I can fix mine."

Gabe says, "I can fix mine, too, I think."

Fernando begins to add again to his structure, only adding to the top to re-create the tower-like structure he had before. He provides running commentary as he says, "Put this over here," as he puts another Lego onto his construction. Fernando moves his over next to Gabe's to again compare and says, "Look at mine bigger."

Gabe furrows his brow and says, "Hey! Stop doing yours bigger! Start doing like me do mine smaller." Then, as he goes to pick up another Lego, Gabe accidentally bumps his structure and it falls over again.

Gabe: Hey!

Fernando: I not do nothing.

Gabe: Yes you did. You broke it!

Fernando: Look it. I not do nothing!

Gabe: Yes, you did you broke my structure!

Fernando shows that he did not do anything with Gabe's structure because he was just working with his own and he hardly moved it. Fernando picks up a Lego (as if trying to change the nature of the conversation) and says, "Oh, I have an idea," and tries to help Gabe rebuild his structure. Gabe says no and works on his structure on his own. Moments later, he again breaks his own structure. Fernando shrugs his shoulders and says, "See? I told you."

Analysis 3

As Fernando and Gabe work on their own structures, some interesting shifts occur. Although they both continue to add to their structures, they are no longer comparing heights and they return to having separate goals. They seem to be more interested in constructing and creating their own structures at this point. They work separately on their individual structures and initially remain unflustered as each one in turn knocks his own structure down. A possible reason for the collapses is that instead of adding to the bottom of the structures as they were previously, they have both shifted to adding the Lego bricks to the top of the structures and the added pressure is making them buckle and fall to the floor. However, because they are not competing at this point, neither one of them is irritated when their respective structure breaks.

As Fernando and Gabe continue to work separately and rebuild their structures, a notable change occurs. Initially, it seems that once Fernando's structure was the same height as Gabe's, they are both satisfied and want to return to playing without any apparent goal beyond creating an interesting structure. They both play happily with their own structures, rebuilding them after the collapses that occur. Fernando, however, apparently never loses this interest in height comparisons as suddenly he moves his back over next to Gabe's and says, "Look at mine bigger!" This minor comparison suddenly shifts the nature of their interaction.

Although Fernando is still being pleasant and seems to be more interested in creating a bigger structure rather than competing specifically with Gabe, Gabe does not seem to feel the same way. Instantly, Gabe's mood changes and he becomes upset that Fernando now has the bigger structure. He now begins to blame Fernando when his own structure breaks and begins to become agitated. Fernando, however, is still not feeling directly competitive and tries to show this by offering to help Gabe rebuild his structure. Gabe refuses the offer, as he clearly does not like in any way to feel like the "loser."

Episode 4

Fernando picks up his structure and moves it away from Gabe to be over by Ronny. He says, "Ronny, I'll help you." Fernando begins to give Ronny Legos, picks up Ronny's structure and puts it next to his own, saying, "This is big. Look at mine. It's big. You want mine like yours? Huh, Ronny?"

Ronny says, "Yes."

Fernando begins to add Legos to the bottom of Ronny's tower of blocks saying, "Over here and over there," as he adds blocks. He stands it up next to his, and observing that it's still not as tall, says, "More," and starts adding more blocks to the bottom of Ronny's structure. Fernando says, "Stand up yours, Ronny. I want to see yours." He then mumbles, "I'm bigger. I'm bigger."

They join the two halves of Ronny's structure together and stand them up next to Fernando's. Seeing that Ronny's is now a bit taller than his is, Fernando says, "Oh, you . . . We both end up bigger!"

The teacher walks by, and Fernando says, "Ms. Morris, look at what we made!"

Gabe says, "Look at mine. It's bigger. Bigger than yours."

Ms. Morris says, "That's beautiful," and she walks away.

Fernando's tower falls over, and he says, "Look it. I break mine myself" [not upset].

Analysis 4

Fernando seems to detect Gabe's mood shift, so he decides to move away and instead sit by Ronny. Still interested in the topic of magnitude and creating bigger structures, Fernando offers to help make Ronny's structure as big as his own. Ronny makes a mild protest and does not seem to want help at first, but Fernando takes over anyway and begins to build another high stack of Legos. Fernando is still interested in the process of adding and creating more height. However, unlike Gabe, Fernando is still not competitive at this point. Although he is the one adding to Ronny's structure, he still considers it Ronny's and does not take it over for himself. He also does not get upset when he stands them up and sees that he has actually made Ronny's taller. In fact, Fernando is still proud of both structures and shows them off to the teacher as she walks by.

As he is calling the teacher's attention to his handiwork, however, Gabe also wants to show off how big his structure is. This shifts Fernando's attention away from Ronny and back to Gabe. However, the mood shift that Gabe undergoes still does not seem to affect Fernando. He has a very even temperament, and even though he is clearly concerned with being "more bigger," he does not get upset when his structure falls over yet again and does not seem to have entered the competitive mode that Gabe is in.

Episode 5

Katie comes over the block area and wants to take some "people" toys to play with. Fernando says, "No. This is our people!" Katie points out that they need to share, but Fernando says no and tells her to go over there because these are "our people." He finally picks out a "girl" and gives it to her. Katie then walked away satisfied. While this is going on, Gabe knocks his structure over again but says nothing and does not get upset.

Ronny says, "Hey, this is not bigger."

Fernando replies, "Yes, it is!" They all resume working on their own structures, and Fernando says, "Let's do it more bigger," as he adds to his structure.

Gabe says, "Huh?"

Fernando repeats, "Let's do it more bigger," and moves his structure over next to Gabe's.

Gabe replies, "This is going to be very bigger than yours."

Fernando goes to the block bin to retrieve more blocks and says, "Mine bigger," as he adds some more to the top of his structure. Gabe continues to add to his, but again he accidentally knocks his structure over as he tries to add a section to the top of his original structure [he does not get upset]. Fernando says, "You see? I told you . . . I did nothing."

Gabe says, "I will make it bigger than yours. Mine's going to be bigger than yours," and repeats this one more time as he adds to his structure.

Fernando replies, "Want to see mine? It's bigger." They continue adding to the tops of their respective structures. Fernando picks up a block.

Gabe: Hey, I had that first!
Fernando: No, Ronny had it first.
Gabe: Ronny had it first?
Fernando: Yes.
Gabe: Why you took it away from him?

Fernando and Gabe go over to the bin to get more Legos. Ronny, who has been sitting next to the block bin for this whole segment, moves slightly across the floor toward Fernando's structure, which is standing about six inches away. Fernando steps over and says, "No, no, Ronny. We're making robots." Ronny mumbles something about his; Fernando takes Ronny's and says, "Look, Ronny. Put yours next to mine," as he actually adds it to the top of his own. By this point, he has to stand up so he can work on it.

Ronny says no in mild protest and then says, "I want to make mine more bigger."

Fernando says, "Look, Ronny. It's more bigger."

Ronny puts his hands on the tower as if he were going to take his part back so he could have his own, but Fernando stops him from doing this. He says, "No, no, Ronny! Look it. We are bigger." Ronny continues to make an inaudible protest as Fernando still adds more to the top. Fernando repeats, "Look. We are bigger!"

Ronny is holding a Lego, and it is unclear what he wants to do. Fernando takes the Lego out of Ronny's hand and begins to add it to the structure himself, but accidentally breaks off a piece of the tower. Fernando says, "Uh, oh" Ronny attempts to gather the Legos up off the floor as Fernando plays around with the tower. Fernando takes part of the top off and asks Ronny to hold his structure. Ronny does not respond, so Fernando says, "That's okay," and adds some more to the top.

Analysis 5

Despite the distraction provided by Katie's quest for a "people" toy to play with, Fernando remains undeterred in his goal to create something that is "more bigger." The boys all continue to work on their own structures, but it seems that Fernando is not one to enjoy playing alone, so he tries to enlist Gabe and create a mutual goal. Gabe, however, apparently still feeling competitive when he first notices Fernando's taller structure, is steadfast in making a "bigger" structure. Gabe clearly prefers that they work on their own structures, and he is focused on having a bigger structure than Fernando's.

It is at this point that Fernando begins to become competitive with Gabe. No longer interested in everyone having something bigger, Fernando is heading into direct competition with Gabe. To that end, when Ronny comes over with his structure to compare, Fernando takes it away and puts it on top of his own, not allowing Ronny to take it back. At this point, both Fernando and Gabe have to stand to work on their structures, yet they both continue undeterred as they work to be the tallest. Ronny again retreats to become a secondary figure in the interaction as he begins to quietly work on the floor to create a new structure of his own.

Episode 6

Fernando moves over to the block bin and says something to Gabe about his structure. They each walk back over to their own respective structures as Ronny continues to play by himself on the floor with his own Legos. Gabe has put together a separate tall piece that he now adds to the top of his tower, already about two and a half feet tall. Fernando looks over at Gabe's and says, "Why you make that more bigger? Yours is funny."

Gabe stands back to look at his and then at Fernando's and says with satisfaction, "Ha, ha. Yours so small."

Fernando replies, "I don't care," as he adds more to the top. They both walk over to the block bin to get more pieces, and suddenly Fernando says, "Hey. I had that blue!" Gabe adds the blue Lego to the top of his structure, and Fernando says, "I'm telling." He walks over to the table where the teacher, Ms. Mann, is sitting with the aide. Fernando tells the teacher how he had the blue one and Gabe took it. Gabe complains that Fernando does not share, but the teacher says if Fernando had it first, then that is all right. They go back over to the block area.

Analysis 6

At this point, both boys are engaged in competitive play. At the same time, they both seem to be querulous as they strive to exceed the other's height. Their quest to create tall structures is not something that either one of them wants to share with the other, as they each strive to have the "biggest" structure. This is an interesting part of the observation because it is the only time that Fernando seems to be as competitive as Gabe is. They take turns making disparaging remarks about the other's structure and then bicker about who can have the blue Lego. This is clear evidence that it is no longer fun and games and each boy's goal has shifted. Whereas previously their goal was to create a tall structure, the goal now is determining who can create the *taller* of the two structures. Before, their interest seemed to lie in the creative pursuit of making something higher and in the exploration of the process of construction, but that is now a secondary characteristic as they compete to have the taller and better structure.

Episode 7

Gabe goes to the block bin to get more Legos, and Fernando stands and looks at their structures. Fernando says, "Gabe, look. This was yours. This was mine," as he points to the top of each of their constructions.

Gabe says, "Mine's a very big. Mine's bigger." He adds more Legos to the top, standing on his toes to do this.

Fernando says, "Watch out. Yours fall." Fernando begins to play with his structure, picking up a toy person and moving it to the top of his construction as he says, "A man. A man."

Gabe is still adding to the top of his structure, and Fernando goes over to the block bin and grabs a handful of blocks from it. When Gabe asks him why he took all those pieces, Fernando replies that it is "so I can make it more bigger." He begins to add more to the top.

At this moment, Gabe's structure buckles and falls down to the floor in several pieces. He and Fernando both look over to Ms. Mann (the teacher), and she says, "It just happened. No, he didn't make it fall down, it just happened. It was very tall."

Fernando begins to add more, and then his falls. Gabe says, "Ha, ha. Yours fall, too!" They are both now on the floor as they start to rebuild. They hurry to put them together.

Gabe: Mine's getting bigger.
Fernando: Mine is getting bigger, too.
Gabe: Mine is getting very big. Mine's getting very big.
Fernando: Is yours funny?
Gabe: No. [Gabe's new structure is now very tall and he has to stand to work

on it. He looks at Fernando's.] Ha, ha, ha, ha, ha. Yours is too small. Mine
is too big. Ha, ha, ha, ha, ha.
Fernando: Up and up . . .
Gabe: You're going to knock it down. Ha, ha, ha, ha, ha.

Then, as Gabe goes to add a Lego to the bottom of his structure, he
knocks his own structure down. Fernando says, "You see?" This time, Gabe
does not get irritated but simply begins to rebuild his structure again. Gabe
adds large sections at a time while Fernando adds to his structure one piece
at a time. Even though his just fell, Gabe's is already bigger again. Fernando
says, "I'm going to make mine over there," but does not really move. He
says, "You want to see something?"

Gabe says, "Look at mine." Gabe is difficult to hear at this point, but he
does say again, "Ha, ha, ha, ha, ha. Mine's more bigger." He is still adding
sections at a time while Fernando continues to add to his structure one
piece at a time.

Ronny comes over and places his next to Fernando's. Gabe says about a
piece, "I had that first," so Fernando puts it back down and goes over to the
block bin to get another piece. Gabe adds more to the top of his, standing
on his toes to do so, and Fernando is walking around colleting more pieces.
This is how the segment ends.

Analysis 7

It seems at this point that the rivalry has subsided a bit, though not completely. Although the boys are still interested in creating taller and bigger
structures, it seems as if Fernando's desire to beat Gabe has waned. The
same cannot be said for Gabe, who continues to try to disparage Fernando's
structure. It is notable, however, that he does not get upset when his structure falls, so perhaps they are not really competing anymore but rather the
competition has become a part of their play. Fernando's goal no longer
seems to be to beat Gabe; he does not fight him for the Lego but seems
content to return to engage in his own parallel activity, ignoring Gabe. He
even threatens to move his structure away so he does not have to listen to
Gabe boast about his structure.

Another clue that suggests Fernando is no longer competing is that he
has returned to putting the Lego bricks together one at a time rather than
stacks at a time as Gabe is doing. This makes it appear that Fernando is no
longer racing to construct his first but is interested again in the process of
creating something tall—the means to an end—rather than simply being
the taller of the two structures.

Discussion I

Social Interaction as a Determinant of Mathematical Activity

The popular public generally does not perceive young children as having very long attention spans. This very idea makes this observation and those of the previous chapter particularly striking. For over eighteen minutes, Fernando, Gabe, and Ronny play with Legos, and at the end of the observation, they show no signs of quitting. Add to this the fact that we have no idea how long they were playing with the Legos before the videotaping began, and the children's play and persistence are really quite remarkable.

It is not merely their persistence, however, that is so important but rather the underlying factors that motivate them to be so focused in their play. Fernando and Gabe seem keenly attentive in exploring and asking new mathematical questions as they play with the Legos. At the beginning of the observation, they have each discovered new ways to play with the Legos, although we do not know what kind of prior knowledge or activities led them to play with the Legos in this manner. Nevertheless, the content of their play is still an important factor as they explore the Legos in a way surely not intended by the manufacturer.

Fernando's play is particularly the focus of this observation. Although we cannot say for certain what prior experiences led Fernando to play with the Legos in this way, it still seems that this is a new experience for him. Fernando conducts several different trials exploring the dynamics of what happens when he flips the beam and Legos over. Fernando's interest seems to span several factors. The fact that he frequently wants to show off his discovery to Gabe, making Gabe watch what Fernando can do, leads one to infer that part of Fernando's fascination has to do with his mastery of this newly acquired skill. He seems to relish his ability and control at flipping the Legos. Beyond this, Fernando is interested in the process and results of flipping, as evidenced by the variations on the behavior that he performs.

Fernando, however, seems to run out of motivation to play with the Legos like this, so he turns to play with Gabe and help him with his structure. As he begins to do this, however, he notices Ronny come over for a second time to compare his structure to Fernando's. This is the most important role Ronny plays throughout the entire observation: he is the driving force behind the shift in Fernando's, and ultimately Gabe's, interests. Although Fernando is not keenly attentive to Ronny's structure, he is suddenly concerned that Ronny's structure is almost as tall as his own. He does not, however, seem to be concerned with this but immediately picks his structure up to see how it compares with Gabe's structure. For the next sixteen minutes of the observation, Gabe and Fernando will focus on a series of magnitude comparisons as they become motivated to have the tallest structure.

Fernando places his structure next to Gabe's and says, "Gabe, why you make that? You know I'm bigger." He then asks Gabe to hold his structure while he begins to add Legos to the bottom. Gabe willingly complies with this and seems interested in what Fernando is doing. Most fascinating, however, is that without asking, Gabe understands that Fernando is not actually trying to be bigger; rather, he is simply trying to become the same size. Thus, as Fernando keeps putting his structure next to Gabe's and saying "What are you doing up there?" Gabe begins to infer what Fernando's goal is in this episode. In fact, Gabe begins to share the goal of equality and even takes over to become the one who actually makes the structures the same height.

Once this goal is achieved, Fernando and Gabe return to their own play. As they work independently on their own structures, Fernando continues to add Legos to his and it appears that his objective is still to create something taller. During this episode, Gabe's structure breaks twice as he plays with it and Fernando's structure breaks once. After rebuilding, Fernando places his next to Gabe's to compare heights again and comments that now his is bigger. This does not make Gabe happy; it actually serves to shift the nature of their interaction for the rest of the observation. Throughout the remaining minutes, Gabe works diligently to make his structure bigger than Fernando's structure.

This shift in interaction is significant for two reasons. First, earlier in the observation, it seems that the social interaction between Fernando, Gabe, and Ronny is the impetus for the shift in attention to height. Fernando is happily assisting Gabe with his structure when he notices Ronny comparing the height of his own structure to that of Fernando's structure. At this moment, Fernando shifts his attention, picks up his structure, and is suddenly concerned with the fact that his structure is shorter than Gabe's is. Fernando and Gabe, then, work together in order to make Fernando's structure taller than Gabe's. Here, the shift in mathematical goals is created by the social environment.

However, as the episode progresses, this somehow changes. In fact, the persistent interest in size and comparing heights creates a major turn in the social interaction. Up to a point, Gabe and Fernando play peacefully and even cooperatively for some time, but as soon as Fernando's structure becomes taller than Gabe's structure, their play gradually becomes more competitive as Gabe clearly does not like to have the smaller structure. The mathematical content and concern with height comparisons actually becomes the driving force of the interaction. Thus, a switch occurs in the direction of influence between mathematics and social interaction.

Secondly, for the duration of the observation, Fernando and Gabe are fixated on creating the tallest structure. Fernando becomes engrossed in this and even goes so far as to take Ronny's structure and put it on top of his own, just so his structure can be bigger than Gabe's. In terms of language and affect, Gabe seems more competitive than Fernando, but this might not be entirely the case. Even though Fernando remains even-tempered and does not go so far as to laugh at Gabe's structure (as Gabe laughs at Fernando's), Fernando's persistence with trying to build a tall structure adds to the querulous relationship between the two boys, causing Gabe's competitive attitude to persist.

Fernando's social environment can be considered a driving force behind the emergence of his mathematical goals. Although Ronny is primarily a peripheral player in this videotaped case study, he is actually the inspiration for Fernando's interest in magnitude comparisons and emerging desire to create the tallest structure. Initially, Fernando and Gabe work together to create an equal starting point, and their play is friendly and cooperative. Apparently, however, this is only because Gabe still perceives that he has the taller structure. His dramatic mood change once Fernando creates a taller tower fuels the rest of the observation. It is possible that Fernando would have moved on to another way to play with the Legos (although this is purely speculative), but Gabe becomes fixated on comparing their structures, which motivates Fernando's interest in magnitude comparisons. More research needs to be conducted in order to gain further insight into the complex relationship between social interaction and preschoolers' spontaneous mathematical activities.

Fernando and Gabe's Spatial and Scientific Thinking

Based on our observations, there seems to be clear evidence that social interaction is at least one determinant of the type of mathematical activity that occurs. In Fernando and Gabe's case, the mathematical activities seemed to focus primarily on magnitude comparisons and, to a lesser extent, on dynamics, particularly when Fernando was flipping Lego pieces off his vertical structure. But so far, little has been said about the means to these ends—in order to flip Legos or compare the heights of towers, one must use spatial relations and scientific reasoning to construct the tower in the first place. How do Fernando, Gabe, and Ronny do this?

Based on our observations, Fernando and Gabe construct skyscrapers in two different ways. As discussed in chapter 3, Fernando is quite adept in constructing skyscrapers for longevity whereas Gabe is not. We see this in the bases or foundations and even the upper "levels" of both Fernando's and Gabe's structures. Additionally, we know that throughout history, professional architects have centered on three criteria while engaged in devising any type of construction: strength, usefulness, and aesthetic quality. In Fernando's structure, strength played a greater role than aesthetic quality and usefulness, evident in Fernando's method for building his foundation (see figure 7.2).

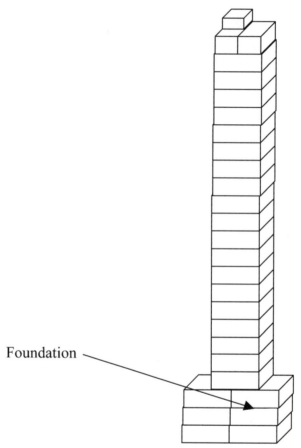

Figure 7.2.   Fernando's skyscraper structure

In Gabe's case, however, it seemed as if aesthetic quality was of primary concern, while strength played a subordinate role and usefulness perhaps had no role at all. In fact, Gabe's overwhelming concern for aesthetics at the expense of strength more than likely contributed to the several collapses of his numerous structures. Gabe's skyscraper structure was asymmetric, due to the numerous cantilevers he had mounted onto the general structure (see figure 7.3).

CASE 4: SPATIAL-ARCHITECTURAL ACTIVITY AS A DYNAMIC ENTERPRISE—THE CASE OF CECIL

This case investigates young children's spontaneous mathematics during free play in the preschool classroom based on Cecil, a boy from a low-

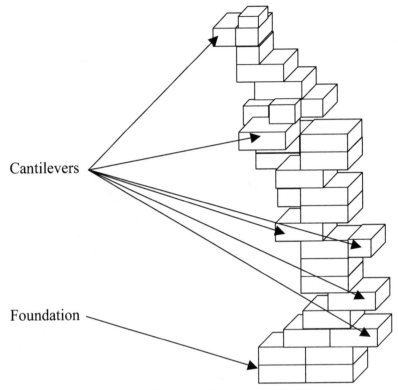

Figure 7.3.   Gabe's asymmetric skyscraper structure prior to collapse

income family who was four-and-a-half years old. Although his activity takes place during an open, free-play period in his classroom, Cecil is invested in his work and takes it quite seriously. He uses Legos and a plastic wheel hub to create various colors, and it is obvious that this is not the first time he has used these manipulatives. Cecil attaches individual Lego pieces to each other and to the hub. He then spins the hub on the table and thus blurs the separate colors into a new mixed color. He essentially creates a wheel of color. He not only forms new colors, much to the amazement of his viewers, but predicts which colors he can make.

As in the previous case studies, the videotaped segment of this study does not show how Cecil's activity first developed, but it seems that the children came upon it on their own. The teachers in the classroom did not introduce this as an activity and, as mentioned above, Cecil's tape was taken during free play when he can choose what he will play, where he will play, and with whom he will spend his play time. On a social level, the tape is interesting because Cecil often is quite aloof toward the children who come to watch him. It is as if he is a magician who knows he does not have to reveal his secrets to an audience of his peers, even though they have the opportunity to observe his prestidigitation over his color wheel. He briefly helps his classmate, Harry, who asks questions about certain color combinations, but Cecil is just as happy to mix his own colors and spends most of the segment in solitary play.

This color experimentation has actually become a class-wide activity. Some students have taken off with it more than others. Cecil seems to have spent a lot of time learning about the dynamics of the spinning wheel through his constructive play. He has also explored which patterns of Legos will create certain new colors as the wheel spins across the table. As Saxe (1991) points out, children's goals in play are never fixed constructions. Rather, they change and evolve in the process of the play itself. Thus, individuals shape their own play and learn through this play, which in turn leads to new discoveries and new goals.

Cecil has discovered his interest in the dynamics of the color wheel by playing with it over time. In this particular segment, it seems his goal is to create new colors and to predict certain color combinations he already knows while exploring new combinations of Legos around the wheel hub. He may also maintain a social goal of remaining the "expert" on this activity. It is clear that Harry in particular is impressed with Cecil's knowledge of this project. At an age when children are beginning to be fairly concerned with others and aware of their role in relationship to others, this feeling of power could also be a motivating factor in Harry's work. Thus, it is important to consider the context in which an individual, in this case a preschool-age child, shapes and reshapes his own activity.

The context here refers to Cecil's immediate surroundings and those stimuli to which he is exposed. For instance, he can choose which objects to incorporate into his play. He, however, only has one wheel hub and the Legos available in the room. He has chosen to play alone, as opposed to taking part in parallel or associative play with peers. His context changes when Harry arrives, asks many questions, and offers suggestions about which Legos Cecil could choose in creating new colors. The context here becomes more interactive and the goal in his play is slightly different. He now is exploring color for himself, but he is also explaining his own method to Harry. This is interesting from an observer's point of view because at first one could only interpret his goals and use of mathematics through actions, and now there is more speech.

Just as Cecil's context has influenced his play and the forming of goals, his activity has influenced the context in which he plays. Saxe's (1991) emergent model of goal formation offers four parameters which both limit and advance the goals an individual constructs in practice. These parameters are as follows: 1) The structure of the activity that consists of the general tasks that must be accomplished in the practice-linked motives; 2) The social interactions between participants in this practice; 3) Cultural forms that have emerged over the course of social history; and 4) The prior understanding that individuals bring to bear on cultural practices will influence the goals that individuals address. The goals that individuals bring to their practices (which in turn stimulate further goals) are interwoven with these four parameters. Saxe's model of emergent goals can be used to explore children's play and may shed light on certain mathematical concepts that are seen as the children work with various media.

As far as the structure of Cecil's environment is concerned, he is participating in free play. His activity requires that he have a hard, flat space for the wheel to spin fast enough and for a long enough time to view new colors, which is his goal, so the manipulative table is more conducive than the rug. The structure of his environment works with his goal of producing these colors with the wheel. Cecil is extremely aware that he also needs the wheel hub itself. When Cecil stops what he is doing to answer the teacher's questions or to accompany Harry on his search for another wheel, he takes the wheel he was using with him, holding it close to his chest as if he is protecting a prized possession. He is aware that losing these pieces would mean he could no longer support his goal in play. His context would not remain conducive to creating color the way he wants.

Episode 1

Harry: [walks up to Cecil's table] Hey, how did you find that spinning thing?
Cecil: [continues to add certain Legos to the Lego wheel] Oh, it was in the doll
    area. There was only one there.
Harry: Only one left?
Cecil: Yup, only one there.

Cecil continues to play with the Legos. Harry asks, "Which area, which area?" Cecil points to the kitchen area. Harry walks over to look for a wheel but does not find one. He then sits down to watch Cecil make colors with his wheel constructed of a hub and surrounding Legos.

Analysis 1

Cecil seems to be actively trying to monopolize the Lego wheel play in this segment. Although it cannot be proven by observing the tape, he sends Harry on a brief futile in-class journey. The whole time Harry looks for the wheel, Cecil continues to work on creating color with his wheel. Sometimes he is not even looking at what he is doing as he attaches the Legos, but he seems to intuitively identify that balance is a necessary factor in the successful spin of the Lego wheel. He looks down only to choose the right colors for his plan (see figure 7.4) and continues his conversation with Harry who is across the room.

Episode 2

Cecil spins the wheel as Harry watches. Cecil is specific in terms of which colors he selects, as he has been throughout the segment. He also shows that he is aware of the certain patterns of Legos that produce new colors. After his statement, "I wonder what green and blue makes," Cecil adds the green and blue Legos to the hub. In the process of doing this, he takes the time to answer Harry's question about what red and yellow make. After he quickly answers "Orange," Cecil spins his wheel, points to the Lego wheel as it spins and enthusiastically says, "Jungle green, green, green, green." When the wheel stops spinning, Cecil turns to Harry, points to the wheel and says, "And look, it's the sixth one."

Analysis 2

Cecil and Harry's interaction and the classroom context (where children must share objects such as Lego wheels) adds a profound social dynamic to free play and to goal formation. In order for Cecil to maintain the context in which he formed his first goal, he must hold on to the wheel hub. Cecil must also decide whether or not to include Harry in his goal. He seems to first include him to boost his own feeling of control as "possessor of the wheel" and therefore of the power of color creation. But, as time passes, he seems to at least show concern for what questions Harry has about color combinations and how to achieve them with the Lego wheel.

At a certain point, Cecil seems to lose some interest in being the one and only color wheel expert and begins to help Harry. Although his tone of voice is still brusque and slightly condescending, he does explain what he is doing as he works and, in fact, eventually turns the wheel hub over to Harry. Perhaps Cecil has acknowledged Harry's persistence. Or perhaps he simply decided it was time to move on.

Cecil must be remembering the order of the Legos from when he had put them on the wheel originally or had them lined up before placing them on the hub. He could not refer to one Lego as the sixth one on a wheel because there is no apparent first Lego as they follow one another in a circle around the hub. There is evidence of a well-developed sense of the ordering or patterning of colors. Cecil is using a mathematical concept of order as part of his play to fulfill his goal. He is not simply guessing. Cecil's next goal in the subsequent episode is to explain his precise method to Harry and perhaps to emphasize his own method for himself. If he was simply trying to create random colors, he would certainly not be concerned with or even notice the position of one Lego in a series.

Lego™ Hub with No Legos™

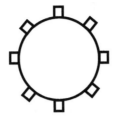

Lego™ Hub with Four Equally Spaced Legos™

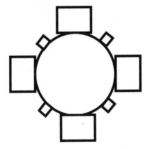

Lego™ Hub with All Legos™ Attached

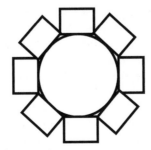

Figure 7.4. Cecil's Lego wheel orientations

As for his disposition, Cecil exhibits confidence. Whether or not Harry even cares about the sixth spot on the wheel, Cecil has verbalized a point regarding his goal and his method of achieving it. A teacher in Harry's place would perhaps have been able to probe further into why this piece was the sixth and why this held such relevance in Cecil's mind. Cecil shows a deep understanding of number as he is in the process of answering Harry's questions about certain colors on the wheel.

Episode 3

Cecil and Harry are still at the table and Cecil is spinning the wheel as Harry asks questions about certain color combinations.

Harry: What's blue and green?
Cecil: [tersely] Jungle green.
Harry: What is yellow and blue?
Cecil: White. [Cecil has shown that he knows that it is green and is perhaps teasing Harry here after having already answered many of his questions.]
Harry: So what's two blues, three reds, and three blues?
Cecil: [immediately] That can't be that much. Only, I'll put three blues and three reds. That makes purple I think.

He starts to put together his necessary colors—the blue and red Legos.

Analysis 3

Here we see yet another example of mathematics directly related to Cecil's goal. He wants to make purple when he spins the wheel, but he has found through his experience with this activity that only seven Legos will fit around the wheel. When Harry suggests a combination of Legos that exceeds this number, Cecil immediately knows that he needs to change the number. While maintaining the colors, he says, "three and three" meaning six pieces in all. He is showing that he knows that the numbers "two," "three," and "three" together will be longer than the distance around the wheel. Even if he is not adding these numbers to a total of eight, he shows that he has learned that certain combinations of numbers will fit around and others will not. He knows that three and three is not too long.

As Cecil takes three reds and three blues and puts them together in a line, he realizes that six Legos is not a perfect number for the wheel either. He says, "I might need one more," before he has actually put the line of Legos around the hub. He is estimating the distance in relation to the number of Legos. He takes one more and adds it to the rest and says, "It makes purple. You need four blues and three yellows, I mean reds, and it makes purple."

After spinning the wheel once, he quickly seizes it and says, "Oh, I messed up. I did it wrong." Cecil's goal was not met because the colors, separated in an order of all three reds then all four blues, did not blend to his satisfaction. He demonstrates his knowledge of the relationship between the mathematical concept of pattern or ordering and the color he can achieve on his wheel. Also, in order to maintain his goal, he must adjust his method. He automatically knows what to do to achieve this desired purple color. Cecil removes the Legos, reorders them in an AB pattern, and then spins them again. He has thus achieved his goal. He actually reorders and tests the patterns of the reds and blues at least two more times while still talking to Harry and to another child, Sidney, who comes to the table.

When Cecil decides to give up his wheel, he makes a point of giving it to Harry. When he is handing the wheel over to Harry, Cecil still turns it back and forth looking at the purple he was able to put together. He says, "Use green and red and you'll get brown," as he gives the color wheel construction to Harry and walks away from the table. It seems like he is passing on his knowledge of color and the dynamics of the wheel like an expert would impart to an apprentice. His genuine enthusiasm for the activity is seen in this action more accurately, perhaps, than in his off-hand way of speaking to Harry when he is actually involved in working with the Lego wheel.

Discussion II

There are a number of different goals that have evolved in Cecil's play. These goals incorporate methods, which often involve spontaneous mathematics. As his situation changes, he has certain social goals that become intertwined with the original motive for the activity—the ability to produce different colors by combining them through the dynamic change made possible by the wheel's movement. As Saxe (1991) makes quite clear, the goals change the contextual factors as the contextual factors must in turn affect the goal and the motives that lead to it. Cecil has shown that genuine interest based on personal initiative can foster an incredibly strong desire to proceed with an activity, explore different perspectives, and eventually meet a goal. Although this activity was not teacher directed, having no specific guidelines other than those that Cecil creates himself, there is evidence of informal mathematics. This segment clearly illustrates that free play should never be construed as free from learning.

This case is the only one of the four case studies that does not show explicit spatial or geometric thinking. There are at least two possibilities for this. First, Cecil and Harry do not use blocks, nor do they use the rectangular-shaped Legos exclusively. Although they do use Legos, the children also use a plastic circular hub, a Lego product rarely used during children's elaborate constructions. Second, we have found that spatial, geometric, and architectural thinking of young children is most evident during the period in which they are engaged in construction. When we think of means versus ends, the means almost always exhibit evidence of cognitive processes, while the ends rarely do. In fact, there is good potential for one to observe spatial, geometric, or any intellectual propensity during the time in which the child is engaged in a particular Lego or block project (the means). In contrast, the ends to a particular Lego or block project is rarely, if at all, demonstrative of a child's spatial and geometric development. We posit, then, that the shorter the duration of the means to a particular Lego or block activity, the less one will observe or tap with regard to cognitive or intellectual activity. Based on our observations of Cecil and Harry's videotaped excerpt, we conclude that the means to the particular end in this situation is relatively short in duration; the constructive process only involves the attachment of four, five, six, seven, or eight Legos to a plastic circular hub. The ends (time spent watching the final product) are relatively long and represent the children's interest in dynamic processes—not spatial, geometric, or architectural ones.

Despite the lack of explicit spatial, geometric, or architectural activity, it would also be inaccurate to portray this videotaped excerpt as having no evidence of spatial and geometric concepts. Take into account the intuitive notion that to generate the "perfect" spin of the spinning color wheel, one must balance the wheel with Legos in such a way that makes it rotationally symmetric. Cecil, in each of the three episodes of this study, develops a geometric product that works for the two children to look at and thus become mentally stimulated by what the product—the Lego wheel—can do. In fact, his Lego production reveals his spatial and geometric propensities very clearly and transparently. To begin with, he never constructs his wheel in a way that Lego pieces of different colors are solely on one side of the hub. Indeed, this would not make the resulting Lego "wheel" spin at all. Further, the Legos that are attached are almost always snug, or equally spaced so that there is little to no space between each Lego piece. So, we argue that Cecil seems to know about the importance of balance at least on an intuitive level, which can only be achieved through a rotationally symmetric construction.

On a not so explicit level, spatial relations are evident in the two boys' verbal exchange when Harry asks Cecil where a Lego hub can be found. Again, one's observation of children's use of mathematical language is extremely important. We also cannot underestimate the environment which will be conducive to Cecil's Lego wheel. He clearly has identified the significance of adequate flat space so that the Lego wheel will be free from obstructions.

CHAPTER TOPICS FOR DISCUSSION

1. Based on your readings of the two case studies discussed and analyzed in this chapter, compare and contrast the spatial, geometric, and

architectural activities of Fernando with those of Cecil. Determine whether other factors—like similarities or differences in terms of social interaction, location or environment, play activity, or type of object—affect each child's engagement in mathematical activity.

2. Observe young children, preferably between the ages of three and six years, during free play. The setting should preferably be within the preschool, although observation of young children's free play outdoors will suffice. Then, select one of the case study children in this chapter, and compare that child with your observational analysis of the child (or children) you have observed in terms of each child's spatial and architectural propensities.

3. Does the process of building a Lego skyscraper or building a Lego wheel have anything to do with the purpose of each child's construction? Explain.

8

Beyond the Blocks: Implementing Praxis

[T]here are individual differences in elementary and secondary students' school performance that probably derive from a complex of ability and motivational, social, cultural, sociopolitical, and other factors and that these have important educational implications.

James H. Borland (2005, 1)

We hope readers will recognize the value of informal play and how it relates to cognitive development and future successes in formal schooling. In this chapter, we identify the relationship between free play activities and the development of mathematical and scientific concepts. Goldhaber's article (1994) "If We Call It Science, Then Can We Let Them Play?" demonstrates the debate between developmentally appropriate early childhood education and the pressure felt by many teachers from parents to meet competitive academic goals. The case study analyses in chapters 6 and 7 highlight the importance of recognizing young children's mathematical and scientific behaviors. The uninitiated person may assume that there was little value in Nat's (case 1), Kathryn's (case 2), Fernando's (case 3), and Cecil's (case 4) activities. However, we provide evidence of advanced conceptual understanding that occurred during the children's free play activities. So, for the children, play served as the vehicle in which they can experiment, demonstrate, and test the boundaries of their understanding.

PLAY AS THE WORK OF CHILDREN

In the previous chapters of this text, our primary concern was to examine the spatial and geometric propensities of young children through the lens

207

of everyday free play. Yet the act of play itself may have been taken for granted by the reader. We now consider the realm of play because it is essentially the primary vehicle by which young children exhibit their cognitive and intellectual levels of understanding. Teachers and parents, therefore, must consider the act of play as a primary period of activity for the child and not a mere afterthought or intervals of time full of trivialities.

Historically, play, with regard to children, follows two essential strands. In one strand, play revolves around the notion of flippancy or nonsensical behavior. In the other, play is a serious, constructive, thought-provoking, and perhaps most important, contemplative enterprise, filled with aspects of learning, development, and eventual progress (Sutton-Smith 1997, 1999). Anecdotal evidence of play exists as early as the ancient Greek and Hellenic periods. The subject of play, in fact, assumed an important role in the writings of Aristotle, particularly in his treatise on *Eudamian Ethics*. His concept of "Eudaimonia" refers to the notion of someone excelling and flourishing in a particular area of interest—it leads to contentment, happiness, and fulfillment in engaging in an activity for the sake of the activity itself. Friedrich Schiller, the author of "An die Freude," which Beethoven incorporated as the text of the fourth movement of his ninth symphony, wrote a fascinating collection of essays under the title *Letters on the Aesthetic Education of Man* (1795). In this essay, Schiller writes that the genuineness of an individual is seen most clearly when at play. Schiller's perspective on the authenticity of play is that its roots are in freedom and in the action of play for its own sake. Like Schiller's discussion on play, the children in our case studies are thoroughly and seemingly happily engaged in their free play activities.

Although it may seem to be an enjoyable or satisfying state, play is by no means an effortless venture. People consume far more energy when at play than when at work; as adults, we take play extremely seriously. Find an individual who has a passion for something, who sculpts, paints, plays a musical instrument, writes poetry or prose, goes hiking, or plays chess. There are some people who would take early retirements, quit their jobs, or even lose their jobs over these activities and pursuits. And here lies the irony of play: As adults, we use play to escape the workaday routines of life and gain the experience of freedom. For many adults, play represents the sine qua non of a successful lifestyle. But at the same time, we (adults) attempt to structure or restrict children's free play. Some adults don't even think of children's play as a beneficial component of everyday life for the child. That is, they have negative perceptions of children engaging in play altogether (e.g., play as a trivial endeavor).

So, what are the characteristics of play? They consist of something we do when we are free of responsibilities (at least for a period of time). Freedom allows play, and play allows us to discover our authentic selves. To use Aristotelian terminology, the act of free play represents the children's version of a Eudaimonic lifestyle; free play is the renaissance of their overall social development. It provides them with a stage to express their developing social orientations of moral development, social connectivity and affiliations, cognitive development, and nurturing behaviors. Mead (1934) and Piaget (1965) argue that play provides the foundation of social development during the early school years. Roeper describes the importance of play for the development of science-related skills of the young child. She states

> Play and exploration remain the best learning tools for the young child. Children develop a sense of inner freedom and permission to reach out if they (and their goals and idiosyncratic ways of learning) are supported by the adults at the school. This security and freedom requires a flexible atmosphere with much opportunity for discovery, individualized and group learning, play, and stimulating enthusiastic adults who are learners themselves. (1988, 133)

Through play, the child can interact with his or her environment and increase cognitive and social awareness. Roeper suggests "through playful interaction children develop many concepts of science" (1988, 123). Piaget believes that play serves an important cognitive function. It supplies the child with numerous opportunities and materials to explore his or her environment, allowing greater opportunities to assimilate and accommodate new information.

We know play is essential for cognitive development, and there exists a plethora of research and theoretical perspective to support this (Copple, Cocking, and Matthews 1984; Jackowitz and Watson 1980; Sutton-Smith 1997, 1999; Vygotsky 1978). We also are aware that a number of studies show that the resources (e.g., blocks, Legos, continuous play materials), in addition to play, not only engage children for many minutes at a time, but also contribute to intellectual development.

Wolfgang and Stakenas (1985) examine the toys children use during free play. They suggest that the nature of the toy contributes to the child's cognitive development, dividing the toys into categories based on their physical properties. The first category, which we call "continuous play materials," refers to toys containing continuous objects like paints, clay (play dough), and sand. These objects contribute to perceptual performance (e.g., puzzle formation, right-left orientation, and drawing). The second category, which we refer to as "countable play objects," are blocks, Legos, puzzles, and dominoes. These objects have been shown to contribute to memory development and verbal, perceptual, and quantitative skills. The third category, "microsymbolic toys," consists of dolls, miniature trucks and cars, small buildings, and people and are said to enhance memory. The fourth category, "macrosymbolic toys," includes "child-size play equipment" or any props for dramatic play, such as dress, hats, shoes, costumes, and toy houses; they are said to influence memory, quantitative skills, and perceptual performance. The combination of these skills can lead us to a definite conclusion that play has a purpose in the realm of cognitive development. Vygotsky suggests that "as play develops, we see a movement toward the conscious realization of its purpose" (1978, 103). For all play, there is a series of rules that delimits the play activity (e.g., game, block construction) and justifies how it will be conducted. "In play," Vygotsky says, "a child always behaves beyond his average age, above his daily behavior; in play it is as though he were a head taller than himself" (1978, 102).

We have seen from our research that environments consisting of blocks, Legos, and the like are not only conducive to arithmetic development but also (even more important) to spatial and geometric development. The discussion of play and more specifically game play and its relationship to acquiring new knowledge and complex skills has refocused the nation's attention on the importance of playing to learn. The Federation of American Scientists reports that video games can provide compelling visuals, complex plot structures, opportunities for strategic thinking, and problem solving (Federation 2006). These games and simulations can provide contextual bridging to enhance young children's spatial and geometric thinking by extending block play. The digital environment allows children to further manipulate the block activities in an alternate format. The children easily adapt technical skills to move from the concrete medium of blocks to the more abstract digital computer-based medium. The analogies of the young child as scientist, mathematician, and architect can be expanded by the enhancement of digital skills in training surgeons, automotive mechanics, and engineers. The games' structures are complete with scaffolding to increase the likelihood of the child obtaining specific skill sets. Unfortunately, some individuals who work with young children are not aware of this reality.

Teachers who are concerned with maximizing the potential of children recognize the opportunity that play affords in overall development. It is vital for teachers to tap children's abilities and help them construct understanding from experience. In a number of respects, the public perception of preschool education is babysitting and daycare. Popular belief has supported the notion that young children are not capable of complex thought or action. Therefore, the role of the preschool teacher was one of caretaker instead of an educator who facilitates learning. Works such as *The Scientist in the Crib* (Gopnik, Meltzoff, and Kuhl 1999) highlight the advances in cognitive science and infant and child development. These works inform us that infants and young children are much more capable at intellectual activities than has previously been thought. In order to cultivate these natural propensities in language and mathematics, we cannot emphasize enough the importance of having well-educated teachers at the early childhood level.

Unfortunately, research suggests that many preschool and early childhood providers are the least educated of the teaching force (Bellm 2005; CCSSO 2002; Gilliam and Marchesseault 2005; Globalization and Schools 2006; Herzenberg, Price, and Bradley 2005). This is due to many factors, primarily one of economics. From our experience, parents will entrust the care of their children to an individual but not lend that same individual their luxury automotive vehicle to transport their children. This example highlights the conundrum of the value placed on early childhood education.

GETTING THE TEACHING RIGHT

The children's work from the case studies clearly demonstrates their "performances of understanding" (Salomon and Perkins 1996, 116). In other words, the children's products demonstrate the idea that thinking and experience are intertwined. According to Eisner, "No form of experience is possible without cognitive activity and that such activity is itself what we mean by thinking" (1982, 36). Eisner's view stresses the importance of quality experiences, which broaden the definition of education and may increase academic achievement.

Elkind (1999) identifies three barriers that need to be overcome before effective instruction in mathematics and science can take place. The first barrier is overcome by recognizing that young children do not think in the same way as adults. Children have preconceived ideas about how the physical world works before entering formal educational settings and hold on to their beliefs steadfastly. Many of the children's naïve conceptions are unique to each child and lack logical consistency by adult standards. Therefore, using reflective or logical analysis to discover how children learn is futile.

The second is overcome by recognizing the transductive nature of children's thinking. Children exhibit transductive thinking when they relate object to object or event to event rather than using inductive or deductive methods. Elkind (1999, 64–65) extends Piaget's viewpoint on young children's conceptions of the world by reporting that children exhibit animism, purposivism, and phenomenalistic causality as characteristics of transductive thinking.

The third barrier is overcome by recognizing that children's motivations are different from those of adults, and they have different priorities for the things that they wish to study or what is important to them. Young children need to first respond to fundamental environmental stimuli such as sensory learning, temporal sequencing, and spatial relationships.

Teachers need to be aware of the developmental importance of Elkind's (1999) concerns to make meaningful use of observations and conclusions emanating from children's free play activities. Although Elkind (1999) raises legitimate concerns, our emphasis is not to quicken the rate of development (if even possible) but to be prepared to meet the needs of each child. Key to this point is the ability to recognize the demonstrated natural abilities of young children and how these abilities relate to formal understanding. This requires better educated and experienced early childhood teachers rather than a highly scripted and structured preschool mathematics and science curriculum. We suggest a method of teaching known as adaptive inquiry (Farenga, Joyce, and Ness 2002, 2006), which requires educators to demonstrate a wide variety of content knowledge, pedagogical content strategies, and understanding of childhood development. These three qualities are our basic requirement for teacher competence. The curriculum exists as a mental construction in the mind of the teacher, called into existence by the readiness of the children.

The competent teacher not only observes what the child is doing but understands its importance to the development of literacy, mathematics, and science skills. When observing children during free play, can the teacher recognize examples of symmetric relations (e.g., point, line, rotational, and other point-group symmetries, or patterning and other forms of space-group symmetries) that a child demonstrates during block play? Drawing on our experience in teacher training and field-based observations, we notice that many early childhood educators would have difficulty in identifying these and related concepts. The situation is not limited to mathematics; the same argument could be made for science because early childhood educators do not have a basic understanding of motion, buoyancy, magnetism, and sound. If concepts such as these cannot be recognized by teachers, how can they accurately evaluate the child's abilities in these areas? This calls into question the purpose and accuracy of formative assessment. In fairness, this situation is not limited to early childhood educators; it extends across the grade levels, even into college, university, and graduate school (Annenberg Media 2006).

LESSONS LEARNED FROM BLOCK PLAY

What do we see in block play? In figure 8.1, we identify the protomathematical and protoscientific experience model. We argue that play forms the core of basic and complex forms of understanding. Protobehaviors are the observed subskills for basic process skills. The adult (teacher, parent, educa-

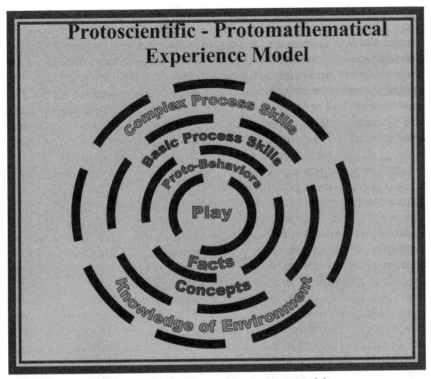

Figure 8.1. Protoscientific–Protomathematical Experience Model

tor) must see these subskills demonstrated by the individual child. Proto-mathematical and protoscientific behaviors are those subskills that purport to both mathematical and scientific thinking. Through play, children have the opportunities to act out protobehaviors such as manipulating objects, recognizing and identifying patterns, identifying attributes of phenomena such as color, texture, shape, and size, and making one-to-one correspondences. The recognition and identification of the attributes of particular objects become basic to more advanced behaviors, such as classifying, communicating, ordering, and sequencing. The basic process skills (e.g., classifying, identifying variables, communicating results) can be combined to form more complex process skills, such as manipulating and identifying variables, hypothesizing, and logical reasoning (see table 8.1).

Lewin's work (1935) illustrates that children are bound by situational constraints. The nature of the objects with which children come in contact are the motivational stimuli that promote understanding. In order for this understanding to take place, the child needs to develop facts and conceptual knowledge about an object. When working with an object such as a block, the child may ascertain its measurement properties of length, width,

Table 8.1. Protobehaviors, basic process skills, and complex process skills

Sample Protobehaviors	*Sample Basic Process Skills*
Manipulating objects in the physical environment	Exploring
Recognizing and identifying patterns Identifying attributes of particular phenomena, such as color, texture, shape, size, letters, or numbers	Observing
Grouping based on attributes, such as color, texture, shape, or size	Classifying
Building language concepts Developing an understanding of verbal or written symbolism	Communicating
Being aware of the spatial orientation of objects (high/low/right/left/next to)	Locating
Knowing the number words Making 1:1 correspondences	Counting
Recognizing objects in quantity or magnitude Recognizing large, small or near, far	Measuring

Sample Basic Process Skills	*Sample Complex Process Skills*
Communicating Observing Predicting Classifying	Manipulating and identifying variables
Communicating Observing Predicting Classifying	Hypothesizing
Communicating Sequencing Measuring Drawing	Proof (in mathematics)
Communicating Sequencing Observing	Logical reasoning
Observing Classifying Measuring	Comparing and contrasting

and height. What knowledge can the child possibly obtain? The example offers the child a preliminary understanding of a three-dimensional object or possibly the contrast between the perceived two-dimensional object and the actual three-dimensional object. For Lewin, objects, depending on their physical properties, may only be used in a limited number of ways and therefore will affect the learning experience and the direction of understanding. The object is a stimulus that may determine the child's actions and behaviors. If we combine Lewin's premise with Vygotsky's zone of proximal development, teachers are more able to identify cognitive propensities in ways that go beyond the young child's expected level of behavior.

We have identified a number of concepts and processes that teachers should be aware of when observing young children engaged in block play (see figures 8.2, 8.3, and 8.4).

Bruner (1966), in *Toward a Theory of Instruction*, discusses the importance in designing ways to improve learning. For Bruner, it is imperative to identify the key features that affect the solution of a problem and to make those features more memorable. In essence, teachers need to present a learning situation in which they demonstrate the features of a problem that are relevant to the solution. Using a Vygotskyan centered approach, teachers who are aware of the child's natural mathematical and scientific inclinations may be able to introduce a larger framework to help the child bridge the gap between her spontaneous understanding and formal concepts to be learned in later years. The critical concern at this point is the teacher's abil-

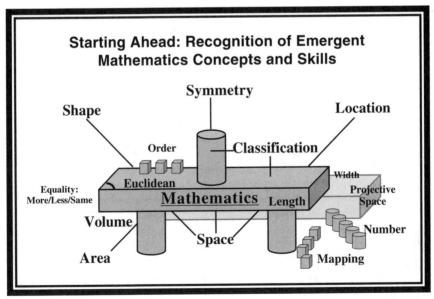

Figure 8.2.   Starting ahead: Recognition of emergent mathematics concepts and skills

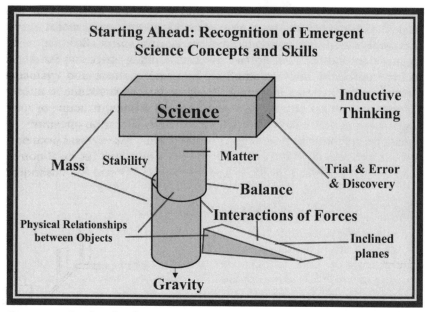

Figure 8.3. Starting ahead: Recognition of emergent science concepts and skills

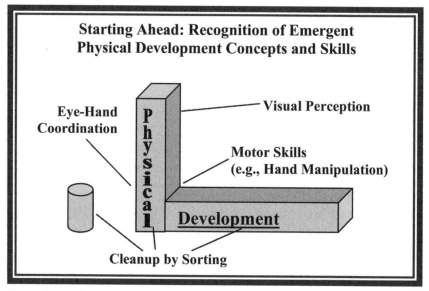

Figure 8.4. Starting ahead: Recognition of emergent physical development concepts and skills

ity to assess the confluence of stimuli from the environment and the child's capacity for understanding and level of motivation. A teacher without this ability will likely fall prey to the issues raised by Elkind.

An important part of this process is giving the child the opportunity during free play to engage in reflective awareness as a means of interpreting real-life three-dimensional representations in other formats—for example, verbally (through speech or written language) or through two-dimensional drawings or diagrams. The preparation for science and mathematics in school should include the attempt to make children aware of the multifaceted perspectives of a given concept. For instance, many children involved in block play may have come from homes where they have not had the experience of looking at the properties of the three-dimensional objects, like the unit block, in terms of perspective taking. In fact, children will not realize for years that the actual three-dimensional block can be represented in numerous ways and that spatial representation is by no means static; it is a much more dynamic enterprise than one would think. We notice this by representing the physical unit block in numerous ways: 1) verbal discourse, 2) in writing, or 3) as a diagram. In terms of a diagram, we realize that the three-dimensional block can be represented in a two-dimensional manner, whereby specific symbolic referents, usually dotted lines, indicate the object's depth, or third dimension.

The key point here is that children should be exposed to these other types of discourse. This exposure to multiple discourse types serves to mediate between the children's experiences at home and what Vygotsky would refer to as "scientific" concepts that are formally discussed in the school setting. Donaldson (1978), in *Children's Minds*, basically makes a similar argument with regard to children's processes in learning to read. Her explanation discusses the importance of the psychology of learning a language and the nature of the correspondence system that should be expressed to children as soon as possible in order to optimize transfer and promote understanding.

CORRESPONDENCE SYSTEMS IN MATHEMATICS AND SCIENCE: THE CASE OF LEGOS AND BLOCKS

Thus far, we have considered the essential vehicle of play and discussed the importance of the early introduction of a correspondence system when young children are learning a new concept. What follows are concepts we have observed young children demonstrating during active free play that we believe educators need to consider for each child's intellectual development. An educator's role is to help individual children bridge the gap between spontaneous actions and scientific concepts. Although we do not embrace the implementation of a formal preschool mathematics or science curriculum, we do advocate the teacher's role in facilitating each child's intellectual curiosities in mathematics and science in a rich knowledge-centered environment in which young children's motivation serves as a springboard for questioning and inquiry (Lay-Dopyera and Dopyera 1986; Piaget 1972). This contributes to the aesthetic quality of the early childhood educator and requires a great deal of background knowledge, not only in mathematics, science, and language concepts, but in the field of child development itself.

We therefore identify common topics in mathematics and science that have emerged from children's questions. We suggest components of mathematically and scientifically related correspondence systems that the educator should convey to young children in a transparent manner as a means of developing intellectual curiosities. We are aware that at this level, most children will not understand all the material that is presented to them. However, teachers can use the experience to plant the seeds of understanding for later intellectual discourse and discovery and base appropriate objectives on children's natural inclinations. The teacher's role is to explain to others the concepts, processes, and attitudes that each young child is capable of during free play.

Mathematical and Scientific Concepts and Processes

Through questioning, a technique that we refer to as "tacit dialoguing," the children inform us of their level of understanding. In discussing the structures the child has created, we note specific mathematical and scientific concepts used in the design process and the proper terminology. Even if it appears futile, it is not surprising to see the child replicate the structure and repeat parts of the conversation at a later time. Further, many children often demonstrate the use of their new knowledge when communicating with classmates, creating a pictorial representation, or writing a story.

Figure 8.2 identifies the emergent mathematical concepts and skills that are evident during block play. Some concepts that are apparent include symmetry, location, classification, number concepts, mapping, measurement concepts (e.g., area, capacity, length, width, height), Euclidean geometric concepts (e.g., parallelism, perpendicularity, congruence, similarity), and projective space. Process skills in science and mathematics are like action verbs in language. They involve the "doing" of science and mathematics. Process skills evident in mathematical thinking are abundant: problem solving, measuring, communicating, conjecturing, proving, representing objects or ideas in different ways, locating objects or places, classifying or ordering, making comparisons that involve magnitude, and operating on numerical quantities.

An example of a classroom-based activity which connects protomathematical behaviors with basic and complex process skills is daily clean-up: placing the same color Legos back in their bins, matching shapes and putting them in the same place, or identifying the shapes of blocks when cleaning up.

What do we call these spontaneous (informal) activities that children are doing while putting the blocks away during clean-up? These are samples of process skills in mathematics and science: sorting, grouping, and classifying. The purpose of the activity determines the cognitive level of the behavior. Further, groups of classifications form the basis for identifying and recognizing patterns. The repetition of patterns forms relationships, which take time to develop and must be fostered. The awareness of repetition and relationships can lead to the development of cause and effect and a great deal of algebraic thinking. This is a cognitively complex task representative of higher level thinking.

Parallel to emergent mathematics concepts, figures 8.3 and 8.4 identify the emergent science concepts and physical and motor skills that are evident during block play. These concepts include but are not limited to forces found in nature (e.g, gravity, friction); physical properties of objects (matter, mass, size, shape recognition, and balance); the discrimination between materials; notions of horizontal and vertical; visualizing objects from different perspectives; concepts of conservation of weight, area, and volume; representational models for investigating problems and relationships; and understanding how form and structure of materials relate to their function.

Within the domain of science, teachers will notice process skills that emerge: engaging in trial and error, inductive thinking, making predictions, building models, making observations, gathering data, manipulating tools and materials, measuring properties of materials, and classifying objects.

Science-related activities provide an opportunity for young children to test their ideas. Although not always noticed by adults, children are experimenting (e.g., dropping, shaping, poking, pushing, building) and using trial and error to develop an understanding of the physical world. Many times, these experiences occur simultaneously with language experience (e.g., communicating interests, difficulties, or outcomes with friends, parents, or teachers). The integration of language occurs naturally as a result of the stimulus provided by these experiences. These informal experiences provide the opportunities for children to explore and express what was learned in their own language.

The following examples of common out-of-school activities may help the reader appreciate some of the ways that young children are introduced to science-related concepts. Children learn many laws of physics intuitively.

They come to school with concepts of the physical world firmly in place. Some of their concepts are correct, but most often, many of their naïve understandings need to be adjusted.

- A child on a swing knows that the harder the push, the higher the swing goes.
- Likewise, with a ball, the child learns that the harder the push down on the ball, the higher the bounce.
- A child drops something from a table. Where does the child look? At the floor.
- A child can experiment with various angles and heights when using a ramp or incline to determine the distance that objects can travel when released. Completed enough times, the child begins to develop an understanding of the relationship between the angle of the incline and the distance the car or ball travels.

The adult's responsibility is to determine if the child can make sense of the experience. If not, the adult needs to set up the activity again or a parallel activity that allows the child to experience the relationship. Therefore, when deciding on an activity, select one in which the variables are visible and can be easily manipulated.

Examples of experimenting and manipulating variables may be done with a simple activity of hand washing. The teacher may try the activity in a number of ways. The first objective may be to emphasize the importance of using soap. Here, the teacher may establish trials in hand washing with or without the use of soap. In a second attempt, the teacher may have children rub or not rub their hands while washing. Further, the teacher may decide to change the temperature of the water using cold, warm, or hot. The teacher's objective is to set up different conditions to help the child answer the question: What is the best way to clean our hands? The hand washing activity provides ample opportunity to explore children's inquiry-related behavior. The preschool classroom is a natural setting for numerous inquiry-based mathematics and science-related activities.

Recognizing Inquiry in Preschool

The inquiry indicators that we have listed below are to serve as a guideline to help foster developmentally appropriate practices for young students. The guidelines are for educators who work with diverse early childhood populations. The children that we observed were all involved in free play activities. The educational goals that we stress below are designed to complement and provide support for the continuation of such free play activities rather than creating a more formal learning environment for the child. The observed complex behaviors serve as rich examples of mathematics and science skills. The intrinsic interest in science and mathematics demonstrates the children's intuitive spatial, geometric, and scientific abilities. However, we realize in many situations that parents, teachers, and administrators are being pressured to increase formal instruction at younger ages. There is an increase in private education centers that provide readiness training for four- and five-year-old children prior to kindergarten. Many parents are worried that when their children enter kindergarten that they will not have the pre-literacy skills for success in reading and mathematics. Consequently, we provide a guideline that any individual who works with young children can use to justify the importance of free play to enhance cognitive abilities.

Early childhood classrooms can be natural environments for inquiry-based learning. Children enter the classroom with numerous questions about the natural world and the objects in their environments. How young children learn should determine how teachers instruct. Appropriate practices for four- and five-year-old children include environments where children learn through active exploration, select their own activities from learning centers provided by the teacher, are physically and mentally active, and are allowed time for individual expression, for a variety of interactions with others, and for problem solving and experimentation. The components of appropriate practice in early childhood education fit naturally with motivation in mathematics and science and inquiry-based teaching strategies, which help to promote cognitive, physical, and aesthetic development. Examining our case studies, we look at how children are naturally inclined to display inquiry-based behaviors. Ash and Kluger-Bell (1999) identified inquiry indicators in K-5 classrooms: What are the children doing? What are the teachers doing? What does the environment support?

Although we agree with the inquiry-based guidelines, we have learned from our fieldwork with teachers that many of the statements in the guidelines are nebulous; certain statements are clouded with non-descriptive, mentalistic terminology. For example, the statement "They exhibit curiosity and ponder observations" contains terms that are too broad when assessing young children's behaviors with regard to skill and concept development. That is to say, in what way is curiosity shown? In addition, what evidence does the teacher have that indicates that a child is pondering observations? How is *ponder* defined here? Accordingly, we have modified the inquiry indicators by Ash and Kluger-Bell (1999, 80–84) below so that teachers will find it easier to assess more observable behaviors. At the same time, we kept their framework for studying inquiry by examining what the children are doing, what the teacher is doing, how the environment supports inquiry, and major conceptual headings for inquiry-related activities. Each of the bold headings is followed by a series of bulleted statements, which are inquiry-related actions.

WHAT ARE THE CHILDREN DOING?

The observer can check whether the child demonstrates the behavior with a short description. This sample of behavior serves as physical evidence of the child's cognitive abilities across content, process, and product (outcome).

Children view themselves as active participants in the process of learning.

Children's Behaviors	Evident	Not Evident	Samples of the Behavior
• They are engaged in mathematics and science-related activities.			
• They engage in the activities for a greater amount of time.			
• They collaborate and work cooperatively with their peers.			
• They modify ideas, take risks, and question or challenge ideas.			
• They listen to differing points of view.			

Children accept an "invitation to learn" and readily engage in the exploration process.

Children's Behaviors	Evident	Not Evident	Samples of the Behavior
• They make observations and ask questions.			
• They challenge their ideas through experimentation and testing.			

Children plan and carry out investigations.

Children's Behaviors	Evident	Not Evident	Samples of the Behavior
• They design a fair test as a way to try out their ideas.			
• They verify, extend, or discard ideas.			

• They conduct investigations by observing, measuring, and recording data.			

Children communicate using a variety of methods.

Children's Behaviors	Evident	Not Evident	Samples of the Behavior
• They express ideas verbally, in writing, drawing, or through modeling (e.g., block play).			
• They listen, speak, and write about mathematics and science-related activities with parents, teachers, and peers.			
• They use the language of the processes of mathematics and science.			

Children propose explanations and solutions and build a store of concepts.

Children's Behaviors	Evident	Not Evident	Samples of the Behavior
• They offer explanations before, during, and after the activity is completed.			
• They classify information (what does and does not work).			
• They are willing to revise explanations based on observations and results.			

Children raise questions.

Children's Behaviors	Evident	Not Evident	Samples of the Behavior
• They ask questions—verbally or through actions.			
• They redefine questions to test ideas.			

Children use observations.

Children's Behaviors	Evident	Not Evident	Samples of the Behavior
• They see details, seek patterns, detect sequences and events; they notice changes, similarities, and differences.			
• They identify patterns based on previously held ideas.			
• They draw conclusions based on observations.			

WHAT IS THE TEACHER DOING?

Teachers model behaviors and skills.

Teachers' Behaviors	Evident	Not Evident	Samples of the Behavior
• They show children how to use new tools or materials.			
• They guide children in working independently.			
• They encourage children to question, test, and revise ideas.			

Teachers support content learning.

Teachers' Behaviors	Evident	Not Evident	Samples of the Behavior
• They help children form tentative explanations while moving toward content understanding.			
• They make tools and materials available for children that support mathematical and scientific ideas appropriate to content learning.			
• They use appropriate content terminology, as well as scientific and mathematical language.			

Teachers use multiple means of assessment.

Teachers' Behaviors	Evident	Not Evident	Samples of the Behavior
• They use multiple formative assessment strategies.			
• They use multiple summative assessment strategies.			
• They interact with parents to determine the child's level of out-of-school mathematics and science-related activities.			
• They help children go to the next stage of learning with appropriate clues and prompts. They are aware of the child's zone of proximal development.			

Teachers act as facilitators.

Teachers' Behaviors	Evident	Not Evident	Samples of the Behavior
• They use open-ended questions that initiate investigation, observation, and thinking.			
• They listen to children's ideas, comments, and questions, in order to help them develop their skills and thought processes.			

HOW DOES THE ENVIRONMENT SUPPORT INQUIRY?

Children work in an appropriate and supportive physical environment.

Environmental Conditions	Evident	Not Evident	Samples of the Behavior
• The room is set up to support small-group interaction and investigation.			
• Lists of student questions are prominent and available for all to see.			

• A variety of general supplies are available, both at desks and in easily accessed cabinets.			
• A variety of materials specific to the area being explored are easily accessible.			
• Student work is displayed in a variety of ways in order to reflect their investigations.			

Children work in an appropriate and supportive emotional environment.

Environmental Conditions	Evident	Not Evident	Samples of the Behavior
• Their thinking is solicited and honored.			
• They express ideas and opinions.			
• They interact with one another and with the teacher.			
• They share information and ideas with each other—as individuals or in groups.			

Children work in a variety of configurations to encourage communication.

Environmental Conditions	Evident	Not Evident	Samples of the Behavior
• Work may be done individually, in student pairs, small or large groups, or in whole-class situations.			
• Children respond to feedback.			

The importance of the inquiry indicators is to help teachers identify what is important in doing inquiry and what the environment of an inquiry-based classroom may look like. This information is provided for teachers to help guide their instruction and assessment strategies. The teacher should feel free to modify the checklists. Like all lists, it is limited because it attempts to make finite a creative process that has infinite possibilities.

CONCLUSION

For early childhood educators, teaching and assessment are inseparable entities. Well-designed preschool programs provide teachers with the opportunities to assess each student's progress in a performance-based setting. The assessment techniques described in our research go well beyond traditional evaluation procedures, which only rank what children have learned. That is, the evidence for the judgment of what the children have learned is usually based on multiple forms of standardized measures. In our discussions with teachers, parents, and other school personnel, one notices that these measures—outcomes of multiple forms of high-stakes tests—are likely to produce value comparisons and competitiveness among parents at the expense of the children's well-being (D. D. Johnson and B. Johnson 2006). Often parents mistakenly assume that high scores on their children's evaluations relate to conceptual understanding, problem solving ability, or an advanced developmental level.

The integration of the assessment measures that we used increases the variety of data when making decisions about young children's cognitive propensities. The information about what children know is supported by what they are able to do. This information is more evidence-based and less judgmental and can be seen in Alejandro's, Fernando's, and Tina's excerpts regarding knowledge of symmetry (see chapter 3) in the construction of symmetrical, three-dimensional objects. The children are providing examples that demonstrate that they not only can recognize symmetrical properties but can create examples of each. In these performance-based assessments, the children have the opportunity to naturally integrate content, process, and product in terms of measures of their abilities. As Copley states, "Assessment can and should occur everywhere, specifically in small groups, play centers, individual interviews and large groups or on the playground. In fact, the most authentic situations occur in everyday places when children are using mathematics to solve problems" (1999, 185).

From birth, humans have a propensity to learn. From the earliest years, children interpret their environment by observing phenomena, asking questions, and pursuing investigations as they attempt to construct knowledge. We have supported this notion through research and have drawn parallels among the work associated with scientists and mathematicians and the intrinsic cognitive inclinations of young children. From our experiences with young children, it was natural to discuss inquiry-based learning environments, multiple forms of assessment, especially assessments that are performance-based and linked to the demonstration of complex cognitive concepts (see symmetry in chapter 3, tension and compression in chapter 6, or patterns in chapter 7).

All young children manifest the potential to start ahead in science and mathematics. However, it is critical that their caretakers identify emergent behaviors to foster literacy in science and mathematics. Moreover, they should be flexible enough to take a specific free play scenario, for example, one with Legos or blocks, and engage young children's interest in multifaceted aspects of a structure, design, or pattern. For example, some children might focus on geometric configurations. But suppose the structure contains an enclosure for other types of play and that there are scientific concepts that account for the structure to remain standing. The adult must be versatile enough to engage the children's minds with regard to other mathematical or scientific phenomena occurring simultaneously. She needs to be flexible with the content because each child will have an alternative perspective with any given activity. Moreover, the process of a child's active engagement may lead from construction of a structure such as a bridge to the actual use of that bridge for dramatic play. In sum, the art of teaching is achieved if one knows when to change the objective from discussing the symmetry of a lattice truss to the traffic passing over the bridge.

CHAPTER TOPICS FOR DISCUSSION

1. It has been suggested by some individuals who work in the field of child development that play is the work of children. Select two such people and explain how their theories support our position in this chapter.
2. Is a mathematics and science curriculum necessary for preschool children? Based on the discussion in the present chapter, identify the strengths and weaknesses of developing a mathematics and science curriculum for the preschool level.
3. Concrete experience involves using materials to allow young children to explore and develop a purpose. In doing so, the children become aware of characteristics of the materials by handling and working with them. Some might say that the resulting structure that the children form could be used as a means of assessment. Explain how the child's product can be used as a form of embedded assessment—that is, as an indicator of the child's cognitive level.

References

Abhau, M., R. Copeland, and G. Greenberger. 1986. *Architecture in education: A resource of imaginative ideas and tested activities.* Philadelphia: Foundation for Architecture.

Acredolo, L. P. 1978. Development of spatial orientation in infancy. *Developmental Psychology* 14 (3): 224–34.

———. 1981. Small- and large-scale spatial concepts in infancy and childhood. In *Spatial representation and behavior across the life span: Theory and application,* ed. L. S. Liben, A. H. Patterson, and N. Newcombe, 63–81. New York: Academic Press.

———. 1982. The familiarity factor in spatial research. *New Directions for Child Development* 15: 19–30.

Allen, E. 1995. *How buildings work: The natural order of architecture.* 2nd ed. New York: Oxford University Press.

Anderson, J. R. 1983. *The architecture of cognition.* Cambridge, MA: Harvard University Press.

Anderson, N. H., and F. Wilkening. 1991. Adaptive thinking in intuitive physics. In *Developmental,* vol. 3 of *Contributions to information integration theory,* ed. N. H. Anderson, 1–42. Hillsdale, NJ: Lawrence Erlbaum Associates.

Annenburg Media. 2006. A private universe. Harvard-Smithsonian Center for Astrophysics, Science Education Department, Science Media Group. www.learner.org (accessed August 7, 2006).

Anooshian, L. J., and D. Young. 1981. Developmental changes in cognitive maps of a familiar neighborhood. *Child Development* 52: 341–48.

Archer, J., and B. Lloyd. 1982. *Sex and gender.* New York: Pelican.

Ash, D., and B. Kluger-Bell. 1999. Identifying inquiry in the K–5 classroom. *Monographs of the National Science Foundation* 2 (serial no. 99): 148.

Baenninger, M., and N. Newcombe. 1989. The role of experience in spatial test performance: A meta-analysis. *Sex Roles* 20: 327–44.

Baillargeon, R. 1993. The object concept revisited: New directions in the investigation of infant's physical knowledge. In *Carnegie Symposium on Cognition: Visual perception and cognition in infancy,* ed. C. Granrud, 265–315. Hillsdale, NJ: Lawrence Erlbaum Associates.

Bakeman, R., and J. M. Gottman. 1997. *Observing interaction: An introduction to sequential analysis.* 2nd ed. New York: Cambridge University Press.

Bakker, D. J. 1990. *Neuropsychology treatment of dyslexia.* New York: Oxford University Press.

Baldwin, J. 1961. *Nobody knows my name.* New York: Doubleday.

Balfanz, R. 1999. Why do we teach young children so little mathematics?: Some historical considerations. In *Mathematics in the early years,* ed. J. V. Copley, 3–10. Reston, VA: National Council of Teachers of Mathematics.

Barnett, W. S. 1996. Lives in the balance: Age-27 benefit-cost analysis of the High/Scope Perry Preschool Program. *Monographs of the High/Scope Educational Research Foundation,* 11. Ypsilanti, MI: High/Scope Press.

Baroody, A. J. 1987. *Children's mathematical thinking: A developmental framework for preschool, primary, and special education teachers.* New York: Teachers College Press.

Baroody, A. J., and J. L. M. Wilkins. 1999. The development of informal counting, number, and arithmetic skills and concepts. In *Mathematics in the early years,* ed. J. V. Copley, 48–65. Reston, VA: National Council of Teachers of Mathematics.

Battista, M. T., and D. H. Clements. 1988. A case for a Logo–based elementary school geometry curriculum. *Arithmetic Teacher* 36: 11–17.

Battista, M. T., D. H. Clements, J. Arnoff, K. Battista, and C. Van Auken-Borrow. 1998. Students' spatial structuring of two-dimensional arrays of squares. *Journal for Research in Mathematics Education* 29 (5): 503–32.

Bellm, D. 2005. Establishing teacher competencies in early care and education: A review of current models and options for California. In *Building California's preschool for all workforce.* Berkeley, CA: Center for the Study of Child Care Employment.

Bem, S. L. 1981. Gender schema theory: A cognitive account of sex typing. *Psychological Review* 88: 354–64.

Benbow, C. P., and J. C. Stanley. 1992. Sex differences in mathematical ability: Fact or artifact? In *Options for girls: A door to the future,* ed. M. Wilson, 109–14. Austin, TX: Pro-Ed.

Berlin, B., and P. Kay. 1969. *Basic color terms: Their universality and evolution.* Berkeley: University of California Press.

Berry, J. W. 1971. Ecological and cultural factors in spatial perceptual development. *Canadian Journal of Behavioral Science* 3: 324–36.

Bishop, A. J. 1983. Space and geometry. In *Acquisition of mathematical concepts and processes,* ed. R. Lesh and M. Landau, 175–227. New York: Academic Press.

———. 1988. Mathematics education in its cultural context. *Educational Studies in Mathematics* 19: 179–91.

———. 1991. *Mathematical enculturation: A cultural perspective on mathematics education.* Boston: Kluwer Academic Publishers.

Blackwell, W. 1984. *Geometry in architecture.* Berkeley, CA: Key Curriculum Press.

Blaut, J. M., and D. Stea. 1974. Mapping at the age of three. *The Journal of Geography* 73 (7): 5–9.

Block, J. H. 1973. Conceptions of sex role: Some cross-cultural and longitudinal perspectives. *American Psychologist* 28: 512–26.

———. 1983. Differential premise arising from differential socialization of sexes: Some conjectures. *Child Development* 54: 1335–54.

Bock, R. D., and D. Kolakowski. 1973. Further evidence of sex-linked major-gene influence on human spatial visualizing ability. *American Journal of Human Genetics* 25: 1–14.

Boles, D. B. 1980. X–linkage of spatial ability: A critical review. *Child Development* 51: 625–35.

Bolger, K., C. Patterson, W. Thompson, and J. Kupersmidt. 1995. Psychosocial adjustment among children experiencing persistent and intermittent family economic hardship. *Child Development* 66: 1107–29.

Borland, J. H. 2005. Gifted education without gifted children: The case for no conception of giftedness. In *Conceptions of giftedness*, 2nd ed., ed. R. J. Sternberg and J. E. Davidson, 1–19. New York: Cambridge University Press.

Bransford, J. D., A. L. Brown, and R. R. Cocking, eds. 2000. *How people learn: Brain, mind, experience, and school.* Washington, DC: National Academy Press.

Bredekamp, S., and C. Copple. 1997. *Developmentally appropriate practice in early childhood programs.* Rev. ed. Washington, DC: NAEYC.

Brosterman, N. 1997. *Inventing kindergarten.* New York: Harry N. Abrams Publishers.

Bruner, J. 1966. *Toward a theory of instruction.* Cambridge, MA: Harvard University Press.

Brush, L. R. 1978. Preschool children's knowledge of addition and subtraction. *Journal for Research in Mathematics Education* 9: 44–54.

Bryant, P., and S. Squire. 2001. Children's mathematics: Lost and found in space. In *Spatial schemas and abstract thought*, ed. M. Gattis, 175–200. Cambridge, MA: MIT Press.

Carpenter, T. P., J. M. Moser, and T. A. Romburg. 1982. *Addition and subtraction: A cognitive perspective.* Hillsdale, NJ: Lawrence Erlbaum Associates.

Carraher, T. N., D. W. Carraher, and A. D. Schliemann. 1985. Mathematics in the streets and in schools. *British Journal of Developmental Psychology* 3: 21–29.

Casati, R., and A. C. Varzi. 1999. *Parts and places: The structures of spatial representation.* Cambridge, MA: MIT Press.

Cassirer, E. 1944. *An essay on man: An introduction of the philosophy of human culture.* New Haven, CT: Yale University Press.

———. 1953–1957. *The philosophy of symbolic forms.* 3 vols. New Haven, CT: Yale University Press.

Ceglowski, D. 1998. *Inside a Head Start center: Developing policies from practice.* New York: Teachers College Press.

Chang, K. 1986. A purely geometric module in the rat's spatial representation. *Cognition* 23: 149–78.

Chantrell, G., ed. 2002. *The Oxford dictionary of word histories.* New York: Oxford University Press.

Chiang, A., and R. C. Atkinson. 1976. Individual differences and interrelationships among a select set of cognitive skills. *Memory and Cognition* 4: 661–72.

Ching, F. D. K. 1996. *Architecture: Form, space, and order.* New York: Wiley.

Chodorow, N. J. 1978. *The reproduction of mothering.* Los Angeles: University of California Press.

———. 1989. *Feminism and psychoanalytic theory.* New Haven, CT: Yale University Press.

Church, E. B., and K. Miller. 1990. *Learning through play: A practical guide for teaching young children/blocks*. New York: Scholastic.

Clark, H. 1973. Space, time semantics, and the child. In *Cognitive development and the acquisition of language*, ed. T. E. Moore, 27–63. New York: Academic Press.

Clements, D. H. 1999. Geometric and spatial thinking in young children. In *Mathematics in the early years*, ed. J. V. Copley, 66–79. Reston, VA: National Council of Teachers of Mathematics.

Clements, D. H., and M. T. Battista. 1989. Learning of geometric concepts in a Logo environment. *Journal for Research in Mathematics Education* 20: 450–67.

———. 1992. Geometry and spatial reasoning. In *Handbook of research on mathematics teaching and learning*, ed. D. Grouws, 420–64. New York: MacMillan.

Clements, D. H., S. Swaminathan, M. Z. Hannibal, and J. Sarama. 1999. Young children's concepts of shape. *Journal for Research in Mathematics Education* 30 (2): 192–212.

Clements, M. A. 1983. The question of how spatial ability is defined and its relevance to mathematical education. *Zentralblatt für Didaktik der Mathematik* 15: 8–20.

Coe, M. D., and R. Koontz. 2002. *Mexico: From the Olmecs to the Aztecs*. 5th ed. New York: Thames and Hudson.

Cogan, S., F. Eberhart, J. Krawchuk, J. Mauer, and L. Shapiro. 1988. *The community as classroom: A teacher's manual*. New York: Historic Districts Press.

Cohen, E. 2000. Equitable classrooms in a changing society. In *Handbook of the sociology of education*, ed. M. T. Hallihan, 265–83. New York: Kluwer.

Cohen, R., and T. Schuepfer. 1980. The representation of landmarks and routes. *Child Development* 51: 1065–71.

Coleman, J. W. 1994. *Foundations of social theory*. Cambridge, MA: Harvard University Press.

Copley, J. V. 1999. Assessing the mathematical understanding of the young child. In *Mathematics in the early years*, ed. J. V. Copley, 182–88. Reston, VA: National Council of Teachers of Mathematics.

Copple, C. E., R. R. Cocking, and W. S. Matthews. 1984. Objects, symbols, and substitutes: The nature of the cognitive activity during symbolic play. In *Child's play: Developmental and applied*, ed. T. D. Yawkey and A. D. Pellegrini, 105–24. Hillsdale, NJ: Lawrence Erlbaum Associates.

Council of Chief State School Officers (CCSSO). 2002. *Key state education policies on PK–12 education: 2002*. Washington, DC: U.S. Department of Education.

Cousins, D., and E. Abravanel. 1971. Some findings relevant to the hypothesis that topological spatial features are differentiated prior to Euclidean features during growth. *British Journal of Psychology* 62: 475–79.

Crain, W. 1992. *Theories of development: Concepts and applications*. 3rd ed. Englewood Cliffs, NJ: Prentice Hall.

Culp, R. E., A. S. Crook, and P. C. Housley. 1983. A comparison of observed and reported adult-infant interactions: Effects of perceived sex. *Sex Roles* 9: 475–79.

D'Ambrosio, U. 1984. *The socio-cultural bases of mathematics education*. Boston: Birkhauser.

———. 1985. Ethnomathematics and its place in the history and pedagogy of mathematics. *For the Learning of Mathematics* 5 (1): 44–48.

Darke, I. 1982. A review of research related to the topological primacy thesis. *Educational Studies in Mathematics* 13: 119–42.

Dasen, P. R. 1972. Cross-cultural Piagetian research: A summary. *Journal of Cross-Cultural Psychology* 3: 23–29.

Dewey, J. 1924. *John Dewey on education. Ed. R. D. Archambault.* Chicago: University of Chicago Press.

DiSalle, R. 1994. On dynamics, indiscernibility, and spacetime ontology. *British Journal for the Philosophy of Science* 45: 265–87.

Donaldson, M. 1978. *Children's minds.* New York: Norton.

Downs, R. M. 1981. Maps and mappings as metaphors for spatial representation. In *Spatial representation and behavior across the life span: Theory and application*, ed. L. S. Liben, A. H. Patterson, and N. Newcombe, 143–66. New York: Academic Press.

Downs, R. M., and L. S. Liben. 1987. Children's understanding of maps. In *Cognitive processes and spatial orientation in animal and man*, ed. P. Ellen and C. Thinus-Blanc, 202–19. Dordrecht, Holland: Martinus Nijhoff.

Downs, R. M., and D. Stea, eds. 1973. *Image and environment: Cognitive mapping and spatial behavior.* Chicago: Aldine Publishing.

Dretske, F. I. 1971. Perception from an epistemological point of view. *Journal of Philosophy* 66: 584–91.

Duncan, G. J., and J. Brooks-Gunn. 1997. *Consequences of growing up poor.* New York: Russell Sage Foundation.

Eccles, J. S. 1985. Why doesn't Jane run? Sex differences in educational and occupational patterns. In *The gifted and talented: Developmental perspective*, ed. F. D. Horowitz and M. O'Brien. Washington, DC: American Psychological Association.

Eccles Parsons, J. 1984. Sex differences in mathematics participation. In *Women in science*, ed. M. W. Steinkamp and M. L. Maehr, 93–138. Greenwich, CT: JAI Press.

Einstein, A. 1954. Foreword to *Concepts of space: The history of theories of space in physics*, by M. Jammer. Cambridge, MA: Harvard University Press.

Eisner, E. W. 1982. *Cognition and curriculum: A basis for deciding what to teach.* New York: Longman.

Ekman, G., R. Lindman, and W. William-Olsson. 1961. A psychophysical study of cartographic symbols. *Perceptual and Motor Skills* 13: 355–68.

Elkind, D. 1999. Educating young children in math, science, and technology. *Dialogue on early childhood science, mathematics, and technology education.* Washington, DC: American Association for the Advancement of Science.

Erikson, E. 1963. *Childhood and society.* 2nd ed. New York: Norton.

Farenga, S. J. 1995. Out of school science related experiences, science attitudes, and the selection of science mini-courses by high-ability upper elementary students. EdD diss., Columbia University.

Farenga, S. J., and B. A. Joyce. 1997. What children bring to the classroom: Learning science from experience. *School Science and Mathematics* 97 (5): 248–52.

———. 1998. Science related attitudes and science course selection: A study of high-ability boys and girls. *Roeper Review* 20 (4): 247–51.

———. 1999a. Informal science experience, attitudes, future interest in science, and gender of high-ability students: An exploratory study. *School Science and Mathematics* 99 (8): 431–37.

———. 1999b. Intentions of young students to enroll in science courses in the future: An examination of gender differences. *Science Education* 83: 55–75.

———. 2002. Teaching youngsters science in a culturally diverse urban classroom. In *Commitment to excellence: Transforming teaching and teacher education in inner-city and urban settings,* ed. A. Catelli and A Diver-Stamnes, 149–70. Cresskill, NJ: Hampton Press.

Farenga, S. J., B. A. Joyce, and D. Ness. 2002. Reaching the zone of optimal learning: The alignment of curriculum, instruction, and assessment. In *Learning science and the science of learning,* ed. R. Bybee. Arlington, VA: National Science Teachers Association.

———. 2006. Adaptive inquiry as the silver bullet: Reconciling local curriculum, instruction, and assessment procedures with state mandated testing in science. In *Assessment in science: Practical experiences and educational research,* ed. M. McMahon, P. Simmons, R. Sommers, D. DeBaets, and F. Crawley, 41–51. Washington, DC: National Science Teachers Association.

Feingold, A. 1988. Cognitive gender differences are disappearing. *American Psychologist* 43: 95–103.

Feldman, S., and S. C. Nash. 1977. The influence of age and sex on responsiveness to babies. *Developmental Psychology* 16: 675–76.

Fennema, E., and T. P. Carpenter. 1981. Sex-related differences in mathematics: Results from national assessment. *Mathematics Teacher* 74: 554–59.

———. 1998. New perspectives on gender differences in mathematics: An introduction. *Educational Researcher* 27 (5): 4–5.

Fennema, E., T. P. Carpenter, L. Levi, M. L. Franke, and S. Empson. 1997. *Cognitively guided instruction: Professional development in primary mathematics.* Madison: Wisconsin Center for Education Research.

Fennema, E., and J. Sherman. 1977. Sex-related differences in mathematics achievement, spatial visualization and affective factors. *American Educational Research Journal* 15: 51–71.

Fennema, E., and L. A. Tartre. 1985. The use of spatial visualization in mathematics by girls and boys. *Journal for Research in Mathematics Education* 16: 184–206.

Flavell, J. H. 1982. On cognitive development. *Child Development* 53: 1–10.

———. 1999. Cognitive development: Children's knowledge about the mind. *Annual Review of Psychology* 50: 21–45.

Fodor, J. 1983. *Modularity of mind: An essay on faculty psychology.* Cambridge, MA: MIT Press.

Forman, G. E. 1975. *Transformations in the manipulations and productions performed with geometric objects: An early system of logic in young children.* Amherst: Center for Early Childhood Education, School of Education, University of Massachusetts, Amherst. (ERIC No. ED 142-276).

Fox, L. H., and S. J. Cohn. 1980. Sex differences in development of precocious mathematical talent. In *Women and the mathematical mystique,* ed. L. H. Fox, L. Brody, and D. Tobin, 94–111. Baltimore: John Hopkins University Press.

Freudenthal, H. 1973. *Mathematics as an educational task.* Dordrecht, The Netherlands: Reidel Publishing.

Fuys, D., D. Geddes, and R. Tischler. 1984. *English translation of selected writings of D.*

van Hiele-Geldof and P. M. van Hiele. Brooklyn, NY: Brooklyn College School of Education.

Galanter, E. 1992. The quadrate mind. *New Ideas in Psychology* 10 (3): 285–301.

Gao, F., S. C. Levine, and J. Huttenlocher. 2000. What do infants know about continuous quantity? *Journal of Experimental Child Psychology* 7: 67–87.

Gattegno, C. 1973. *The universe of babies*. New York: Educational Solutions.

Gattis, M., ed. 2003. *Spatial schemas and abstract thought*. Cambridge, MA: MIT Press.

Geary, D. C. 1994. *Children's mathematical development: Research and practical applications*. Washington, DC: American Psychological Association.

Geertz, C. 1973. *The interpretation of cultures*. New York: Basic Books.

Gelman, R., and C. R. Gallistel. 1978. *The child's understanding of number*. Cambridge, MA: Harvard University Press.

Genkins, E. F. 1971. A comparison of two methods of teaching the concept of bilateral symmetry to young children. EdD diss., Teachers College, Columbia University.

———. 1975. The concept of bilateral symmetry in young children. In *Children's mathematical concepts: Six Piagetian studies in mathematics education*, ed. M. F. Rosskopf, 3–41. New York: Teachers College Press.

Gerdes, P. 1988. On culture, geometric thinking, and mathematics education. *Educational Studies in Mathematics* 19 (3): 137–62.

———. 1995. *Une tradition géométrique en Afrique: Les dessins sur le sable*. 3 vols. Paris: L'Harmattan.

———. 1998. On some geometrical and architectural ideas from African art and craft. In *Nexus II: Architecture and mathematics*, ed. K. Williams, 75–86. Firenze: Edizioni dell'Erba.

———. 1999. *Geometry from Africa: Mathematical and educational explorations*. Washington, DC: Mathematical Association of America.

———. 2003. *Awakening of geometrical thought in early culture*. Minneapolis, MN: MEP Publications.

Gilliam, W. S., and C. M. Marchesseault. 2005. Part 1: Who's teaching our youngest students? Teacher education and training, experience, compensation and benefits, and assistant teachers. In *From capitols to classrooms, policies to practice: State-funded prekindergarten at the classroom level*. New Haven, CT: Yale University Child Study Center.

Gilligan, C. 1982. *In a different voice*. Cambridge, MA: Harvard University Press.

Ginsburg, H. P. 1972. *The myth of the deprived child: Poor children's intellect and education*. Englewood Cliffs, NJ: Prentice Hall.

———. 1989. *Children's arithmetic: How they learn it and how you teach it*. Austin, TX: Pro-Ed.

———. 1997. *Entering the child's mind: The clinical interview in psychological research and practice*. New York: Cambridge University Press.

Ginsburg, H. P., N. Inoue, and K. H. Seo. 1999. Young children doing mathematics: Observations of everyday activities. In *Mathematics in the early years*, ed. J. V. Copley, 88–99. Reston, VA: National Council of Teachers of Mathematics.

Ginsburg, H. P., C. L. Lin, D. Ness, and K. H. Seo. 2003. Young American and Chinese children's everyday mathematical activity. *Mathematical Thinking and Learning* 5 (4): 235–58.

Ginsburg, H. P., S. Pappas, and K. H. Seo. 2001. Everyday mathematical knowledge: Asking young children what is developmentally appropriate. In *Psychological perspectives on early childhood education: Reframing dilemmas in research and practice*, ed. S. L. Golbeck, 181–219. Mahwah, NJ: Lawrence Erlbaum Associates.

Ginsburg, H. P., and R. L. Russell. 1981. Social class and racial influences on early mathematical thinking. *Monographs of the Society for Research in Child Development* 46 (serial no. 193, 6).

Gleitman, H. 1995. *Psychology*. 4th ed. New York: Norton.

Globalization and schools. (2006, October 11). *The Washington Post*, p. A18.

Goldberg, S., S. L. Blumberg, and A. Kriger. 1982. Menarche and interest in infants: Biological and social influences. *Child Development* 53: 1544–50.

Goldhaber, J. 1994. If we call it science, then can we let the children play? *Childhood Education*: 24–27.

Gopnik, A., A. N. Meltzoff, and P. K. Kuhl. 1999. *The scientist in the crib: What early learning tells us about the mind*. New York: Harper Perennial.

Gould, S. J. 1996. *The mismeasure of man*. New York: Norton.

Greeno, J. G. 1980. Some examples of cognitive task analysis with instructional implications. In *Aptitude, learning, and instruction*. Vol. 2, *Cognitive process analyses of learning and problem solving*, ed. R. E. Snow, P. Federico and W. E. Montague, 1–21. Hillsdale, NJ: Lawrence Erlbaum Associates.

Halpern, D. F. 1989. The disappearance of cognitive gender differences: What you see depends on where you look. *American Psychologist* 44: 1156–57.

Hargittai, I., and M. Hargittai. 1994. *Symmetry: A unifying concept*. Bolinas, CA: Shelter Publications.

———. 1996. The universality of the symmetry concept. In *Nexus: Architecture and mathematics*, ed. K. Williams, 81–95. Fucecchio (Florence): Edizioni dell'Erba.

Harlen, W., ed. 1985. *Primary science: Taking the plunge*. Oxford: Heinemann.

Harris, L. J. 1981. Sex-related variations in spatial skill. In *Spatial representation and behavior across the life span*, ed. L. S. Liben, A. H. Patterson, and N. Newcombe, 83–125. New York: Academic Press.

Harris, L. J., and E. Strommen. 1972. The role of front-back features in children's "front," "back," and "beside" placements of objects. *Merrill-Palmer Quarterly* 18: 259–71.

Hart, R. A. 1981. Children's spatial representation of the landscape: Lessons and questions from a field study. In *Spatial representation and behavior across the life span: Theory and application*, ed. L. S. Liben, A. H. Patterson, and N. Newcombe, 195–233. New York: Academic Press.

Hart, R. A., and G. T. Moore. 1973. The development of spatial cognition: A review. In *Image and environment: Cognitive mapping and spatial behavior*, ed. R. M. Downs and D. Stea, 248–95. Chicago: Aldine Publishing.

Hermer, L., and E. S. Spelke. 1994. A geometric process for spatial reorientation in young children. *Nature* 370: 57–59.

Herzenberg, S., M. Price, and D. Bradley. 2005. *Losing ground in early childhood education: Declining workforce qualifications in an expanding industry*. Washington, DC: Economic Policy Institute.

Hirsch, E. S. 1996. *The block book*. 3rd ed. Washington, DC: National Association for the Education of Young Children.

Hochberg, J. 1964. *Perception*. Englewood Cliffs, NJ: Prentice Hall.

———. 1988. Perception of objects in space. In *Fifty years of psychology: Essays in honor of Floyd Ruch*, ed. E. Hilgard, 57–73. Glenville, IL: Scott Foresman.

———. 1994. Perceptual theory and visual cognition. In *Cognitive approaches to human perception*, ed. S. Ballestreros, 269–89. Hillsdale, NJ: Lawrence Erlbaum Associates.

———. 1995. The construction of pictorial meaning. In *Advances in visual semiotics: The semiotic web 1992–93*, ed. T. Sebeok and J. Umiker-Sebeok, 109–62. Berlin: Mouton de Gruyter.

Hoffer, A. 1983. Van Hiele–based research. In *Acquisition of mathematical concepts and processes*, ed. R. Lesh and M. Landau, 205–27. New York: Academic Press.

Hoffman, L. W. 1977. Changes in family roles, socialization, and sex differences. *American Psychologist* 32: 644–57.

Hollinger, C. L. 1991. Facilitating career development of young gifted women. *Roeper Review* 13 (3): 135–39.

Howard, I. P., and W. B. Templeton. 1966. *Human spatial orientation*. New York: Wiley.

Hughes, F. P. 1999. *Children, play, and development*. Needham Heights, MA: Allyn and Bacon.

Huttenlocher, J., and N. Newcombe. 1984. The child's representation of information about location. In *The origins of cognitive skills: The eighteenth annual Carnegie symposium on cognition*, ed. C. Sophian, 81–111. Hillsdale, NJ: Lawrence Erlbaum Associates.

Huttenlocher, J., N. Newcombe, and E. H. Sandberg. 1994. The coding of spatial location in young children. *Cognitive Psychology* 27: 115–48.

Huttenlocher, J., N. Newcombe, and M. Vasilyeva. 1999. Spatial scaling in young children. *Psychology Science* 10: 393–98.

Jackowitz, E. R., and M. W. Watson. 1980. The development of object transformations in early pretend play. *Developmental Psychology* 16: 543–49.

Jammer, M. 1954. *Concepts of space: The history of theories of space in physics*. Cambridge, MA: Harvard University Press.

Johnson, D. D., and B. Johnson. 2006. *High stakes*. Lanham, MD: Rowman and Littlefield.

Johnson, D. D., B. Johnson, S. J. Farenga, and D. Ness. 2005. *Trivializing teacher education: The accreditation squeeze*. Lanham, MD: Rowman and Littlefield.

———. Forthcoming. *Stop high stakes betting now: An appeal to America's conscience*. Lanham, MD: Rowman and Littlefield.

Johnson, E. S., and A. C. Meade. 1987. Developmental patterns of spatial ability: An early sex difference. *Child Development* 58: 725–40.

Johnson, H. M. 1996. The art of block building. In *The block book*, 3rd ed., ed. E. S. Hirsch, 9–25. Washington, DC: National Association for the Education of Young Children.

Johnson, S. 1984. Girls need a science education too. *The Australian Science Teachers Journal* 30 (2): 18–23.

Johnson-Laird, P. N., P. Legrenzi, and M. Sonino Legrenzi. 1974. Reasoning and a sense of reality. *British Journal of Psychology* 63: 395–400.

Kahle, J. B. 1990. Why girls don't know. In *What research says to the science teacher: The process of knowing*, ed. M. Budd Rowe, Vol. 6, 55–67. Washington, DC: National Science Teachers Association.

ı Kamii, C., and R. DeVries. 1978. *Physical knowledge in preschool education: Implications of Piaget's theory.* Englewood Cliffs, NJ: Prentice Hall.

Kant, I. 1781/1902. *Critique of pure reason.* 2nd rev. ed. Trans F. M. Müller. New York: MacMillan.

Kapadia, R. 1974. A critical examination of Piaget–Inhelder's view on topology. *Educational Studies in Mathematics* 5: 419–24.

Karmiloff-Smith, A., and B. Inhelder. 1974. If you want to get ahead, get a theory. *Cognition* 3: 195–212.

Kohlberg, L. A. 1966. A cognitive-developmental analysis of children's sex-role concepts and attitudes. In *The development of sex differences*, ed. E. Maccoby, 82–173. Palo Alto, CA: Stanford University Press.

———. 1978. Revisions in the theory and practice of moral development. *New Directions for Child Development* 2: 83–88.

Kritchevsky, M. 1988. The elementary spatial functions of the brain. In *Spatial cognition: Brain bases and development*, ed. J. Stiles-Davis, M. Kritchevsky, and U. Bellugi, 111–40. Hillsdale, NJ: Lawrence Erlbaum Associates.

Kuczaj, S. A., II, and M. P. Maratsos. 1975. On the acquisition of front, back and side. *Child Development* 46: 202–10.

Kuhn, D. 2002. What is scientific thinking and how does it develop? In *Blackwell handbook of childhood cognitive development*, ed. U. Goswami, 371–93. Malden, MA: Blackwell Publishers.

Landau, B., and R. Jackendoff. 1993. "What" and "where" in spatial language and spatial cognition. *Behavioral and Brain Sciences* 16: 217–65.

Landau, B., H. Gleitman, and E. Spelke. 1981. Spatial knowledge and geometric knowledge in a child blind from birth. *Science* 213: 1275–78.

Landau, B., E. Spelke, and H. Gleitman. 1984. Spatial knowledge in a young blind child. *Cognition* 16: 225–60.

Lansky, L. M., V. J. Crandall, J. Kagan, and C. T. Baker. 1961. Sex differences in aggression and its correlates in middle-class adolescents. *Child Development* 32: 45–58.

Laurendeau, M., and A. Pinard. 1970. *The development of the concept of space in the child.* New York: International Universities Press.

Lay-Dopyera, M., and J. Dopyera. 1986. Strategies for teaching. In *Early childhood curriculum: A review of current research*, ed. C. Seafeldt. New York: Teachers College Press.

Lean, G., and M. A. Clements. 1981. Spatial ability, visual imagery, and mathematical performance. *Educational Studies in Mathematics* 12: 267–99.

Leeb-Lundberg, K. 1996. The block builder mathematician. In *The block book*, 3rd ed., ed. E. S. Hirsch, 35–60. Washington, DC: NAEYC.

Lesh, R., and M. Landau, eds. 1983. *Acquisition of mathematical concepts and processes.* New York: Academic Press.

Lesser, G. S., G. Fifer, and D. H. Clark. 1965. Mental abilities of children from different social-class and cultural groups. *Monographs of the Society for Research in Child Development* 20 (serial no. 102, 4).

Lever, J. 1976. Sex differences in the games children play. *Social Problems* 23: 55–62.

Lewin, K. 1935. *A dynamic theory of personality*. New York: MacGraw Hill.

Liben, L. S. 1981. Spatial representation and behavior: Multiple perspectives. In *Spatial representation and behavior across the life span: Theory and application*, ed. L. S. Liben, A. H. Patterson, and N. Newcombe, 3–36. New York: Academic Press.

———. 1988. Conceptual issues in the development of spatial cognition. In *Spatial cognition: Brain bases and development*, ed. J. Stiles-Davis, M. Kritchevsky, and U. Bellugi, 167–94. Hillsdale, NJ: Lawrence Erlbaum Associates.

———. 1997. Children's understanding of spatial representations of place: Mapping the methodological landscape. In *Spatial cognition in the child and adult*. Vol. 1 of *Handbook of spatial research paradigms and methodologies*, ed. N. Foreman and R. Gillett. West Sussex, UK: Psychology Press.

———. 1999. Developing an understanding of external spatial representations. In *Development of mental representation: Theories and applications*, ed. I. E. Siegel, 297–321. Mahwah, NJ: Lawrence Erlbaum Associates.

———. 2001. Thinking through maps. In *Spatial schemas and abstract thought*, ed. M. Gattis. Cambridge, MA: MIT Press.

———. 2002. Spatial development in childhood: Where are we now? In *Blackwell handbook of childhood cognitive development*, ed. U. Goswami, 326–48. Malden, MA: Blackwell Publishers.

Liben, L. S., and R. M. Downs. 1989. Understanding maps as symbols: The development of map concepts in children. In *Advances in child development and behavior*, ed. H. W. Reese, 145–201. San Diego: Academic Press.

———. 1991. The role of graphic representations in understanding the world. In *Visions of aesthetics, the environment, and development: The legacy of Joachim F. Wohlwill*, ed. R. M. Downs, L. S. Liben, and D. S. Palermo, 139–80. Hillsdale, NJ: Lawrence Erlbaum Associates.

———. 2001. Geography for young children: Maps as tools for learning environments. In *Psychology perspectives on early childhood education*, ed. S. L. Golbeck. Mahwah, NJ: Lawrence Erlbaum Associates.

Liben, L. S., and S. L. Golbeck. 1980. Sex differences in performance on Piagetian spatial tasks: Differences in competence or performance? *Child Development* 51: 594–97.

Lin, C.-L., and D. Ness. 2000. Taiwanese and American preschool children's everyday mathematics. Paper presented at the meeting of the American Educational Research Association, New Orleans.

Linn, M. C., and J. S. Hyde. 1989. Gender, mathematics, and science. *Educational Researcher* 18 (8): 17–27.

Linn, M. C., and A. C. Petersen. 1985. Emergence and characterization of sex differences in spatial ability: A meta-analysis. *Child Development* 56: 1479–98.

Locke, J. 1694/1998. *Essay concerning human understanding*. Ed. R. Woolhouse. New York: Penguin.

Lovell, K. 1959. A follow-up study of some aspects of the work of Piaget and Inhelder on the child's conception of space. *British Journal of Educational Psychology* 29: 104–17.

Lunzer, E. A. 1955. Studies in the development of play behavior in young children between the ages of two and six. Unpublished doctoral dissertation, Birmingham University, London.

Lupton, E., and J. A. Miller. 1991. *The ABC's of ▲●■: The Bauhaus and design theory from preschool to postmodernism.* Princeton, NJ: Princeton Architectural Press.

Luria, A. R. 1966. *Human brain and psychological processes.* New York: Harper and Row.

———. 1970. The functional organization of the brain. *Scientific American* 222 (3): 66–78.

MacDonald, S. 2001. *Block play: The complete guide to learning and playing with blocks.* Beltsville, MD: Gryphon House.

Mandler, J. M. 1988. The development of spatial cognition: On topological and Euclidean representation. In *Spatial cognition: Brain bases and development*, ed. J. Stiles-Davis, M. Kritchevsky, and U. Bellugi, 423–32. Hillsdale, NJ: Lawrence Erlbaum Associates.

Mapapá, A. 1994. Symmetries and metal grates in Maputo-Didactic experimentation. In *Explorations in ethnomathematics and ethnoscience in Mozambique*, ed. P. Gerdes, 49–55. Maputo: Instituto Superior Pedagógico Moçambique.

Markus, H., and D. Oyserman. 1989. Gender and thought: The role of the self-concept. In *Gender and thought: Psychological perspectives*, ed. M. Crawford and M. Gentry. New York: Springer-Verlag.

Martin, J. L. 1976. An analysis of some of Piaget's topological tasks from a mathematical point of view. *Journal for Research in Mathematics Education* 7: 8–25.

McCarty, D. 1972. *McCarty scales of children's abilities.* New York: The Psychological Corporation.

McClelland, J. L., D. E. Rumelhart, and the PDP Research Group. 1986. *Psychological and biological models.* Vol. 2 of *Parallel distributed processing: Explorations in the microstructure of cognition.* Cambridge, MA: MIT Press.

McCloskey, M. 1983. Intuitive physics. *Scientific American* 248 (4): 122–30.

McCune, L., and M. B. Zanes. 2001. Learning, attention, and play. In *Psychological perspectives on early childhood education: Reframing dilemmas in research and practice*, ed. S. L. Golbeck, 181–219. Mahwah, NJ: Lawrence Erlbaum Associates.

McGee, M. G. 1979. Human spatial abilities: Psychometric studies and environmental, genetic, hormonal, and neurological influences. *Psychological Bulletin* 86: 889–918.

McLean, J. F., and G. J. Hitch. 1999. Working memory impairments in children with specific arithmetic learning difficulties. *Journal of Experimental Child Psychology* 24: 240–60.

McLeod, J., and J. Nonnemaker. 2000. Poverty and child emotional and behavioral problems: Racial-ethnic differences in processes and effects. *Journal of Health and Social Behavior* 41: 137–61.

McLoyd, V. C. 1997. The impact of poverty and low socioeconomic status on the socioemotional functioning of African-American children and adolescents: Mediating effects. In *Social and emotional adjustment and family relations in ethnic minority families*, ed. R. W. Taylor and M. C. Wang, 7–34. Mahwah, NJ: Lawrence Erlbaum Associates.

———. 1998. Socioeconomic disadvantage and child development. *American Psychologist* 53: 185–204.

McNamara, T. P., and V. A. Diwadkar. 1997. Symmetry and asymmetry of human spatial memory. *Cognitive Psychology* 34: 160–90.

McShane, D., and J. W. Berry. 1988. Native North Americans: Indian and Inuit abilities. In *Human abilities in cultural context*, ed. S. H. Irvine and J. W. Berry, 385–426. Cambridge: Cambridge University Press.

Mead, G. H. 1934. *Mind, self, and society.* Chicago: University of Chicago Press.

Miller, G. A. 1998. *Psychology: The science of mental life.* New York: Adams-Bannister-Cox.

Milner, B. 1974. Hemispheric specialization: Scope and limits. In *The neurosciences: Third research program*, ed. F. O. Schmitt and F. G. Worden, 75–89. Cambridge, MA: MIT Press.

Mitchelmore, M. C. 1976. Cross-cultural research on concepts of space and geometry. In *Space and geometry. Papers from a research workshop*, ed. J. L. Martin and D. A. Bradbard, 143–84. Athens, GA: University of Georgia Center for the Study of Learning and Teaching Mathematics. (ERIC No. ED 132–033).

———. 1980. Prediction of developmental stages in the representation of regular space figures. *Journal for Research in Mathematics Education* 11: 83–93.

Mix, K. S., J. Huttenlocher, and S. C. Levine. 2002. *Quantitative development in infancy and early childhood.* New York: Oxford University Press.

Morris, C. A., and C. B. Mervis. 1999. Williams syndrome. In *Handbook of neurodevelopmental and genetic disorders in children*, ed. S. Goldstein and C. R. Reynolds, 555–90. New York: Guilford Press.

Moss, P. A. 1994. Can there be validity without reliability? *Educational Researcher* 23 (2): 5–12.

Nash, S. C. 1979. Sex role as a mediator of intellectual functioning. In *Sex-related differences in cognitive functioning: Developmental issues*, ed. M. A. Wittig and A. C. Petersen, 263–381. New York: Academic Press.

National Council of Teachers of Mathematics (NCTM). 2000. *Principles and standards of school mathematics.* Reston, VA: NCTM.

National Institute of Child Health and Human Development Early Child Care Research Network. 2005. Duration and developmental timing of poverty and children's cognitive and social development from birth through third grade. *Child Development* 76 (4): 795–810.

National Research Council. 1996. *National science education standards.* Washington, DC: National Academy Press.

Natriello, G. J., E. L. McDill, and A. M. Pallas. 1990. *Schooling disadvantaged children: Racing against catastrophe.* New York: Teachers College Press.

Neisser, U. 1976. *Cognition and reality.* San Francisco: Freeman.

Ness, D. 2001. The development of spatial thinking, emergent geometric concepts and architectural principles in the everyday context. PhD diss., Columbia University.

———. 2002. Helping teachers recognize and connect the culturally bound nature of young children's mathematical intuitions to in-school mathematics concepts. In *Commitment to excellence: Transforming teaching and teacher education in inner-city and urban settings*, ed. L. A. Catelli and A. Diver-Stamnes, 171–90. Cresskill, NJ: Hampton Press.

New York State Education Department. 1982. *Mathematics/architecture related activities*. Albany, NY: The State Department Bureau of Curriculum Development.

Newcombe, N. S., and J. Huttenlocher. 2003. *Making space: The development of spatial representation and reasoning*. Cambridge, MA: MIT Press.

Nisbett, R. E., and T. D. Wilson. 1977. Telling more than we know: Verbal reports on mental processes. *Psychological Review* 84: 231–59.

Norman, D. K. 1980. A comparison of children's spatial reasoning: Rural Appalachia, suburban, and urban New England. *Child Development* 51: 288–91.

Novak, J. 1995. Concept mapping: A strategy for organizing knowledge. In *Learning science in the schools: Research reforming practice*, ed. S. Glynn and R. Duit. Mahwah, NJ: Lawrence Erlbaum Associates.

Oakes, J. 1990. *Multiplying inequalities: The effects of race, social class, and tracking on opportunities to learn mathematics and science*. Santa Monica, CA: The RAND Corporation.

O'Gorman, J. F. 1998. *ABC of architecture*. Philadelphia: University of Pennsylvania Press.

Okamoto, Y., R. Case, C. Bleiker, and B. Henderson. 1996. Cross-cultural investigations: The role of central conceptual structures in the development of children's thought. *Monographs of the Society for Research in Child Development* 61(serial no. 246, 1–2).

O'Keefe, J., and L. Nadel. 1978. *The hippocampus as a cognitive map*. New York: Oxford University Press.

Ondracek, P. J., and G. L. Allen. 2000. Children's acquisition of spatial knowledge from verbal descriptions. *Spatial Cognition and Computation* 2: 1–30.

Opper, S. 1979. Cross-cultural studies in cognition and language: The acquisition of class inclusion by Thai and Swiss children. *Archives de Psychologie* 47 (183): 293–308.

Ormrod, J. 1999. *Human learning*. Upper Saddle River, NJ: Merrill/Prentice Hall.

Page, E. I. 1959. Haptic perception: A consideration of one of the investigations of Piaget and Innelder. *Educational Review* 11: 115–24.

Paulu, N., and M. Martin. 1991. *Helping your child learn science*. Washington, DC: U.S. Department of Education, Office of Educational Research and Improvement.

Peel, E. A. 1959. Experimental examination of some of Piaget's schemata concerning children's perception and thinking, and a discussion of their educational significance. *British Journal of Educational Psychology* 29: 89–103.

Petitto, A. L., and H. P. Ginsburg. 1982. Mental arithmetic in Africa and America: Strategies, principles, and explanations. *International Journal of Psychology* 17: 81–102.

Piaget, J. 1954. *The construction of reality in the child*. New York: Basic Books.

———. 1965. *The moral judgment of the child*. New York: Free Press.

———. 1968. *Structuralism*. New York: Basic Books.

———. 1972. *Science of education and the psychology of the child*. Rev. ed. New York: Viking.

Piaget, J., and R. Garcia. 1989. *Psychogenesis and the history of science*. New York: Columbia University Press.

Piaget, J., and B. Inhelder. 1956/1967. *The child's conception of space*. Trans. F. J. Langdon and J. L. Lunzer. London: Routledge and Kegan Paul.

Piaget, J., B. Inhelder, and A. Szeminska. 1960. *The child's conception of geometry.* Trans. E. A. Lunzer. New York: Basic Books.

Pinar, W. 2001. *What is curriculum theory?* Mahwah, NJ: Lawrence Erlbaum Associates.

Pinxten, R. 1976. *Universalism versus relativism in language and thought.* The Hague: Mouton.

———. 1997. Applications in the teaching of mathematics and the sciences. In *Ethnomathematics: Challenging Eurocentrism in mathematics education,* ed. A. B. Powell and M. Frankenstein, 373–401. Albany: State University of New York Press.

Pinxten, R., E. van Dooren, and F. Harvey. 1983. *The anthropology of space: Explorations into the natural philosophy and semantics of the Navajo.* Philadelphia: University of Pennsylvania Press.

Porter, A. 1989. A curriculum out of balance: The case of elementary school mathematics. *Educational Researcher* 18: 9–15.

Pratt, C. 1970. *I learn from children.* New York: Cornerstone Library.

Presson, C. C. 1982a. The development of map-reading skills. *Child Development* 53: 196–99.

———. 1982b. Strategies in spatial reasoning. *Journal of Experimental Psychology: Learning, Memory and Cognition* 8: 243–51.

Presson, C. C., and S. C. Somerville. 1985. Beyond egocentrism: A new look at the beginnings of spatial representation. In *Children's searching: The development of search skill and spatial representation,* ed. H. M. Wellman, 1–26. Hillsdale, NJ: Lawrence Erlbaum Associates.

Provenzo, E. F., Jr., and A. Brett. 1983. *The complete block book.* Syracuse, NY: Syracuse University Press.

Reid, T. 1764/2001. *An inquiry into the human mind on the principles of common sense.* Ed. D. Brookes. University Park: Pennsylvania State University Press.

Reifel, S. 1984. Block construction: Children's developmental landmarks in the presentation of space. *Young Children* 40 (1): 61–67.

Resnick, L. B. 1989. Developing mathematical knowledge. *American Psychologist* 44: 162–69.

Roe, A. 1951a. A psychological study of eminent biologists. *Psychological Monographs,* 65 (serial no. 331, 14).

———. 1951b. A psychological study of eminent physical scientists. *Genetic Psychology Monographs* 43: 121–235.

———. 1952. A psychologist examines 64 eminent scientists. *Scientific American* 187 (5): 21–25.

———. 1981. A psychologist examines 64 eminent scientists. In *Psychology and education of the gifted,* ed. W. B. Barbe and J. Renzulli, 103–110. New York: Irving Publishers.

Roeper, A. 1988. The early environment of the child: Experience in a continuing search for meaning. In *Gifted young in science: Potential through performance,* ed. P. F. Brandwein and A. H. Passow, 121–39. Washington, DC: National Science Teachers Association.

Rosen, J. 1998. *Symmetry discovered: Concepts and applications in nature and science.* New York: Dover Publications.

Roth, J. L., J. Brooks-Gunn, M. R. Linver, and S. L. Hofferth. 2003. What happens during the school day? Time diaries from a national sample of elementary school teachers. *Teachers College Record* 105 (3): 317–43.

Salomon, G., and D. Perkins. 1996. Learning in wonderland: What do computers really offer education? In *Technology and the future of schooling: Ninety-fifth yearbook of the National Society for the Study of Education, Part II*, ed. S. T. Kerr, 111–30. Chicago: University of Chicago Press.

Salvadori, M. 1980. *Why buildings stand up: The strength of architecture*. New York: Norton.

———. 1990. *The art of construction: Projects and principles for beginning engineers and architects*. Chicago: Chicago Review Press.

Saxe, G. 1991. *Culture and cognitive development: Studies in mathematical understanding*. Hillsdale, NJ: Lawrence Erlbaum Associates.

Schiller, F. 1795/1983. *Letters on the aesthetic education of man*. New York: Oxford University Press.

Schweinhart, L. J. 1994. Lasting benefits of preschool programs. (ERIC Document Reproduction Services No. ED 367 478).

Schweinhart, L. J., H. V. Barnes, and D. P. Weikart. 1993. Significant benefits: The High/Scope Perry Preschool study through age 27. *Monographs of the High/Scope Educational Research Foundation*, 10. Ypsilanti, MI: High/Scope Press.

Schweinhart, L. J., J. Montie, Z. Xiang, W. S. Barnett, C. R. Belfield, and M. Nores. 2005. Lifetime effects: The High/Scope Perry Preschool study through age 40. *Monographs of the High/Scope Educational Research Foundation*, 14. Ypsilanti, MI: High/Scope Press.

Seo, K. H. 1998. Guideline for deep analysis. New York: Unpublished manuscript.

Semrud-Clikeman, M., and G. W. Hynd. 1990. Right hemisphere dysfunction in nonverbal learning disabilities: Social, academic, and adaptive functioning in adults and children. *Psychological Bulletin* 107: 196–209.

Serlio, S. 1611/1982. *The five books of architecture*. New York: Dover Publications.

Shemyakin, F. N. 1962. Orientation in space. In Vol. 1 of *Psychological science in the U.S.S.R.*, ed. B. G. Ananyev, 186–255. Washington, DC: Office of Technical Services, Report #62–11083.

Siann, G. 1977. *Sex difference in spatial ability on children: Its bearing on theories accounting for sex differences in spatial abilities in adults*. PhD diss., University of Edinburgh.

Siegel, A. W., and M. Schadler. 1977. Young children's cognitive maps of their classroom. *Child Development* 48: 388–94.

Siegler, R. S. 1995. Children's thinking: How does it occur? In *Memory performance and competencies: Issues in growth and development*, ed. F. E. Weinert and W. Schneider, 405–30. Mahwah, NJ: Lawrence Erlbaum Associates.

———. 1996. *Emerging minds: The process of change in children's thinking*. New York: Oxford University Press.

Slafer, A., and K. Cahill. 1995. *Why design? Activities and projects from the National Building Museum*. Chicago: Chicago Review Press.

Smith, C., and B. B. Lloyd. 1978. Maternal behavior and perceived sex of infant. *Child Development* 49: 1263–65.

Smock, C. D. 1976. Piaget's thinking about the development of space concepts and geometry. In *Space and geometry*, ed. J. L. Martin, 39–80. Columbus, OH: ERIC/ SMEAC.

Soar, R. S., and R. M. Soar. 1972. An empirical analysis of selected Follow Through programs: An example of a process approach to evaluation. In *Early Childhood Education*, ed. I. Gordon. Chicago: National Society for Study of Education.

Sophian, C. 1984. Developing search skills in infancy and early childhood. In *Origins of cognitive skills: The eighteenth annual Carnegie Symposium on Cognition*, ed. C. Sophian, 27–56. Hillsdale, NJ: Lawrence Erlbaum Associates.

Spelke, E. S., and E. L. Newport. 1998. Nativism, empiricism, and the development of knowledge. In *Handbook of child psychology*. 5th ed. Vol. 1, *Theoretical models of human development*, ed. R. M. Lerner, 275–340. New York: Wiley.

Spiers, P. A. 1987. Alcalculia revisited: Current issues. In *Mathematical disabilities: A cognitive neuropsychological perspective*, ed. G. Deloche and X. Seron, 1–25. Hillsdale, NJ: Lawrence Erlbaum Associates.

Springer, S. P., and G. Deutsch. 1981. *Left brain, right brain*. New York: W. H. Freeman.

Stafford, R. E. 1961. Sex differences in spatial visualization as evidence of sex-linked inheritance. *Perceptual and Motor Skills* 13: 428.

Starkey, P., and A. Klein. 1992. Economic and cultural influences on early mathematical development. In *New directions in child and family research: Shaping Head Start in the 90s*, ed. F. L. Parker, R. Robinson, S. Sombrano, C. Piotrowski, J. Hagen, S. Randolph, and A. Baker, 440–43. New York: National Council of Jewish Women.

Starkey, P., E. S. Spelke, and R. Gelman. 1980. Number confidence in infants: Sensitivity to numeric invariance and numeric change. Paper presented at the meeting of the International Conference of Infant Studies, New Haven, CT.

Stea, D., and J. M. Blaut. 1973a. Some preliminary observations on spatial learning in school children. In *Image and environment: Cognitive mapping and spatial behavior*, ed. R. M. Downs and D. Stea, 226–45. Chicago: Aldine Publishing.

———. 1973b. Toward a developmental theory of spatial learning. In *Image and environment: Cognitive mapping and spatial behavior*, ed. R. M. Downs and D. Stea, 51–62. Chicago: Aldine Publishing.

Stiles-Davis, J., M. Kritchevsky, and U. Bellugi. 1988. *Spatial cognition: Brain bases and development*. Hillsdale, NJ: Lawrence Erlbaum Associates.

Stodolsky, S. S., and G. Lesser. 1967. Learning patterns in the disadvantaged. *Harvard Educational Review* 37 (4): 546–93.

Sutton-Smith, B. 1997. *The ambiguity of play*. Cambridge, MA: Harvard University Press.

———. 1999. The rhetorics of adult and child play theories. In *Advances in early education and day care*, ed. S. Reifel. Stamford, CT: JAI Press.

Tartre, L. A. 1990. Spatial skills, gender, and mathematics. In *Mathematics and gender: Influences on teachers and students*, ed. E. Fennema and G. Leder, 27–59. New York: Teachers College Press.

Teller, P. 1969. Some discussion and extension of Manfred Bierwisch's work on German adjectivals. *Foundations of Language* 5: 151–75.

Thomas, B. 1982. An abstract of kindergarten teachers' elicitation and utilization of children's prior knowledge in the teaching of shape concepts. Unpublished manuscript, School of Education, Health, Nursing, and Arts Professions, New York University.

Tolman, E. C. 1948. Cognitive maps in rats and man. *Psychological Review* 55: 189–208.

Tranel, D., L. E. Hall, S. Olson, and N. N. Tranel. 1987. Evidence for right-hemisphere developmental learning disability. *Developmental Neuropsychology* 3: 113–27.

Tversky, B. 1999. Talking about space. *APA Review of Books* 44 (1): 39–40.

Uttal, D. H. 2000. Seeing the big picture: Map use and the development of spatial cognition. *Developmental Science* 3 (3): 247–86.

Van de Walle, J. A. 1998. *Elementary and middle school mathematics: Teaching developmentally.* New York: Longman.

Van Hiele, P. M. 1986. *Structure and insight.* Orlando, FL: Academic Press.

———. 1999. Developing geometric thinking through activities that begin with play. *Teaching Children Mathematics* 5 (6): 310–16.

Vitruvius. 1914/1960. *The ten books on architecture.* New York: Dover Publications.

Vygotsky, L. S. 1978. *Mind in society: The development of higher psychological processes.* Cambridge, MA: Harvard University Press.

Waber, D. P. 1977. Sex differences in mental abilities, hemispheric lateralization, and rate of physical growth at adolescence. *Developmental Psychology* 13: 29–38.

———. 1979. Cognitive abilities and sex-related variations in the maturation of cortical functions. In *Sex-related differences in cognitive functioning,* ed. M. A. Wittig and A. C. Petersen, 161–86. New York: Academic Press.

Wandersee, J., J. Mintzes, and J. Novak. 1994. Research on alternative conceptions in science. In *Handbook of research on science teaching and learning,* ed. D. Gabel, 131–76. New York: Macmillan Publishing.

Wapner, S., and H. Werner. 1957. *Perceptual development.* Worcester, MA: Clark University Press.

Wason, P. C., and P. N. Johnson-Laird. 1972. *Psychology of reasoning: Structure and content.* London: Batsford.

Wellhousen, K., and J. Kieff. 2001. *A constructivist approach to block play in early childhood.* Stamford, CT: Thomson Learning.

Wellman, H. M., ed. 1985. *Children's searching: The development of search skills and spatial representation.* Hillsdale, NJ: Lawrence Erlbaum Associates.

Wellman, H. M., and S. C. Somerville. 1982. The development of human search ability. In *Advances in developmental psychology,* ed. M. E. Lamb and A. L. Brown, 41–84. Hillsdale, NJ: Lawrence Erlbaum Associates.

Wellman, H. M., S. C. Somerville, and R. J. Haake. 1979. Development of search procedures in real-life spatial environments. *Developmental Psychology* 15: 530–42.

Werner, H. 1948. *Comparative psychology of mental development.* New York: International Universities Press.

———. 1957. The concept of development from a comparative and organismic point of view. In *The concept of development,* ed. D. B. Harris, 125–48. Minneapolis: University of Minnesota Press.

Werner, H., and Kaplan, B. 1956. The developmental approach to cognition: Its relevance to the psychological interpretation of anthropological and ethnolinguistic data. *American Anthropologist* 58: 866–80.

Weyl, H. 1980. *Symmetry*. Princeton, NJ: Princeton University Press.

Wheatley, G. W. 1990. Spatial sense and mathematics learning. *Arithmetic Teacher* 37 (6): 10–11.

Wheatley, G. W., and P. Cobb. 1990. Analysis of young children's spatial constructions. In *Transforming early childhood mathematics education: International perspectives*, ed. L. P. Steffe and T. Wood, 161–73. Hillsdale, NJ: Lawrence Erlbaum.

White, N., A. Green, and R. Steiner. 1995. An investigation of differences between 3 age-groups in verbal and spatial task-performance using the dual-task paradigm. *Brain and Cognition* 28 (1): 59–78.

Whitehead, A. N. 1919. *An enquiry concerning the principles of human knowledge*. Cambridge, UK: Cambridge University Press.

Witelson, S. F., and J. A. Swallow. 1988. Neuropsychological study of the development of spatial cognition. In *Spatial cognition: Brain bases and development*, ed. J. Stiles-Davis, M. Kritchevsky, and U. Bellugi, 373–409. Hillsdale, NJ: Lawrence Erlbaum Associates.

Wolf, R. 1966. The measurement of environments. In *Testing problems in perspective*, ed. A. Anastasi. Rev. ed., 491–503. Washington, DC: Council on Education.

Wolfgang, C. H., and R. G. Stakenas. 1985. An explanation of toy content of preschool children's home environments as a predictor of cognitive development. *Early Child Development and Care* 19: 291–307.

Wolfgang, C. H., L. L. Stannard, and I. Jones. 2001. Block play performance among preschoolers as a predictor of later school achievement in mathematics. *Journal of Research in Childhood Education* 15 (2): 173–80.

Wynn, K. 1995. Infants possess a system of numerical knowledge. *Current Direction in Psychological Science* 4 (6): 172–77.

Yakimanskaya, I. S. 1971. The development of spatial concepts and their role in the mastery of elementary geometric knowledge. In Vol. 5 of *Soviet studies in the psychology of learning and teaching mathematics*, ed. J. Kilpatrick and I. Wirszup, 145–68. Chicago: Chicago University Press.

———. 1991. The development of spatial thinking in school children. In Vol. 3 of *Soviet studies in mathematics education*. Reston, VA: National Council of Teachers of Mathematics.

Zvonkin, A. 1991. Mathematics for little ones. *Journal of Mathematical Behavior* 11 (2): 207–19.

Index